ICSA Study Text

International Finance and Administration Qualifications

Fund Administration

ICSA Study Text

International Finance and Administration Qualifications

Fund Administration

Haley Camp and Jo Carré

icsa
The Governance Institute

First published 2017

Published by ICSA Publishing Limited
Saffron House
6–10 Kirby Street
London EC1N 8TS

Typeset by Paul Barrett Book Production, Cambridge
Printed in Great Britain by Lightning Source, Milton Keynes, Buckinghamshire

British Cataloguing in Publication Data
A catalogue record for this book is available from the British Library.

ISBN 978 186072 700 9

Contents

Acknowledgements

The publisher and authors would like to acknowledge the contribution made by Jonathan Wilson, author of chapters one and two, and the technical reviewer of the text David Loader.

The publisher and author acknowledge the following for the permission to reproduce the figures in this volume:

Figure 9.1 Guernsey Finance, (2015), Typical Guernsey private equity structure [ONLINE]. Available at: *www.guernseyfinance.com/media/593159/uk-private-equity-2015.pdf*

Figure 9.2 Mourant Ozannes, (2016), *Comparison of Offshore Private Equity Holding Structures* [ONLINE]. Available at *www.mourantozannes.com/publications/comparison-of-offshore-private-equity-holding-structures.aspx*

Figure 13.1 FATF, (2016) FATF Website, Copyright © FATF/OECD. Available at *www.fatf-gafi.org/about/fatfsecretariat/*

Figure 13.2 ESMA structure [ONLINE]. Available at *www.esma.europa.eu/about-esma/governance*

Every effort has been made to locate and acknowledge sources and holders of copyright material in this study text. In the event that any have been inadvertently overlooked, please contact the publisher.

How to use this study text

ICSA study texts developed to support ICSA's Level 5 International Finance and Administration Qualifications follow a standard format and include a range of navigational, self-testing and illustrative features to help you get the most out of the support materials.

Each text is divided into three main sections:

- introductory material
- the text itself
- additional reference information.

The sections below show you how to find your way around the text and make the most of its features.

Introductory material

The introductory section of each text includes a full contents list and the aims and learning outcomes for the modules in question.

Where relevant, the introductory section will also include a list of acronyms and abbreviations or a list of legal cases for reference.

The text itself

Each part opens with a list of the chapters to follow, an overview of what will be covered and learning outcomes for the part.

Every chapter opens with a list of the topics covered and an introduction specific to that chapter. Chapters are structured to allow students to break the content down into manageable sections for study. Each chapter ends with a summary of key content to reinforce understanding.

Features

The text is enhanced by a range of illustrative and self-testing features to assist understanding and to help you prepare for the examination. You will find answers to the 'test yourself' and 'worked example' questions towards the end of this text. Each feature is presented in a standard format, so that you will become familiar with how to use them in your study.

These features are identified by a series of icons.

The texts also include tables, figures and other illustrations as relevant.

Reference material

The text ends with a range of additional guidance and reference material, including a glossary of key terms, a directory of web resources and a comprehensive index.

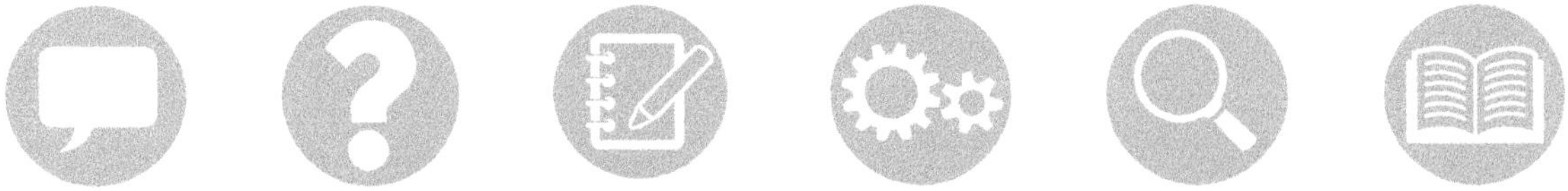

Stop and think | Test yourself | Worked examples | Making it work | Case law | Case study

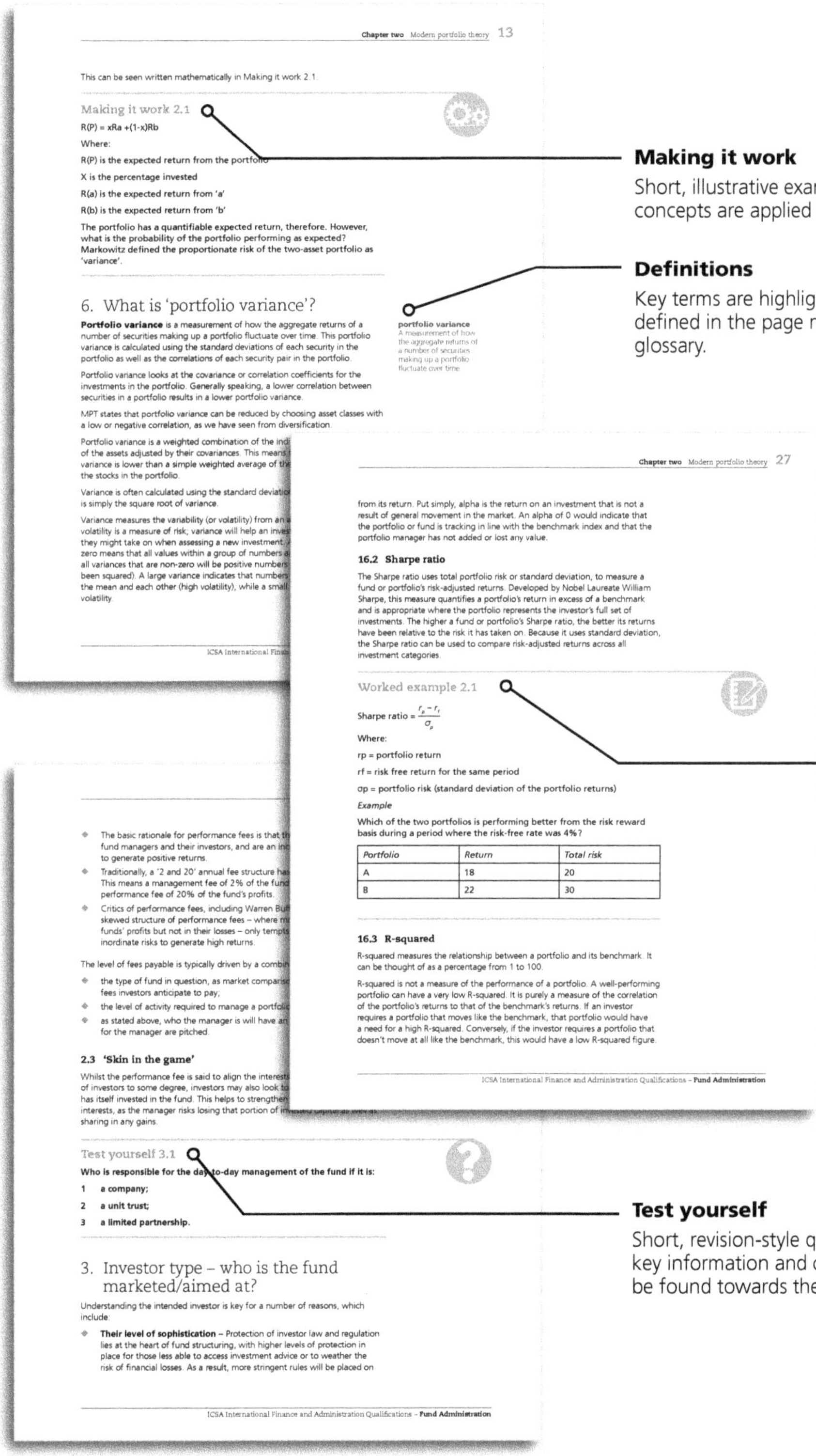

Making it work

Short, illustrative examples which look at how concepts are applied in practice.

Definitions

Key terms are highlighted in bold on first use and defined in the page margins and the end of book glossary.

Worked example

Crucial to an understanding of finance-based modules. Questions and answers allow you to work through a calculation as part of your study. Answers are to be found towards the end of the text.

Test yourself

Short, revision-style questions to help you re-cap on key information and core concepts. Answers are to be found towards the end of the text.

The Fund Administration modules

Aims

These modules provide an understanding of the fund administration and management process.

Subjects covered include investing money and assets, the role and duties of fund administrators and fund managers, how the funds industry and its services are regulated, fund products and services available to investors and characteristics of investment and portfolio management practice.

Learning outcomes

On successful completion of these modules, you will:

- Understand the role of investment in generating wealth
- Know the options available for investors when investing money and assets
- Understand the role of banks and lenders
- Understand the role and duties of fund administrators and fund managers
- Know the tools a fund administrator can use to create the best return
- Understand the impact of regulation and due diligence on the sector
- Understand fund products and services available to investors
- Understand how investors choose the most appropriate fund product to meet their investment needs
- Understand the risk and return created by fund products and services
- Understand the role of portfolio management in wealth management
- Understand portfolio management strategy
- Understand the impact of risk, regulation and due diligence on portfolio management.

Acronyms and abbreviations

AIF	alternative investment fund
AIFM	alternative investment fund manager
AIFMD	Alternative Investment Fund Managers Directive
AUM	assets under management
CAPM	capital asset pricing model
CFTC	Commodity Futures Trading Commission
CIMA	Cayman Islands Monetary Authority
DTAA	double taxation avoidance agreements
ELP	exempted limited partnership
ELP Law	Exempted Limited Partnership Law
ESMA	European Securities and Markets Authority
FATCA	Foreign Account Tax Compliance Act
FCR	financial condition report
FFI	foreign financial institutions
FIO	Federal Insurance Office
GAO	Government Accountability Office
GBC1	Global Business Company
GP	general partners
IFRS	International Financial Reporting Standards
IGA	inter-governmental agreement
IMA	investment management agreement
IPO	initial public offering
IPPA	investment promotion and protection agreement
IRR	internal rate of return
IRS	Inland Revenue Service
LLP	limited liability partnerships
LP	limited partnership
LPA	limited partnership agreement
MAS	Monetary Authority of Singapore
MCMAA	Multilateral Convention on Mutual Administrative Assistance in Tax Matters
MCR	minimum capital requirement
MiFID	Marketing in Financial Instruments Directive
MiFIR	Markets in Financial Instruments Regulation
MPT	modern portfolio theory
NAIF	notified alternative investment fund

NAV	net asset valuations
ORSA	own risk and solvency assessment
PCC	protected cell companies (Guernsey)
PFI	privately funded initiative
PIN	property index notes
PMA	property management agreement
QRT	quantitative report template
SCR	solvency capital requirement
SEC	Securities and Exchange Commission
SFL	Simple Fund Limited
SML	security market line
SPC	segregated portfolio companies (Cayman)
TER	total expense ratio
TRS	total return swaps
UCITS	undertakings for collective investment in transferable securities
UEIF	unregulated eligible investor funds
UETF	unregulated exchange traded funds
UKGAAP	United States Generally Accepted Accounting Principles

Part one

Chapter one
Introduction to investment

Chapter two
Modern portfolio theory

Understanding the investment environment

Overview

Part one will give you an understanding of the world of investment, the drivers behind it and what people seek to achieve through investment. Consideration is also given as to how investment aims can impact on decision making and risk versus reward. It will also examine how to go about constructing a portfolio, the risk considerations when doing so and how modern portfolio theory has evolved to enable the use of a mathematical basis for designing a balanced portfolio that is appropriate for the aims of the investor.

Learning outcomes

At the end of this part, you will be able to:

- Understand the meaning of risk
- Understand how modern portfolio theory defines risk

Chapter one
Introduction to investment

List of topics

1. Markets and participants
2. The meaning of risk
3. Asset allocation

Introduction

Investing is essentially taking risk with a cash pot in order to achieve a return and grow an individual's savings. Cash can either be deposited in an account, perhaps in a bank where it may or may not outpace inflation, or invested where it will be subjected to a level of risk. If inflation grows at a greater rate than a deposit account, the purchasing power of that money is eroded. Similarly, an individual cannot physically work more hours than exist in a week and therefore, if they are drawing the best salary that they can, they will have to invest in order to achieve a lifestyle or wealth beyond that which is available to them by working alone.

This chapter investigates what it is to invest, the conduits through which one can invest and the risks and returns inherent in such an endeavour.

Stock markets are a channel for money between borrowers and lenders, buyers and sellers. Lenders are individuals with savings while borrowers are companies and governments in general. The markets are also where buyers and sellers of different investments compete to get the best returns. The two forces that dominate in this arena are those of supply and demand, which dictate the price of investments, with demand representing the quantity of an asset that investors will buy at a given price and supply being the amount that sellers are prepared to supply to the market at a given price. Also, the greater the expected risk of an investment, the greater the reward likely and the longer that money is tied up, the better the return offered. Often, markets and investors try to look ahead and take into account all of the information they have but sometimes they overreact or overlook possible scenarios. The two main types of investment are debt and equity, debt being money lent and equity being shares in companies which can also be considered part-ownership. Cautious investors should always spread the risk by having a mix of the two in a portfolio as there are diversification of risk benefits to be enjoyed.

1. Markets and participants

The capital markets and the money markets are types of market for dealing in capital. Generally, capital markets are financial exchanges for investing long-term capital (perhaps five years and more) while money markets are for borrowing and lending largely short-term capital (overnight to two years for instance).

Debt can be overdrafts, long-term notes or fixed interest securities which pay a coupon while the cash is lent and are repaid in full at maturity. Generally, debt is considered less risky than equity but offers limited reward. Equity, being part ownership of a company, allows investors to share the profits of a business, which is mostly riskier than fixed interest debt, but offers long-term protection from inflation, amongst other benefits.

The stock market equity is a share in the ownership of the company. The return from shares can vary and investors may lose everything if the company folds. Companies issue shares to raise funds for expansion and investors buy them either directly or through pension funds or other vehicles such as insurance companies or trusts. Shares are never repaid so there exists the secondary market where they can be bought and sold, which is essential as this attracts speculators and creates liquidity for owners. Companies can be very different from each other so to compare like with like, shares are grouped together into sectors of similar businesses, such as miners, utilities, transport, etc.

In Britain the 100 largest companies by market capitalisation (number of shares in issue multiplied by the share price) are quoted as the FTSE 100 whereas the FTSE All Share represents the wider market.

1.1 Bonds

A bond is a debt security, similar to an IOU. Borrowers issue bonds to raise money from investors willing to lend them money for a certain length of time.

When we buy a bond, we are lending to the issuer, which may be a government or corporation. In return, the issuer promises to pay a specified (fixed) rate of interest during the life of the bond and to repay the principal, also known as the nominal or par value of the bond, when it matures, or becomes due after the set period of time.

Types of bonds

- **Corporate bonds** are debt securities issued by private and public corporations.
- **Investment-grade bonds** have a higher credit rating, implying less credit risk, than high-yield corporate bonds.
- **High-yield bonds** have a lower credit rating, implying higher credit risk, than investment-grade bonds and, therefore, offer higher interest rates in return for the increased risk an investor must take on.

corporate bonds
Debt securities issued by private and public corporations.

investment-grade bonds
Have a higher credit rating, implying less credit risk, than high-yield corporate bonds.

high-yield bonds
Have a lower credit rating, implying higher credit risk, than investment-grade bonds and, therefore, offer higher interest rates in return for the increased risk an investor must take on.

sovereign debt or government bonds
Debt securities issued by governments and have set periods to return of capital. Short-term securities generally mature in under five years, medium term bonds mature within ten years and long-term bonds typically mature in excess of 20 years.

- **Sovereign debt or government bonds** (UK Government bonds are called gilts as they used to have gold 'gilt' edges) are debt securities issued by governments and have set periods to return of capital. Short-term securities generally mature in under five years, medium-term bonds mature within ten years and long-term bonds typically mature in excess of 20 years.

The benefits and risks of bonds

Bonds can provide a means of preserving capital and earning a predictable return. Bond investments provide steady streams of income from interest payments prior to maturity.

As with any investment, bonds have risks, including:

- Credit risk where an issuer may fail to make interest or principal payments on time and thereby default on its bonds.
- Interest rate risk. Interest rate changes will affect the bond's value. If bonds are held to maturity the investor will receive the face value, plus the interest. If sold before maturity, the bond may be worth more or less than the face value. Rising interest rates will mean that to sell an older bond with a lower interest rate, it may have to be sold at a discount.
- Inflation risk. Inflation is a general upward movement in prices. Inflation reduces purchasing power, which is a risk for investors receiving a fixed rate of interest.
- Liquidity risk. This refers to the risk that investors won't find a market (buyer or seller) for the bond, possibly preventing them from buying or selling when they would like to.

1.2 The benefits and risks of shares

Shares offer investors the greatest potential for capital appreciation (growth) over the long term. Investors willing to hold shares over long periods of time have generally been rewarded with positive returns.

Equity prices move down as well as up however, and there is no guarantee that the company whose shares are held by an investor will grow and there is always the threat that they can lose money invested in shares.

If a company goes bankrupt and its assets are liquidated, ordinary shareholders are the last to share in the proceeds, behind creditors and bond holders. Even when companies are not in danger of bankruptcy, their share price may fluctuate both up and down.

Market and share fluctuations can be uncomfortable to some investors. A share's price can be affected by many factors both inside the company or by events the company has no control over, such as political or market events.

Lifestyle and investment term horizons usually have a bearing on the amount of risk (fluctuation) in a portfolio and young investors with many years before retirement may choose to hold a greater portion of their portfolio in equities while an older investor approaching retirement may choose to hold more bonds and suffer less volatility ahead of cashing in their portfolio. If they have to sell shares at a time of market retraction, they may get back less than they paid for the investment.

The risks of equity investments can be offset by diversifying across a number of different shares or by investing in other kinds of assets that are not shares, such as bonds. The merits of diversification and its quantifiable reduction are set out in the modern portfolio theory section of this workbook.

2. The meaning of risk

All investments involve some degree of risk. In finance, risk refers to the degree of uncertainty or potential financial loss inherent in an investment decision. The risk is that the investment will not perform as well as we expect. In general, as investment risks rise, investors seek higher returns to compensate for taking such risks.

Each investment has different risks and returns, such as how easily investors can get their money out when they need it, how fast their portfolio will grow and how safe their cash will be. Investors face more than one type of risk.

Investing in shares of a particular company means that we are purchasing part-ownership in that company and with a bond, we are loaning money to a company. Returns from both of these investments means that we are repaid only if the company stays in business. If the company falls into bankruptcy and its assets liquidated, ordinary shareholders are the last in line to share in the proceeds. If there are assets, the company's bondholders will be paid first with shareholders receiving whatever is left, which may be nothing.

2.1 Volatility risk

Even when companies aren't in danger of failing, their stock price may fluctuate up or down. Inflation, interest rate fluctuations and liquidity risk will all impact on share prices as well as bonds but not in the same way.

Valuing shares is not an exact science because shares do not pay a fixed rate of return and have no redemption date as for instance fixed income. Investors use three main measures to assess share values: dividend yield, price-earnings ratio and net asset value. The first two are relative measures and the third is an absolute measure.

- The dividend yield tells investors what kind of income they can expect from a share and can be used to compare shares with each other or different types of investment. As share prices rise, yields fall. Yields can be historic and based on previous years' profits, or prospective and based on estimates of future earnings. Most investors tend to look at future earnings as that will be important in making decisions as to what to include in their portfolios.

- Price-earnings (P/E) ratios give a measure of how high a company's share prices are relative to its earnings; a high P/E ratio means that investors expect earnings to rise sharply. As share prices rise, the P/E ratios rise. P/E ratios can be useful in evaluating how companies compare, although the measure can sometimes be suspect as businesses frequently differ and earnings valuations are sometimes unreliable.
- Net asset value measures what shares in a company would be worth if it was wound up. It is often used in situations where a company seems in danger of going bust and is also used where tangible assets are very important to the firm, particularly investment trusts and property shares. Asset values are regularly far below the share prices. Because investors are concerned with the company's ongoing business they may not give a true representation of what a company would actually fetch if it was wound up. Other measures of company performance include cash flow analysis, liquidity ratios, borrowing ratios and shareholder value analysis, although these tools move in and out of fashion.

2.2 Attitude to risk

When it comes to investing, risk and reward are deemed to have a close relationship. A depositor in a bank where returns are often deemed to be risk-free crosses a line to become an investor and that line is one of risk tolerance. It is often said that 'no pain, no gain' and this comes close to explaining the relationship between risk and reward as all investments will involve some degree of risk. There is often a disclaimer on investment advice documentation that states that 'some or all of the money invested could be lost' and 'returns from historic investment may not be replicated in the future'.

The reward for placing money on risk is the potential for greater investment returns. An investment portfolio with a long time horizon may make more money by investing in higher risk assets, such as equities, than if it was limited to less risky assets such as bonds or cash deposits. Conversely, lower risk cash investments may be more appropriate for short-term financial goals.

A speculative investor, or one with a higher risk tolerance, should be willing to risk losing money to achieve potentially better returns. A conservative investor with a lower risk tolerance, should favour investments that preserve the value original investment, perhaps on an inflation-adjusted basis.

Investment advisers try to help potential investors assess their risk tolerance. Some will even estimate asset allocations based on responses to questionnaires. While the suggested asset allocations may be a useful starting point, it is useful to keep in mind that the results may be biased towards financial products or services sold by companies or individuals with a return to be drawn from particular securities or funds.

3. Asset allocation

Asset allocation involves spreading an investment pot across different assets, such as shares, bonds and cash. Asset allocation is a decision that is particular to an investor given a number of factors, some of which are expanded upon below. The allocation can also change at different times in an investor's life, depending on how long it is to be invested for and the ability to tolerate risk.

3.1 Factors to consider

Time horizon

The time horizon is the number of months, years, or decades an individual or company needs to invest to achieve a financial goal. Investors with a longer time horizon may feel comfortable taking on more volatile or riskier investments. Those with a shorter time horizon may prefer to take on less risk.

Risk tolerance

Risk tolerance is an investor's ability or willingness to lose some or possibly all of their original investment in exchange for potentially greater returns.

3.2 Benefits of diversification

Diversification is the practice of spreading money among different investments to reduce risk. Employment of this strategy can be summed up as 'putting eggs in different baskets'.

A way to diversify risk is to allocate investments across different asset classes. Historically, shares, bonds (fixed interest securities) and cash have not moved up and down at the same time (positive correlation in the modern portfolio theory section of this work book). Scenarios that cause one asset class to perform poorly may create a positive return for another type of asset. Investors adopting this strategy of eggs in different baskets hope that if one is losing money, the others make up for those losses.

Stronger diversification can be achieved if investments are also spread within an asset class. For instance, holding a number of different shares or bonds and investing in different industry sectors. As we saw above with assets classes, if one sector is performing poorly, returns may be offset by other holdings in sectors that are not positively correlated (prices moving up and down in line with one another).

Retail investors (general investing public) often find it easier to diversify by owning managed funds. A managed fund pools money from many investors and invests the money in shares, bonds and other financial securities. Managed funds make it easy for investors to own a smaller amount of many investments. A stock market index fund, or exchange traded fund, often owns shares in hundreds of companies, thereby creating diversification within one investment.

However, a fund won't necessarily provide diversification if it focuses on only one industry sector. Indeed, if narrowly focused funds are invested in, an investor may need to invest in several of them to be adequately diversified in a particular sector or geography. As more investments are added to a portfolio, it is likely that additional fees and expenses will be payable, which will lower investment returns. So these costs need to be considered when deciding the best way to diversify a portfolio.

3.3 Rebalancing the asset allocation

Rebalancing a portfolio will bring it back to its original asset allocation and, hopefully, its original risk profile. Rebalancing is important as, over time, some investments will perform better and grow faster than others. This can skew portfolio holdings out of alignment with investment goals. By rebalancing, an investor can ensure that the portfolio does not overweight a particular asset category, and that it will return the portfolio to the designated level of risk.

For example, a portfolio might start with 50% invested in shares, but over a period that may rise to 75% due to stock market gains. To re-establish the original asset allocation strategy, some shares will need to be sold or more cash brought in to the portfolio to invest in other asset classes.

To rebalance a portfolio, an investor can sell investments where holdings are 'overweight' and use the proceeds to buy investments in the underweighted asset classes.

If they are continuing to add to investments, they can alter contributions so that more goes to underweighted asset categories until the portfolio is rebalanced.

It is always worth considering, when rebalancing, the impact of transaction fees or possible tax consequences. It is outside the scope of this book to discuss further but financial professionals or tax advisers could help identify ways to minimise these potential costs.

How often the portfolio should be rebalanced is something that should be given thought to. As discussed above, regular rebalancing has cost implications so most investors tend to either rebalance at regular intervals, such as every quarter or annually, or when holdings of an asset class increase or decrease more than a certain percentage.

This tends to work best in mean-reverting markets as, psychologically, it can be difficult to sell an asset when it is doing well in favour of an asset class that is doing poorly. It takes discipline therefore but improves chances of buying low and selling high.

Chapter summary

- The capital markets and the money markets are types of market for dealing in capital.
- All investments involve some degree of risk.
- Asset allocation involves spreading an investment pot across different assets, such as shares, bonds, and cash.

Chapter two
Modern portfolio theory

List of topics

Introduction

Modern portfolio theory (MPT) is born out of investment common sense. The rationale is that minimising risk and maximising the potential return should be something that logical humans have in mind when allocating assets across a portfolio. The well-worn tenet that states 'the higher the risk, the higher the potential reward' is cast in an intelligent framework within MPT where the combination of holdings in a portfolio is assessed from how they perform in relation to one another (correlation) and the risk and return characteristics of each, collectively.

modern portfolio theory
An investment framework that is useful in diversifying the risk when allocating assets in a financial, liquid (tradable) portfolio in order to maximise the potential return given a specified level of risk appetite or tolerance.

MPT is essentially an investment framework that is useful in diversifying the risk when allocating assets in a financial, liquid (tradable) portfolio in order to maximise the potential return given a specified level of risk appetite or tolerance. In other words, by spreading risks across multiple investment holdings, the risk of potential loss can be minimised without necessarily reducing the returns from a portfolio.

If only one investment is purchased, the portfolio will have the risk and return characteristics of that holding. Each single investment exhibits is own particular risk and return characteristics. What MPT looks to do is quantify the risk mathematically and eliminate or reduce this specific risk by adding other assets that perform dissimilarly to the investment basket. Put simply, the portfolio is constructed so that when some assets fall in value, other assets rise and balance is maintained. When markets in general rise, the investment portfolio gains in value.

MPT uses mathematics to intelligently construct an investment portfolio. The steps involved include:

- valuing the investments that could be included in the portfolio;
- calculating the asset allocation (or number and type of investments);
- optimising the portfolio to get the maximum amount of return for the minimum amount of risk; and
- monitoring the portfolio to see if it meets performance expectations from both a risk and return perspective, making changes when market conditions warrant a change.

1. History of modern portfolio theory

MPT was first introduced in 1952 in a paper titled *Portfolio Selection*, published by the Journal of Finance and written by Harry Markowitz, an American economist who was awarded Nobel Laureate status for his work. Markowitz's studies demonstrated that investing should not be about trying to pick future high-performing stocks, but that the combination of the investments chosen was more important in terms of reward for the level of risk taken. By adding assets that are uncorrelated or inversely correlated, the overall risk in a portfolio is diversified across all the different 'eggs in the basket' and risk is reduced and can be quantified. This measuring of risk becomes extremely useful when considering purchases and sales within the investment basket.

In 1958 James Tobin added leverage to MPT by including an investment that pays a risk-free rate of return, which allowed the construction of portfolios whose risk-return profiles were capable of outperforming Markowitz's Efficient Frontier.

financial or capital markets
Where governments and companies raise finance via the sale and purchase of fixed income securities, often called bonds or equities, more commonly known as shares via a stock market.

2. Efficient financial markets

Financial or capital markets are where governments and companies raise finance via the sale and purchase of fixed income securities, often called bonds.

The market is used to trade new issues of either bonds or shares, which are known as primary, or already existing securities, known as the secondary market. Typical capital market instruments include: equities, bonds, foreign exchange markets, derivatives (futures and options) as well as insurance contracts, mortgages and other tradable securities.

An efficient capital market is where the prices of these instruments reflect information accurately and in real time. New information about a company will be analysed and the future value of cash flow expected from the security will change the current share price to accommodate this change in fundamental value.

Thus, the prices of securities fluctuate and market participants, such as traders and stockbrokers, will trade them competitively to try to achieve maximum profit. Funds from savers and investors (corporate or individual) are expected to flow into the financial markets intent on seeking out the best places to invest and, therefore, you can see that information available and its ability to impact of share prices is of the utmost importance. If stocks are efficiently priced with all information about the underlying company known, investors can feel confident about the choices they make for their portfolios.

3. Diversification

Diversification is how risk in a portfolio is reduced.

diversification
How risk in a portfolio is reduced.

A portfolio which is constructed of a number of different asset classes such as equities, bonds, cash, property and commodities will blend low-risk cash deposits and bonds with higher risk equities and commodities, for instance. The asset class could then be diversified further with different managers, industry sectors and geographies selected. The proportions allocated will depend upon the investor's risk preference and the prevailing market conditions.

4. Risk – analysis of different types of risk

4.1 Risk

Risk, in its simplest form, can be divided between systematic and unsystematic, or specific, risk. Specific risk is that associated with a particular individual investment. A specific risk is diversifiable by adding other diverse holdings to the portfolio, provided that the risks of the other holdings are not directly correlated. Systematic risk is that of the portfolio or market and cannot be diversified away through the addition of other assets, and is due to outside factors such as the economy performing poorly or international tensions, etc. Systematic risk affects the whole market or 'system'.

4.2 How MPT defines risk

The risk for investors is that the return from an investment will be lower than expected. MPT is interested in the amount that this return deviates from the average return and quantifies this risk accordingly, measuring it as 'standard deviation'. Every holding has its own mean and therefore deviation from it can be measured specifically. MPT assesses the likely profitability of investments from a basis of weighting the expected returns on a 'normal' distribution, the familiar bell-shaped curve when drawn graphically. Therefore, risk is measured by the standard deviation of returns and the expected portfolio return is measured by the weighted average of individual investments within it.

4.3 Correlation

In considering risk, it is the effect that an investment will have on the overall risk of the portfolio that is important, not the risk of the investment in isolation. The amount of diversification of risk available will depend upon the degree to which returns from different investments move in line with each other or the degree to which they are 'correlated'. An investor can reduce the risk in a portfolio by holding several investments that are not perfectly (positively) correlated. Highly correlated shares for instance may occur from companies in the same industry or sector; if the oil price moves, oil companies' shares will tend to move in the same direction. Negative correlation is viewed when prices tend to move in opposite directions. If no discernible relationship can be observed with prices bearing no relationship to each other, there is no correlation between the assets. Correlation is measured on a scale of +1 to –1. A correlation coefficient of 1 between two assets (perfect) means whatever one asset does will predict the movement of the other. One asset's gain of 10% will be matched by the other asset's gain of 10%, therefore. Minus one is perfect inverse and is equally predictive but opposite. This means that if investment 'a' increases by 10%, investment 'b' will decrease by 10%. Ignoring the sign, the greater the number, the greater the strength of the relationship between the two. A correlation of zero means returns are completely independent and no relationship exists between the two. Anything less than 1 means that investors can diversify the risk in portfolios. Proportionate reduction of risk, relative to return is therefore available in almost all portfolios with two or more investments. Eggs (risk) will be in different baskets (investments).

As you may imagine, the correlation between investments varies over time and reassessment of data leading to rebalancing of the investments in the portfolio may be necessary. This is a criticism levelled at MPT but we should remember that theory is often not perfectly replicable in practice.

5. Variance

The expected return from a portfolio is therefore the weighted average of the expected returns of the two investments where the weights are the proportions of the available cash invested in each holding.

This can be seen written mathematically in Making it work 2.1.

Making it work 2.1

R(P) = xRa +(1-x)Rb

Where:

R(P) is the expected return from the portfolio

X is the percentage invested

R(a) is the expected return from 'a'

R(b) is the expected return from 'b'

The portfolio has a quantifiable expected return, therefore. However, what is the probability of the portfolio performing as expected? Markowitz defined the proportionate risk of the two-asset portfolio as 'variance'.

6. What is 'portfolio variance'?

Portfolio variance is a measurement of how the aggregate returns of a number of securities making up a portfolio fluctuate over time. This portfolio variance is calculated using the standard deviations of each security in the portfolio as well as the correlations of each security pair in the portfolio.

portfolio variance
A measurement of how the aggregate returns of a number of securities making up a portfolio fluctuate over time.

Portfolio variance looks at the covariance or correlation coefficients for the investments in the portfolio. Generally speaking, a lower correlation between securities in a portfolio results in a lower portfolio variance.

MPT states that portfolio variance can be reduced by choosing asset classes with a low or negative correlation, as we have seen from diversification.

Portfolio variance is a weighted combination of the individual variances of each of the assets adjusted by their covariances. This means that the overall portfolio variance is lower than a simple weighted average of the individual variances of the stocks in the portfolio.

Variance is often calculated using the standard deviation of the portfolio, which is simply the square root of variance.

Variance measures the variability (or volatility) from an average or mean and volatility is a measure of risk; variance will help an investor determine the risk they might take on when assessing a new investment. A variance value of zero means that all values within a group of numbers are the same and that all variances that are non-zero will be positive numbers (because they have been squared). A large variance indicates that numbers in the set are far from the mean and each other (high volatility), while a small variance indicates little volatility.

7. Covariance – variability of returns around the mean

Covariance is used in portfolio theory to determine what assets to include in the portfolio. Covariance is a statistical measure of the directional relationship between two asset prices. Portfolio theory uses this statistical measurement to reduce the overall risk for a portfolio. A positive covariance means that assets generally move in the same direction. Negative covariance means assets generally move in opposite directions.

Covariance is an important measurement in MPT. MPT attempts to determine an efficient frontier for a mix of assets in a portfolio. The efficient frontier seeks to optimise the maximum return against the degree of risk for all the combined assets in the portfolio. The aim is to select investments for the portfolio that have a lower standard deviation than the standard deviation of the individual assets, thereby helping to reduce the volatility of the portfolio. MPT tries to create an optimal blend of higher-volatility assets with lower-volatility assets and, by diversifying the assets in a portfolio, risk can be reduced but still achieve a positive return.

In the construction of a portfolio, it is important to attempt to reduce overall risk by including assets that have a negative covariance with each other. Analysts use historical price data to determine the measure of covariance between different stocks. This assumes that the same statistical relationship between the asset prices will continue into the future, which is not always the case. By including assets that show a negative covariance, the risk of a portfolio is minimised.

Covariance can be used to maximise diversification in a portfolio by adding investments with a negative covariance to a portfolio which reduces the overall risk. Covariance provides a statistical measurement of the risk for a mix of different investments and is calculated by formulae.

Covariance only measures the directional relationship between two investments. It does not show the strength of the relationship between assets as the correlation coefficient does.

8. Optimum portfolios

Let us consider a portfolio containing just two investments. Markowitz looked to achieve the optimum portfolio from this basis. The two investments generate differing returns in dissimilar environments or market conditions, which we will call scenarios. The returns 'R' from assets 'a' and 'b' are shown in table 2.1 below and are different given scenarios S1 or S2 which could be high inflation against low inflation or high interest rates against a low interest environment etc.

Table 2.1: Returns from assets

	Scenario 1	Scenario 2
Return from investment 'a' (Ra)	20%	10%
Return from investment 'b' (Rb)	10%	20%

The average return of 'a' is therefore 15%. The risk (which can be defined as the range of possible outcomes) is between 10% and 20%. The same figures apply to investment 'b' but you can see that the different scenarios have an impact on which will return greater growth.

So, if the risk is the same and the likely returns are the same, does it matter which investment is chosen?

Markowitz taught that there was an alternative strategy to selecting either investment because their returns do not move in unison (positive correlation) depending on the scenarios present. This relates once again to not putting all eggs in one basket, or all investment money in one holding and produces a portfolio with the same overall return but reduces the risk taken to zero.

9. The optimum portfolio

If both 'a' and 'b' are purchased for inclusion in the portfolio we diversify the risk. If half of the investible cash is used to purchase 'a' and half for 'b', this will still generate the average return of 15% whichever scenario occurs. Due to the opposite nature of returns from 'a' and 'b' being impacted by the two different scenarios, the risk will be reduced to a zero chance of not obtaining the 15% return.

This is an important concept in MPT and, even though it is at a very basic level (Markowitz was operating without computers in 1952), it forms the framework within which to add multiple investment portfolios and forecast a multitude of potential scenarios occurring.

The three significant conclusions that can be derived from Markowitz's two-asset portfolio are as follows:

- Risky investments can be combined into a less risky (or even risk-free) portfolio. This can be viewed as putting 'eggs into different baskets', diversifying the specific risk of each investment.
- Rational investors would not hold one investment exclusively as the return can be maintained but the risk reduced by holding both 'a' and 'b'.
- The risk and return performance data for each individual holding should not be analysed in isolation due to the fact that when one is performing well, the other is performing badly – it can be said that they are inversely correlated.

10. Portfolio theory formulae

Making it work 2.2

There are two main formulae which allow intelligent combining of risks and returns, provided the correlation coefficient is known.

Investment	A	B
Expected return	ra	rb
Risk	σa	σb
Proportion invested	Pa	Pb
Correlation coefficient	Cor ab	

Return of portfolio:

$$r_{a+b} = P_a r_a + P_b r_b$$

Risk of portfolio

$$\sigma_{a+b2} = P_{a2}\sigma_{a2} + P_{b2}\sigma_{b2} + 2P_aP_b\sigma_a\sigma_b Cor_{ab}$$

From these formulae, it can be observed that the return is derived from the combination on a simple weighted average basis, and that the effect of combing risks is attributable to the correlation coefficient.

10.1 The efficient frontier

From the last section, it can be seen that the correlation coefficient is the key to the extent that a portfolio of two investments can achieve diversification of risk. To be able to calculate the proportionate allocation of multiple investments in a portfolio, the risk-return profiles of combinations of investments must be established, given the different correlation coefficients.

10.2 Perfect positive correlation

In this scenario, the two chosen investments move in unison and there is no benefit from diversification. The resulting risk and return performance are the weighted average of the two investment risks and returns.

Figure 2.1: Perfect positive correlation

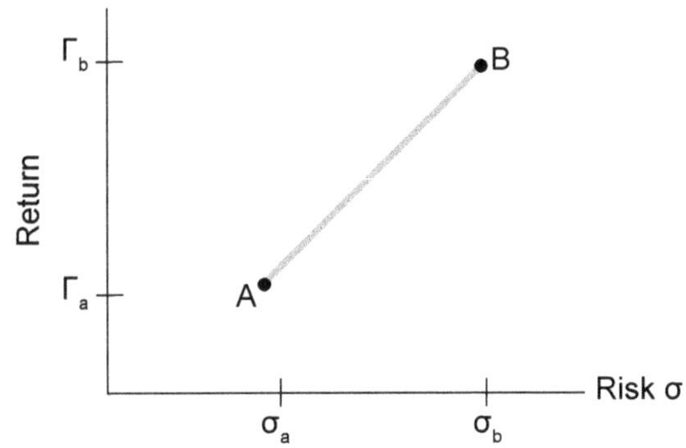

10.3 Perfect negative correlation

As we know that the two investments move in opposite directions to each other, there will be an asset allocation available that completely diversifies away the risk.

Figure 2.2: Perfect negative correlation

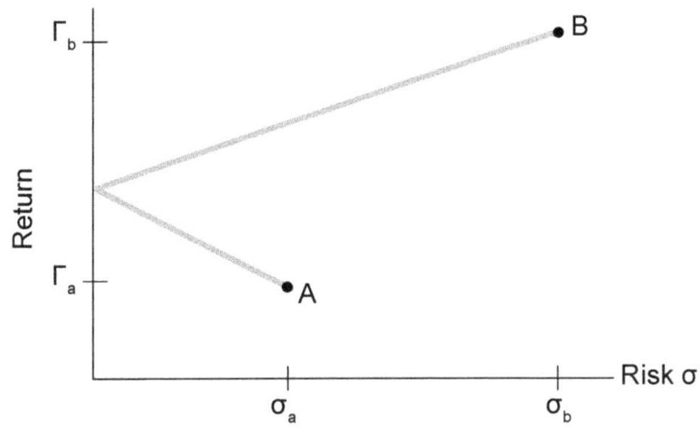

10.4 Imperfect correlation

As previously discussed, it is highly improbable that the two investments are perfectly positively correlated (+1) or perfectly negatively correlated (–1). Imperfect correlation, somewhere between -1 and +1, is the most likely situation.

Figure 2.3: Imperfect correlation

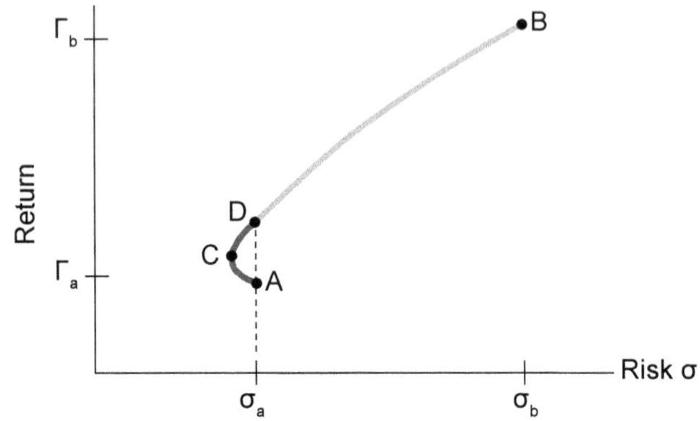

From this graph, it can be seen that some portfolios should be discarded given the rational demand that lower returns for the same risk should not be tolerated. Portfolios on the line A to C have the same risk as C to D but for lower returns and therefore we will only consider portfolios on the curve from C to B as they offer the highest possible returns for the level of risk tolerance.

10.5 Indifference curves

There are many portfolios (combinations of investments A and B) on the curve C to B, so which should be chosen? The answer will be supplied by the risk appetite or utility (satisfaction) of the investor. The investor has no preference for one risk-reward ratio over another on their indifference curve. One can refer to each point on the indifference curve as rendering the same level of utility for the investor. The indifference curve is therefore the locus of various points showing different combinations of A and B providing equal utility to the particular investor.

Figure 2.4: Indifference curves

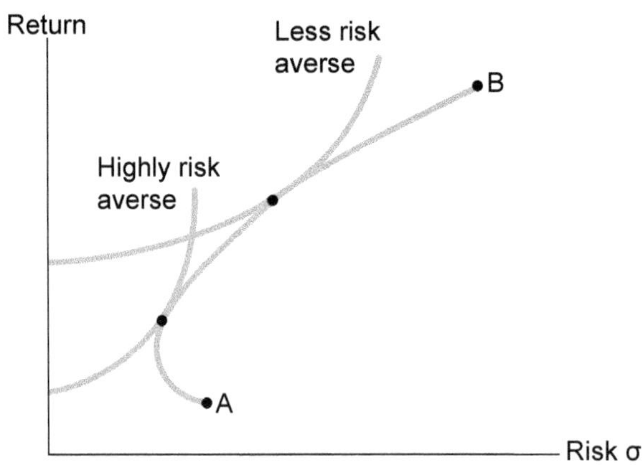

A risk averse investor will prefer to allocate more cash to investment A whereas a less risk averse investor will invest more into B. While this may have been apparent before, it is now measurable with specific allocations to each investment calculated to best suit the investor's indifference curve.

11. Multi-asset portfolios

In efficient capital markets where returns from investments are normally distributed (symmetrical bell curve standard deviation), the rational, risk averse investor can minimise their utility preferences by diversification. Most investors will look to diversify further than the two-asset combination will allow and include numerous investments within a portfolio and therefore the extension of the analysis above must be created for the multi-asset portfolio.

The first point to note is that the possible portfolios now lie within an area rather than on the line from the two-constituent portfolio. The area is constructed by plotting an infinite number of curves similar to AB in the previous diagram.

That said, the rational investor should discard all portfolios that do not appear along the upper boundary between X and Y as, along this frontier, portfolios are efficient in that they produce the highest level of return for the given level of risk. The line X to Y is known as 'the efficient frontier' therefore, as it dominates all other possible portfolios.

Figure 2.5: Multi-asset portfolios

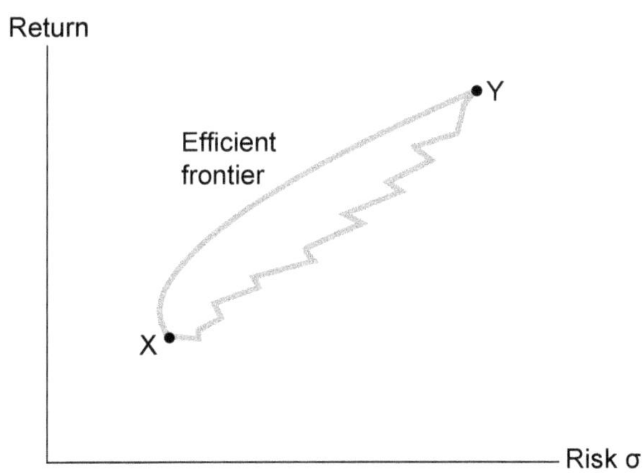

Given the universe of investments that could be included in a portfolio, computer technology is obviously very important in obtaining the possible combinations that could make up the efficient frontier. As mentioned before, Markowitz had proffered the theory in 1952 but the practical application was lengthy and based upon trial and error.

Given that the technology now exists to be able to assess the correlations of securities, how many investments should an investor choose for their portfolio?

We have looked at the benefits of risk reduction through diversification but at what point does the addition of another investment become less attractive as it tends toward the average market risk? Size will be a factor as a small portfolio will incur proportionately higher fees than a large portfolio, in practice. A diversified portfolio of 30 shares has been deemed to diversify away roughly 90% of the average shares' diversifiable risk. Large numbers of holdings do not need to be incorporated into a portfolio therefore and there is little risk reduction in holding 150 shares over a basket of only 50. In fact the costs associated with holding that many investments could start to outweigh the benefits.

12. Risk-free investments

In the preceding paragraphs, the correlation and reward characteristics of risky investments have been assessed and the efficient frontier should be understandable. The risk appetite of different investors has been interpreted by their indifference curves and they will have been able to choose the optimal portfolio for them. Is there a portfolio that all rational investors should prefer?

Not all securities are risky, however. If we assume that developed market governments do not renege on their debt obligations, sovereign fixed income bonds should be redeemable at maturity for the agreed sum and income payments during the period held as they are guaranteed by the state. If the portfolio is constructed from this risk-free investment (rf) and a risky security (rm) then a straight line of possibilities exists (depending on the split of funds between the two components) in much the same way that our two-asset portfolio did before. The difference is that 'rf' makes no contribution to the risk of the portfolio is plotted on a graph, directly on the y axis.

Figure 2.6: Risk free investment

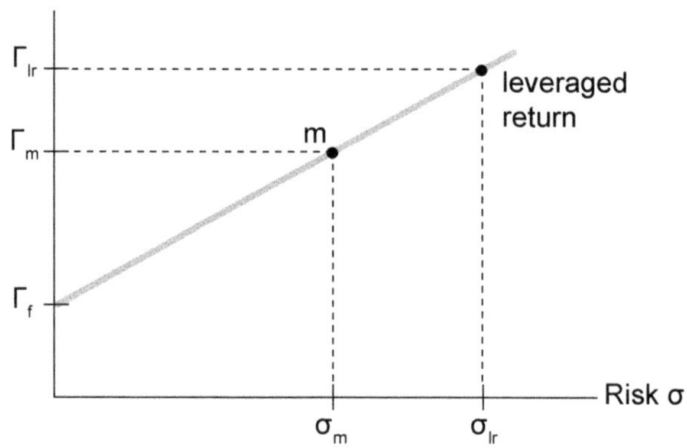

The line is extended from rf through M as theoretically cash could be borrowed at the risk-free rate and invested into the portfolio M giving a geared return further out along the line.

With the inclusion of the possibility of borrowing or lending at the risk-free rate, any point on the line between rf, where it touches the efficient frontier and beyond, is a possible portfolio.

This line is called the capital market line and gives the greatest return at any level of risk. All rational, diversified investors would choose to invest somewhere along this line.

This gives investors the ability to create portfolios with greater returns for their given utility as the capital markets line only touches the efficient frontier at M.

Figure 2.7: Capital markets line

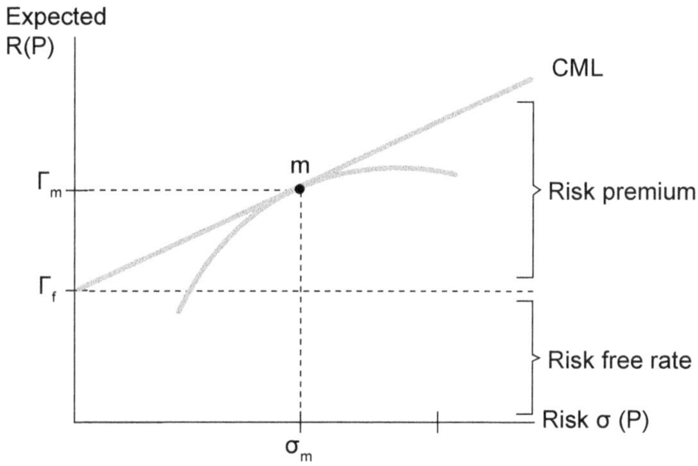

13. The market portfolio

What is portfolio M though? This is called the **market portfolio** and is deemed to hold a proportion of all investments in the market. The assumption is that markets are efficient, as discussed towards the start of this chapter, and therefore the price of all investments will be correctly valued in the market and will be included in the portfolio M.

market portfolio
This is deemed to hold a proportion of all investments in the market.

The market portfolio and risk-free investment are important assumptions in the theory behind the capital asset pricing model.

14. The capital asset pricing model

The **capital asset pricing model** (CAPM) describes the relationship between systematic risk and expected return for assets. CAPM is widely used for the pricing of risky securities, generating expected returns for assets given their risk and calculating costs of capital. You will recall that diversification reduces unsystematic risk and that systematic risk could not be eliminated. In 1964, William Sharpe developed the CAPM that exhibited assumptions in that the efficient portfolio has to be the market portfolio. Based on this, typical investors must keep the market portfolio leveraged or deleveraged to realise their desired risk. This is done with the use of a function of risk named beta (β). The CAPM model states that the expected return of an investment is defined by the rate

capital asset pricing model
Describes the relationship between systematic risk and expected return for assets.

on a risk-free security (such as a government bond) plus a risk premium. If this expected return does not meet or beat the required return, then the investment should not be included in the portfolio.

Table 2.2: Systematic and unsystematic risks

Systematic risk	**Unsystematic risk**
Interest rate changes	Quality of management
Inflation rate changes	Profit margins with companies
Tax rate changes	Supply factors
Economic conditions	Demand factors
Political conditions	Company/investment specific
Undiversifiable	Diversifiable

Systematic or market risk impacts on the economy in general and cannot be eliminated. So a diversified investor, who has constructed a portfolio with the tools discussed so far, will still face some risk and will seek a return commensurate with that level of systematic risk. If the investor has included an investment in a risk-free security such as government bonds, it is possible to calculate the returns achievable and the risks faced.

Making it work 2.3

rm Returns expected from the market portfolio

rf Returns from risk-free investments

β Proportion of funds invested in market portfolio. If the proportion of funds invested in the market portfolio is β – returning rm, then the remainder (1- β) can generate rf.

Using the formulae from Making it work 2.2 on page 16 and rearranged algebraically, the return can be written as:

$$r = r_f + \beta (r_m - r_f)$$

The risk faced by the diversified portfolio investor will only be that of systematic risk and can be written as:

$$\sigma_s = \beta\sigma_m$$

Where

σ_s = the systematic risk in the portfolio, and;

σ_m = the systematic risk in the market portfolio

The risk in the portfolio can be seen to be a function of the proportion of the funds invested in the market portfolio as the other holding, the risk-free security does not contribute any risk. Rearranging this equation will allow us to think of β as the proportion of market risk that the investor is willing to take and can be written as follows:

$$\beta = \frac{\sigma_s}{\sigma_m}$$

Considering these equations, an investor is now able to assess whether a new investment is to be included in the portfolio in place of an existing constituent. If it had the same level of systematic risk, it would be included only if it offered a higher return, and this gives the minimum acceptable return for the investment, based upon its level of systematic risk.

This can be shown graphically with the risk of the market portfolio having a β of 1. This line is called the **securities market line** (SML) which shows the relationship between relative levels of risk (β) and expected returns. The SML is a line drawn on a chart that creates a graphical representation of the CAPM, showing different levels of systematic risk of various investments plotted against the expected return of the whole market. The x-axis of the chart represents risk in terms of beta, and the y-axis of the chart represents expected return. The market risk premium of an investment is determined by where it is plotted on the chart in relation to the SML.

Securities market line
The line which shows the relationship between relative levels of risk (β) and expected returns.

The SML is an investment evaluation tool, therefore, derived from the CAPM, a model that describes risk-return relationships for securities, and is based on the assumptions that investors have to be compensated for both the time value of money (with the inclusion of the risk-free rate) and the corresponding level of risk associated with any investment, referred to as the risk premium.

Making it work 2.4

The formula for plotting the security market line is as follows:

Required Return = Risk Free Rate of Return + (Beta × Market Return – Risk Free Rate of Return)

The SML is employed by investors evaluating an investment for potential inclusion in a portfolio in terms of whether the security offers a higher expected return against its level of risk. When the security is plotted on the SML chart, if it appears above the SML it is considered undervalued because it offers a greater return against its inherent risk. Equally, if the security is plotted below the SML, it is considered overvalued in price because the expected return does not overcome the inherent risk and it should not be included.

The SML is also used in comparing two similar securities offering approximately the same return, in order to determine which of the two securities involves the least amount of market risk in relation to the expected return. Similarly, the SML can be used to compare two investments of equal risk to see which one offers the highest expected return, commensurate with that level of risk.

Figure 2.8: Security market line

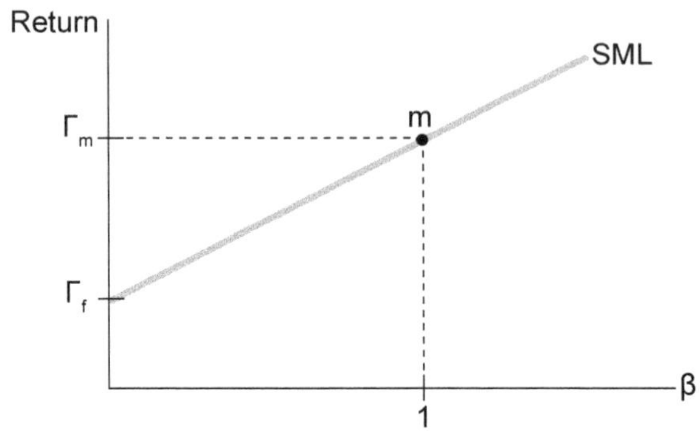

We can therefore observe that for an investment whose risk, relative to the market portfolio, is given by β, the minimum acceptable level of return is given by the CAPM formula:

$r = r_f + \beta(r_m - r_f)$

As an example, if the risk-free rate of return is 3% and the market portfolio is expected to return 12%, a diversified investor would require a return from an investment with a β of 0.5 as follows:

r = 3% + 0.5 × (12%–3%) = 7.5%

If, however, the investor is less risk averse, they may require a return greater than that expected from the market and opt for investments with a β of 1.5. The calculation would therefore give:

r = 3% + 1.5 × (12%–3%) = 16.5%

This latter investor is seeking a higher return and would need to take on high risk in order to have the chance of this higher return. The portfolio should be constructed with a high β (beta factor) to try to achieve this.

All rational investors have portfolios on the CML, relevant to their risk-return preferences. However, the market portfolio and the CML are depicted without reference to the risk-return (indifference) curves of the investors. This result is James Tobin's Separation Theorem. It states that the best blend of risk assets in the market portfolio is determined without considering the risk-return preferences of the investors.

14.1 More about beta

The concept of beta is central to the CAPM and the security market line. As demonstrated above, beta is a relative measure of the systematic risk of an investment. As with correlation coefficients, the sign (+/–) indicates whether the investment's returns move with the market (+) or in the opposite direction (-). The value of the beta defines its relative volatility. From the examples above, we noticed that a beta of 0.5 gave a return that was less than that expected from the market; equally, there would be an expectation than if the market fell, the investment would not fall by as much. A beta of 1 should on average return the same as the market's returns and a beta of greater than 1 will move in the same direction as the market, but to a greater extent. A beta of less than 0 will move in the opposite direction to the market.

Beta factors are calculated for shares quoted on stock markets and are based on the average variability of the returns against those of the market as a whole. This is done graphically with the line of best fit through the data points and the angle of its slope providing the beta figure. This line is known as the security's characteristic line.

The beta from individual components of a portfolio are calculated on the basis of their expected returns and the information can then be used to assess the overall beta of the portfolio, which will be the weighted average of the individual betas. Any proposed new investments can then be assessed against the beta of the portfolio ahead of possible inclusion.

15. Efficient markets hypothesis

This is a theoretical state of the financial markets which states that it is impossible to beat the market due to informational efficiency, which reflects prices at fair value and all known information both priced in and available to all market participants. The theory assumes that shares always trade at fair value, making it impossible for investors to find undervalued company shares. If shares are priced efficiently, then their prices will reflect forecasts of expected benefits from cash flows capitalised at the appropriate discount rates for present purchase. Any new information will be rapidly absorbed into the price to keep it fair.

Evidence suggests that efficient markets can be divided into three potential degrees of efficiency:

15.1 Weak form

All information that can be gleaned from historic price movements has already been incorporated into the current price of the investment. Therefore, it should not be possible to predict future price movements by past price movements. Technical analysis (the use of historical share values, often assimilated on graphs) cannot be used to forecast where excess returns can be achieved. The market will have at least this level of efficiency if an investment pattern of returns cannot be predicted from historical patterns. So prices should have a random walk with variations around the expected return being unpredictable.

15.2 Semi-strong form

This form states that current share prices not only reflect the information available in the weak form but also that they quickly absorb all new publicly available information and that the current price has factored in both market and non-market public information. For instance, if a company releases figures constituting new information, the price will quickly readjust to account for it. This form allows for directors and company insiders to have greater knowledge than the market despite the fact that they will not be able to trade on the information, for instance merger and acquisition knowledge or other private information such as the knowledge of figures and reports ahead of market release. Fundamental analysis cannot be utilised to achieve excess returns.

15.3 Strong form

The strong form of the EMH assumes that all information, both publicly available and private, is reflected in the current share price. This includes market, non-market and insider information, which are all factored in, and alludes to a near-perfect market where excess returns cannot be achieved on a consistent basis. In other words, no investor will ever be able to make better than average returns or outperform the market.

16. Statistical measurement

There are five standard statistical risk measurements used in MPT, two of which we have already discussed, beta and standard deviation, the other three being alpha, R-squared and the Sharpe ratio. These indicators are all intended to help investors determine a potential investment's risk-reward profile.

16.1 Alpha

Often considered the 'active return' on an investment, alpha calculates the performance of an investment against a benchmark such as a market index, since they are considered to represent the market's movement as a whole. The excess returns of a portfolio relative to the return of a benchmark index is the portfolio's alpha.

Alpha measures risk-adjusted return, or the actual return an investment provides in relation to the return you would expect based on its beta; as you will remember, beta measures the security's volatility in relation to its benchmark. If an investment's actual return is higher than its beta, the security has a positive alpha, and if the return is lower it has a negative alpha.

If a portfolio's beta is 1.5 and its benchmark gained 2%, it would be expected to gain 3% (2% × 1.5 = 3%). If the portfolio gained 5%, it would have a positive alpha of 2.

Alpha is most often used for funds and other similar investment types where there is active management. It is often represented as a single number (like 3 or –5), but this refers to a percentage measuring how the portfolio or fund performed compared to the benchmark index (i.e. 3% better or 5% worse).

Using alpha in measuring performance assumes that the portfolio is sufficiently diversified so as to eliminate unsystematic or specific risk. Because alpha represents the performance of a portfolio relative to a benchmark, it is considered to represent the value that a portfolio manager adds to or subtracts from its return. Put simply, alpha is the return on an investment that is not a result of general movement in the market. An alpha of 0 would indicate that the portfolio or fund is tracking in line with the benchmark index and that the portfolio manager has not added or lost any value.

16.2 Sharpe ratio

The Sharpe ratio uses total portfolio risk or standard deviation, to measure a fund or portfolio's risk-adjusted returns. Developed by Nobel Laureate William Sharpe, this measure quantifies a portfolio's return in excess of a benchmark and is appropriate where the portfolio represents the investor's full set of investments. The higher a fund or portfolio's Sharpe ratio, the better its returns have been relative to the risk it has taken on. Because it uses standard deviation, the Sharpe ratio can be used to compare risk-adjusted returns across all investment categories.

Worked example 2.1

$$\text{Sharpe ratio} = \frac{r_p - r_f}{\sigma_p}$$

Where:

rp = portfolio return

rf = risk free return for the same period

σp = portfolio risk (standard deviation of the portfolio returns)

Example

Which of the two portfolios is performing better from the risk reward basis during a period where the risk-free rate was 4%?

Portfolio	*Return*	*Total risk*
A	18	20
B	22	30

16.3 R-squared

R-squared measures the relationship between a portfolio and its benchmark. It can be thought of as a percentage from 1 to 100.

R-squared is not a measure of the performance of a portfolio. A well-performing portfolio can have a very low R-squared. It is purely a measure of the correlation of the portfolio's returns to that of the benchmark's returns. If an investor requires a portfolio that moves like the benchmark, that portfolio would have a need for a high R-squared. Conversely, if the investor requires a portfolio that doesn't move at all like the benchmark, this would have a low R-squared figure.

General ranges for R-squared

A generated R-squared figure between 70 and 100% would indicate good correlation between the portfolio's return and the benchmark's return, 40–70% would be an average correlation between the portfolio's return and the benchmark's return with a figure of less than 40% indicates low correlation between the portfolio's return and that of the benchmark's.

An R-squared figure of 100 indicates that all movements of a portfolio can be explained by movements in the benchmark. Thus, portfolios that invest only in FTSE 100 shares will have an R-squared very close to 100. Conversely, a low R-squared indicates that very few of the portfolio's movements can be explained by movements in its benchmark index. An R-squared measure of 30, for example, means that only 30% of the portfolio's movements can be explained by movements in the benchmark index.

Chapter summary

- MPT shows that, when risks are spread across multiple investment holdings, the risk of potential loss can be minimised without necessarily reducing the returns from a portfolio.
- In efficient capital markets where returns from investments are normally distributed, the rational, risk averse investor can minimise their utility preferences by diversification.
- The market portfolio and risk-free investment are important assumptions in the theory behind the capital asset pricing model.
- The securities market line is an investment evaluation tool derived from the capital asset pricing model, a model that describes risk-return relationships for securities.
- Evidence suggests that efficient markets can be divided into three potential degrees of efficiency: weak form, semi-strong form and strong form.

Part two

Chapter three
Fund structures and legal vehicles

Chapter four
The roles of the fund manager, fund administrator and fund's governing body

Chapter five
Offshore fund administration

Chapter six
Fund accounting

Chapter seven
Net asset valuations

Chapter eight
The role of safekeeping assets

Fund administration and regulation

Overview

This part examines how an investment fund comes together from the spark of an idea through to expertise and structuring. In considering this, the roles of the key principals to any fund are explored. These include the fund manager, the fund administrator and the fund's governing body (such as its board of directors). This part also breaks down the key components of the fund administrator's role. Finally, the over-arching concept of governance is considered, including its growing place in fund administration practice.

Learning outcomes

At the end of this part, you will be able to:

- Identify a number of legal vehicles and their key characteristics
- Identify a number of fund structures and their key characteristics

- Understand the key components when defining a fund's structure
- Understand who and what a fund's governing body, fund manager and fund administrator is
- Consider safeguards in place to regulate the fund's governing body, fund manager and fund administrator and manage conflicts of interest
- Understand the components that make up investment funds
- Know the key parties to the fund and the administrator's role in their operation
- Understand different types of funds
- Understand the differences between a fund accountant and a fund administrator
- Understand the process involved in the production of fund accounts
- Consider how a Net Asset Valuation is produced
- Understand the role the Administrator plays in Net Asset Valuation production
- Understand the potential conflicts of interest and their correlation to Net Asset Valuation
- Understand whose role it is to safeguard assets
- Know the different titles used and how their responsibilities change, and the obligations and oversight that they need in place to ensure that the assets within a fund are safe-guarded
- Explore the provisions in different jurisdictions as to requirements for the safeguarding of assets

Chapter three
Fund structures and legal vehicles

List of topics

1. Investment objective – what does the fund aim to do?
2. Management structure – who will deliver the investment objective?
3. Investor type – who is the fund marketed/aimed at?
4. Legal fund structures
5. By return of capital and/or income
6. By equity or debt interests
7. Upfront or commitment basis
8. Open- or closed-ended
9. Closed-ended fund raising
10. Leveraged or unleveraged
11. Private or public funds
12. Scrutiny and investor protection
13. Custodians
14. Key documents
15. Consolidated structures
16. Competing with onshore jurisdictions
17. Challenges to structure

Introduction

Almost as important as investor capital, the structure of the fund is key both to its success and its attractiveness. As it is so fundamental to success, the structure of the fund is determined very early on in the life of the fund.

Fund structuring is based upon key factors including:

- the specific transaction objectives to be achieved;
- the targeted investor base;

- accounting considerations;
- tax considerations;
- regulatory considerations; and
- commercial considerations.

Figure 3.1: Example of ultimate fund structure

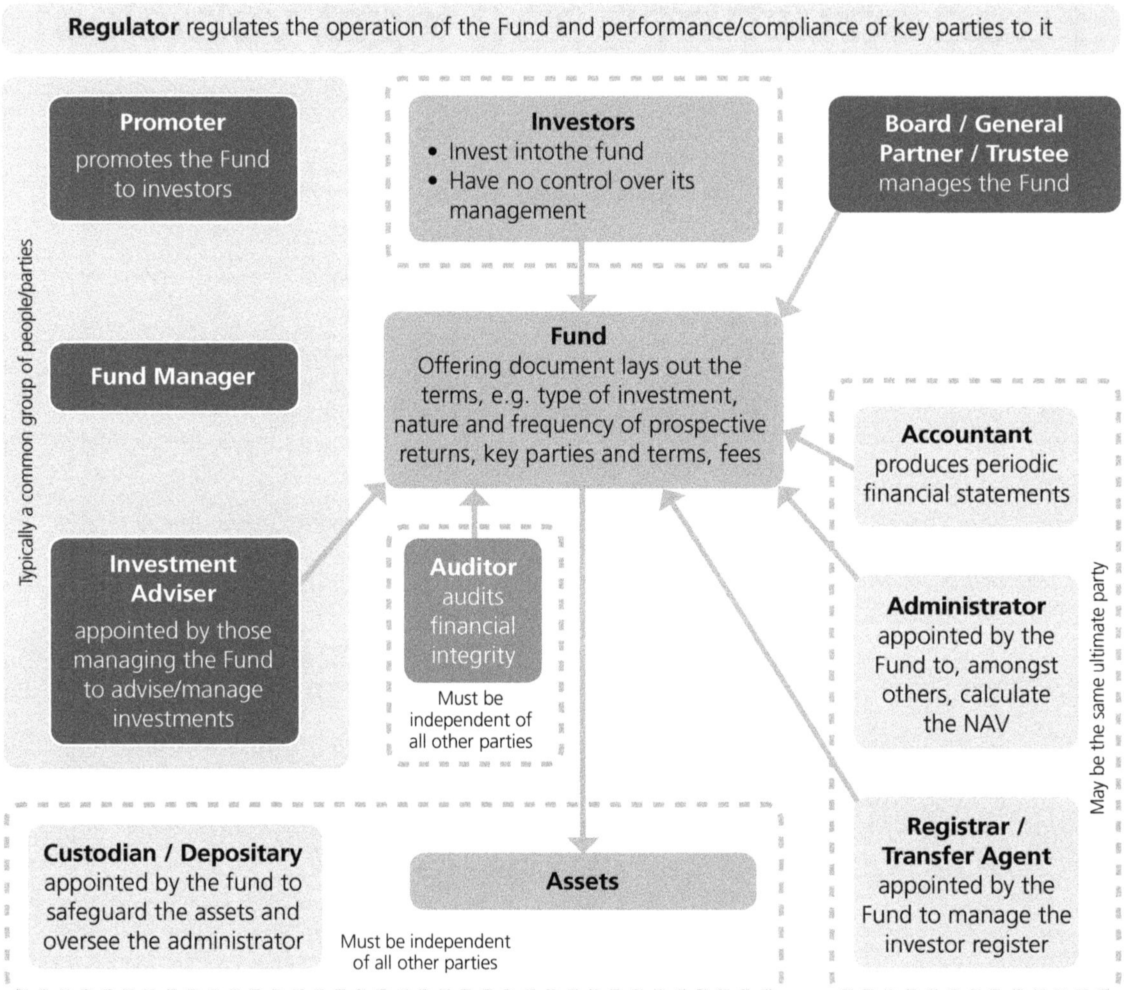

Structuring, then, is a jigsaw puzzle, with each of its component parts being as important as one another. This chapter will consider the following key building blocks:

- investment objective;
- management structure;
- investor type;

- legal structure;
- equity and debt interests;
- leverage;
- levels of scrutiny and investor protection; and
- other fees.

How the building blocks piece together will determine the ultimate fund structure.

1. Investment objective – what does the fund aim to do?

Every fund structure starts with an idea, the concept that investors will buy into. This premise, whatever it may be, will tend to be classified into one of a number of generic categories, including:

1.1 Equity

These are funds that invest in stocks (equity securities).

The investment premise of each fund may be different, but the ultimate weighting of investment in stocks will remain. Typically, **equity funds** have been longer term with the intention of capital growth, though dividends (income) have been an important source of total return.

equity funds
Funds that invest in stocks (equity securities).

1.2 Private equity

These are funds that invest in the equity securities and debt of operating companies that are not publicly traded on a stock exchange.

Private equity funds seek to provide working capital to their target investments to nurture expansion, new product development or restructuring of the company's operations, management or ownership. Private equity funds will typically target businesses:

private equity funds
Funds that invest in the equity securities and debt of operating companies that are not publicly traded on a stock exchange.

- already in distress or those that without clear management are destined to find themselves in distressed positions;
- that are cash generative and which could stand alone or become the anchor business in a series of acquisitions or otherwise an add-on to other acquisitions;
- that with growth capital can expand into new markets, new products etc;
- in need of additional financing through offering mezzanine capital (a form of junior debt that ranks above the common equity), where it has exhausted traditional lending routes (e.g. banks); or
- in need of venture capital (see below).

1.3 Venture capital

venture capital funds
Funds that invest into private companies with a view to financing and managing their growth, improvement, etc.

Similar to private equity, **venture capital funds** invest into private companies with a view to financing and managing their growth, improvement etc. Target businesses will typically be those in their infancy but identified as early-stage, emerging firms. They have also typically tended to be those in more innovative areas of trade, such as technology businesses, whether social media or technology intended for more scientific use.

The nature of all of these target businesses means that they present a higher risk of failure than other businesses and so a venture capital firm will invest on the basis of high returns in the event of success, ordinarily driven through an 'exit' event, such as an initial public offering or a merger and acquisition (trade sale).

1.4 Real estate

Though private equity and venture capital funds may invest in real estate, real estate is typically viewed as an asset class in its own right, due to the varying nature of investment premises that funds holding real estate may adopt.

real estate
Can include many different types of property for many different purposes, such as residential, office space and commercial property as well as funds investing in care homes or student accommodation etc.

Real estate can include many different types of property for many different purposes, such as residential, office space and commercial property as well as funds investing in care homes or student accommodation etc.

Varied too may be the fund's purpose when dealing with real estate, including construction (funding the development of the properties), buying and owning property with a view to generating rental income or the sale of property for the purpose of capital appreciation and return. A fund may intend to deal with the real estate through all or a combination of those phases.

1.5 Infrastructure

As governments face more competition for state funds but increasing demand for public services, they have looked to private sources of funding to participate in the building and maintenance of numerous public facilities, such as schools, prisons, hospitals and transport infrastructure. A number of infrastructure funds have developed in the wake of that requirement, able to provide funding (whether alone or part of consortia) and facilities management during the construction and operation of those assets.

Due to the long-term nature of the assets held, the purpose of infrastructure funds is to provide long-term income yield through dividends rather than focusing on capital return, though some do retain an objective of returning some capital return at the end of the contract term for those assets with remaining economic lives ahead of them.

A number of infrastructure funds exist today, with the earlier ones tending to be more focused on typical public infrastructure whilst later funds have developed into areas of renewable energies, in recognition of increasing government interest in that area.

1.6 Esoteric

This is a generic name for those investment premises that sit outside of the norm, such as litigation funds and forestry funds. As the asset classes are not those long trodden by investment funds, the terms of the investment objective and how investors realise returns tend to be more fluid. As a result, the prospective investor base tends to be smaller and somewhat limited to those with an interest in that area or with control over a large fund (institutional investors) who may invest a proportion of monies available to them in more **esoteric** offerings.

esoteric
An unusual and out of the ordinary asset class for a fund.

The above are not exhaustive but are illustrative of the first question relevant when structuring any fund – that is, what does the fund aim to do? This purpose will be established by a core group of people that we typically name the promoter.

The first stage of the fund for the promoter is to gauge interest, which it will typically achieve through a round of meetings or roadshows with prospective investors at which it will unveil its 'deck'. The deck is a brief presentation setting out what the investment objective is, who will manage it and over what timeframe and how investor returns might be driven. These are informal conversations but assist the promoter in gauging interest for their concept and its feasibility for continuing.

2. Management structure – who will deliver the investment objective?

Often the promoter and the fund manager will be the same group of people. This is so because an idea requires the people with the relevant skills and access to investor funding to drive it. Ultimately it is the people with the know-how and ability to make it happen that investors are buying into rather than the idea itself.

When considering the manager, investors will have specific regard to:

- the track record of the manager;
- the track record of its key people;
- proposed management and performance fees; and
- whether the manager will have 'skin in the game'.

2.1 Track record

Track record is a key piece of the structuring puzzle, with investors more likely to invest in a fund managed by someone with a good history of success and returns. This doesn't stop new managers from successfully raising funds, but may have an impact both on the regulatory appetite in the preferred jurisdiction of the fund and the management and performance fees a manager can command.

We live in a highly regulated environment, with both onshore and offshore fund jurisdictions globally putting in place ever greater levels of investor protection in the form of investment fund and fund management regulation.

The Global Financial Crisis of 2007/2008, threw a global spotlight on the level of risk some were willing to take to gain great rewards amidst a culture that was viewed by many as placing those rewards above the protection of their customers (e.g. investors). Many commentators have likened this risk-taking attitude to the roll of a dice at the blackjack table and so as economies and governments have recovered and continue to recover from this crisis, greater scrutiny has been placed on the controls governing third party management of people's money.

Applications to be approved as fund promoters have, accordingly, become more scrutinised, with regulators requiring sight of the skills and experience of the fund promoter demonstrated in a tangible way, such as financial results, investor return profiles and successfully completed investment projects.

For example, the Guernsey Financial Services Commission 'regards the 'Promoter' of a fund as the party ultimately responsible for its success. The Commission welcomes approaches from promoters of the first rank who have a favourable track record in the establishment and/or management of investment funds.' Whilst other jurisdictions do not state it so plainly as this, this treatment of the promoter/manager as being ultimately responsible for the fund rings true.

Demonstrating track record may be through a combination both of the fund manager's track record and that of its individual principles, the latter becoming more important where a fund manager has not been in existence very long and so has little or no ostensible track record to declare.

From an investor perspective, the track record of the individual people can often be more important than that of the manager as a whole. Though somewhat of a cliché, it is so often true that people buy into people.

2.2 Management and performance fees structures

The manager gets paid through management and performance fees.

- A management fee is a charge levied by an investment manager for managing an investment fund. The management fee is intended to compensate the managers for their time and expertise for selecting fund assets and managing the portfolio. It can also include other items such as investor relations expenses and the administration costs of the fund.
- Management fee structures vary from fund to fund, but they are typically based on a percentage of assets under management (AUM). For example, a mutual fund's management fee could be stated as 0.5% of AUM.
- A performance fee is a payment made to a fund manager for generating positive returns. The performance fee is generally calculated as a percentage of investment profits, often both realised and unrealised.

- The basic rationale for performance fees is that they align the interests of fund managers and their investors, and are an incentive for fund managers to generate positive returns.
- Traditionally, a '2 and 20' annual fee structure has been fairly typical. This means a management fee of 2% of the fund's net asset value and a performance fee of 20% of the fund's profits.
- Critics of performance fees, including Warren Buffett, opine that the skewed structure of performance fees – where managers share in the funds' profits but not in their losses – only tempts fund managers to take inordinate risks to generate high returns.

The level of fees payable is typically driven by a combination of factors:

- the type of fund in question, as market comparisons establish the range of fees investors anticipate to pay;
- the level of activity required to manage a portfolio; and
- as stated above, who the manager is will have an effect on where the fees for the manager are pitched.

2.3 'Skin in the game'

Whilst the performance fee is said to align the interests of the manager to those of investors to some degree, investors may also look to see that the manager has itself invested in the fund. This helps to strengthen that alignment of interests, as the manager risks losing that portion of invested capital as well as sharing in any gains.

Test yourself 3.1

Who is responsible for the day-to-day management of the fund if it is:

1 a company

2 a unit trust

3 a limited partnership

3. Investor type – who is the fund marketed/aimed at?

Understanding the intended investor is key for a number of reasons, which include:

- **Their level of sophistication** – Protection of investor law and regulation lies at the heart of fund structuring, with higher levels of protection in place for those less able to access investment advice or to weather the risk of financial losses. As a result, more stringent rules will be placed on a fund aimed at less sophisticated investors, generally requiring less risky investment objectives and means of realising them. This may become particularly apparent through the types of fund eligible for use for such investors and the high levels of regulation and continuing obligations required of them.

- **Legal obligations** – Many fund investors are not natural persons but instead are legal or other entities investing as part of structured investment parameters. As a result, these investors may have restrictions placed on them as to the type of investments they may make, e.g. quoted versus non-quoted investments, or other forms of prescription.
- **Geographical location** – Where the investor is from will have a bearing on the structuring of funds including from a tax efficiency perspective but also from a stance of recognition, with certain legal forms of entity being favoured over others dependent upon the geographic origins of the investor.
- **Religious codes** – Funds may be structured such that they follow certain rules laid down by religious followings. The most prevalent example is Islamic financing, which typically follow the Sharia code, barring investors from generating certain types of profit, from investing in certain areas (e.g. gambling) and may require a separate committee to oversee the fund's adherence to the code.

3.1 Investor sophistication

Fund investors are generally divided into three generic categories.

- **Retail** – Individual investors who buy and sell securities for their personal account, and not for another company or organisation.

  Retail investors typically trade in much smaller amounts than institutional investors and, as such, do not exert much, if any, control over corporate decisions.

  Funds targeting retail investment are less common in offshore markets. Due to the high level of investor protection they are afforded in those jurisdictions they are regulated by, whether through domicile or promotion into that jurisdiction, and the relatively low amounts of money being invested by retail investors, the obstacles to entry are often deemed too high to make a structure feasible.

  Retail investors may invest into many different types of funds, however often they will be prohibited from doing so unless they have received targeted investment advice warning them of the potential risks as well as explaining the prospective rewards resulting in making an investment. Typically, therefore, much retail investing occurs through broker advisery accounts and independent financial advisers (IFAs).

  In this way, it is the IFA who takes on the majority of the investor protection measures, such as a requirement to understand the general circumstances of the investor, their risk attitude and their ability to bear losses.

For many retail investors, the minimum subscription amounts mandated by investment funds create a barrier to entry, thus effectively preventing retail investment in most cases. Even if the minimum subscriptions amount can be met, often this represents a large proportion of personal wealth, making investment too risky. One answer is to invest in a clubbed manner, through various routes, but perhaps the most utilised method to enter a number of investments in a clubbed manner is through pension, insurance and investment specialists. These specialists offer products directly to retail investors based upon risk parameters and then utilise the combined fire-power to take positions in various investment types, including investment funds, thus delivering a diversified pool of investments and spreading risk.

- **Institutional** – An institutional investor is a non-bank person or organisation that trades securities in large enough share quantities or currency amounts that it qualifies for preferential treatment and lower commissions. Institutional investors face fewer protective regulations because it is assumed they are more knowledgeable and better able to protect themselves. Examples of institutional investors include pension funds and life insurance companies.
- **Sophisticated** – Is a type of investor who is deemed to have sufficient investing experience and knowledge to weigh the risks and merits of an investment opportunity.

4. Legal fund structures

Legal structuring is a combination of factors, including:

- choice of entity type(s);
- efficiency of taxation;
- nature of return required (capital, income or both); and
- the structure of the return (equity, debt or both).

4.1 Choice of entity type

Invariably, all fund structures are made up of a combination of the same core building blocks (by whatever legal name known), these being:

- companies;
- partnerships; and
- unit trusts.

4.2 Companies

Companies are distinct from other entity types as under domestic laws they automatically gain legal personality and, in the absence of exemption, are opaque for taxation purposes.

Typical company types and their characteristics

Companies can be broken down into the following types:

- **Limited liability**

  Fund structuring typically favours companies with limited liability.

  Investors favour a limited liability structure, as it provides them with certainty as to the amount of capital they will need to pay in to the fund and thus the extent of their liability (maximum financial outlay) to the fund.

  Other company types are available, such as those with unlimited liability (where the maximum financial outlay is not limited) or those limited by guarantee of its members (where the members guarantee financial outlay or assistance in defined terms). It is rarer to find these company types in fund structures.

- **Non-cellular**

  Whilst shareholder rights can be carved out to determine rights to capital and/or income and the priority in which they will be paid out, a non-cellular company will always have a single pool of assets over which people may seek to assert certain rights and obligations. This means that, as well as investors, other parties can obtain rights in respect of the entire asset pool, such as a lending institution or other creditors.

Figure 3.2: Non-cellular company structure

- **Cell companies**

  The use of cellular structures brought about an innovative new way to utilise companies when structuring funds. Since their introduction in Guernsey in the late 1990s, a number of offshore jurisdictions have followed suit introducing their own equivalent legislation.

  Cell companies have allowed a single over-arching legal structure to be created, below which multiple segregated pools of assets may exist, each one capable of being classified as a fund.

The ability to have multiple funds under management in one overriding structure existed prior to cellular companies through the use of unit trusts, but its creation added another weapon in the arsenal. For those countries and/or investors more familiar with a corporate structure, a cellular company provides that familiarity whilst allowing a flexibility not available in standard corporate structures.

The attraction of cellular companies is that they create a legally recognised form of non-recourse between their individual cells, whereby the assets of one cell are segregated from, and so are legally distinct from, those of the core and all other cells. In this way, the assets of one cell are ring-fenced from those of the other cells.

Cellular companies now exist in two distinct forms, being those with unincorporated cells (e.g. the protected cell company/segregated portfolio company) and those with incorporated cells (e.g. the incorporated cell company).

Unincorporated cells

In the case of both protected cell companies (e.g. Guernsey) or segregated portfolio companies (e.g. Cayman), there is one legal entity in law, being the protected cell company (PCC) or segregated portfolio company (SPC) itself (referred to as the core). Protected cells or portfolios created within the legal entity are not in themselves incorporated and so do not gain their own separate legal identity.

Figure 3.3: Cellular company structure

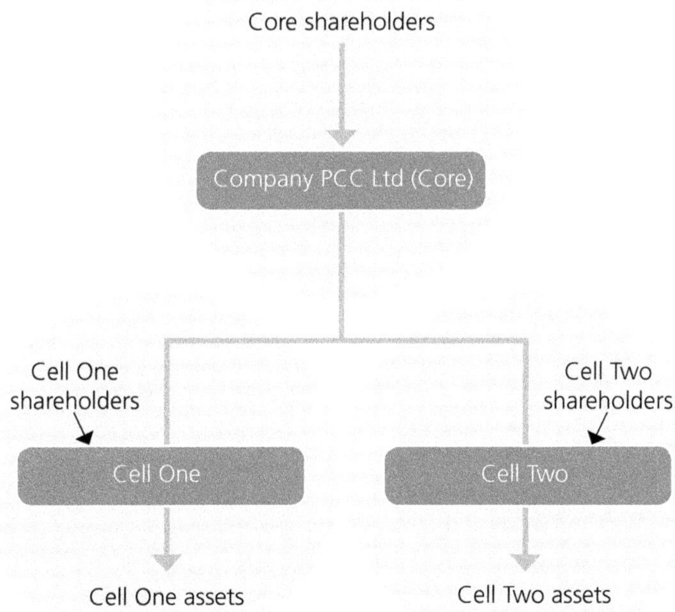

Features of a PCC/SPC include:

- A common board for both the core and all of its cells.
- Cells within the same structure cannot transact with one another.
- Each cell has limited recourse, meaning that a creditor or other party with an interest in one cell may only seek to perfect that interest in respect of that cell. There is no recourse to any other cell within the structure nor to assets of the core.

Incorporated cell companies

Though less used for investment fund purposes, the Companies (Guernsey) Law 2008 also permits cellular companies to be formed whereby each of the cells created thereunder are incorporated and thus gain their own separate legal identity. Malta also has a form of incorporated cell company (ICC), the société d'investissement à capital variable (SICAV).

In many respects, an ICC operates and looks like a PCC, however its main differences are:

- cells are separately incorporated and so gain their own legal personality;
- incorporated cells may transact directly with other incorporated cells within the same ICC; and
- incorporated cells may be incorporated as non-cellular entities in their own right whilst still sitting within the umbrella of the incorporated cell company.

Figure 3.4: Cellular company structure

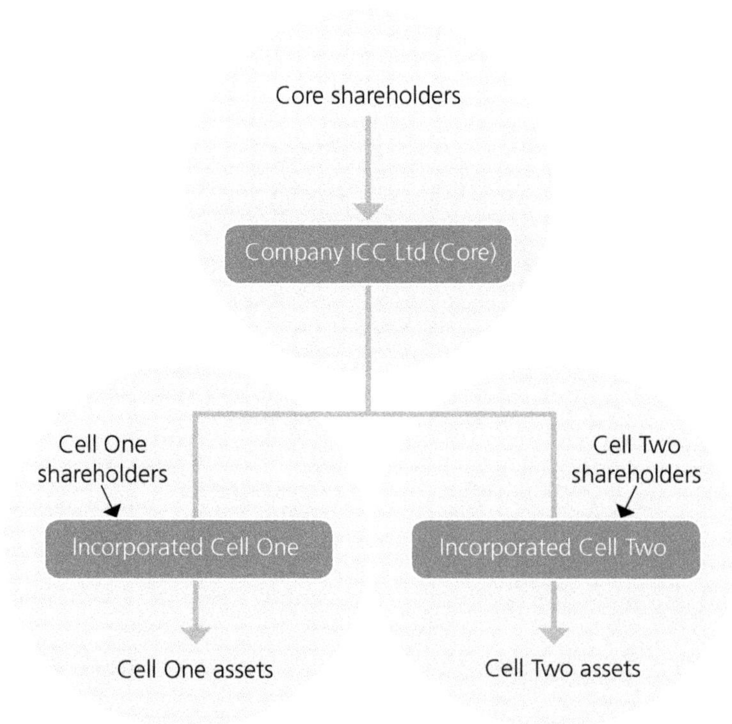

The core

Common throughout all cellular entities is the concept of the core, that being the part of the legal entity distinct from its segregated/protected cells.

The core governs both the company and all cells created thereunder and, in legislation, the board of the company is required also to be the board of the cells.

Formation

Cellular companies enjoy success in several offshore jurisdictions including Guernsey, Cayman, Mauritius and BVI. In most cases, specific legislation controls the circumstances in which they may be formed making them less accessible than non-cellular forms of company. However, as long as the purpose of formation is sound, permission will generally be granted. Once formed, it is the board who determines which segregated cells exist within that structure and its responsibility to manage them in the best interests of the company.

- Guernsey PCCs may only be formed with the consent of the Guernsey Financial Services Commission and for specific purposes, which includes authorisation or registration as a collective investment scheme. (Section 437, Companies (Guernsey) Law 2008).
- Similarly, applications to form Mauritius PCCs must be submitted to the Financial Services Commission in accordance with the requirements of the Protected Cell Company Act 1999, the Companies Act 2001 and the Financial Services Act 2007.
- The creation of Caymans SPCs is governed by Part XIV of the Companies Law of the Cayman Islands. Since 2002, SPCs have been capable of being utilised for mutual fund structures.

Flexibility

Ultimately, cellular companies can afford a greater level of flexibility than non-cellular companies in a number of ways:

- The core will typically be owned by the manager, which generally will be issued with management shares or similar, granting core shareholders voting rights but no rights to share in the profits. The core can create value of its own, but this is rare in fund structures, with the costs of the core being met by its underlying cells on a pro-rata or other agreed basis because it does not generate cash itself.
- Cells will then issue cellular shares, granting various rights only in respect of that cell and, to the extent desired, the core. As a result, investors in one cell do not have to gain rights to determine the outcome of matters in relation to other cells or in relation to the overall management of the structure through the core.
- Cells can be created as different funds. Dependent upon the fund's overriding scheme documents, each cell could, in theory, be created for entirely different purposes for different asset classes with varying portfolio requirements, restrictions etc.

- Whilst each cell will typically be required to register and to be approved as funds by their respective regulator, some efficiencies of timescale may be available to cellular structures creating new funds with similar investment and other parameters as the regulator will be familiar with the fund premise and the documentation required to be published by the fund may be easily replicated and amended on a rolling basis.
- As the prevalence of manager-led fund regulation increases globally, this requirement to separately register each fund may fall away entirely, making a cellular company a very quick way of creating new funds, as incorporation times are eliminated; a cell may be created through a board resolution alone.
- The costs of rolling out multiple funds within one legal structure may be significantly reduced when compared to the costs of creating each fund as a separate legal structure. Commonality may be achieved through hiring the same third party service providers across the entire structure, which should result in cost savings. The costs of maintaining legal standing with the company's registrar and of meeting regulatory fees should also be reduced. Ultimately this can be delivered to investors in the form of a lower total expense ratio (TER), which may either lessen the effect of dilution on profits that the fund's expenses have or may allow funds to become feasible despite a lesser level of investment (i.e. lower AUM) than a standalone structure may have required.

4.3 Partnerships

Legal forms of partnerships are frequently used in private equity and hedge fund structures but they may also form part of the structuring of many different types of funds, including infrastructure funds.

There are generally two forms of partnerships available in fund structuring, by whatsoever name called:

- **Limited partnerships (LP)**
- **Limited liability partnerships (LLP)**

On the face of it, the two can appear very similar and so the differences can often come down to subtle nuances. Some jurisdictions recognise only one form of partnership, typically the LP, whilst others will recognise both forms of partnership, formed under different legislation and thus with differing legal characteristics.

Limited partnerships

LPs are a long-recognised legal structure, and have been replicated, to a greater or lesser degree, in multiple jurisdictions, such as:

- Guernsey's limited partnerships are formed in accordance with The Limited Partnerships (Guernsey) Law, 1995. Whilst this law has remained relatively untouched since then, Guernsey anticipates a new limited partnership law in the near future to bring concepts more in line with those established by the companies law.

  - The Cayman Islands enacted the Exempted Limited Partnership Law, 2014, repealing all previous law in this area. The aim of the 2014 law is to appeal to private equity and other investment funds and goes some way towards bridging the gap between companies and partnerships by adopting many of the concepts used in Cayman's companies law.
  - Mauritius introduced the Limited Partnership (LP) Act 2011, allowing global funds to be structured in Mauritius without the need for complex master-feeder structures.
  - Jersey limited partnerships are formed in accordance with The Limited Partnerships (Jersey) Law, 1994 and, subject to the consent of the Jersey Financial Services Commission, are commonly used in structuring collective investment schemes.
  - In the BVI, limited partnerships are formed in accordance with Part VI of The Partnership Act, 1996.
  - Malta has enacted a partnership en commandite (LP).

Of course, onshore solutions do also exist:

- The United Kingdom has long recognised the limited partnership, which is presently governed by the Limited Partnerships Act 1907.
- Luxembourg offers two limited partnership structures:
  - Société en commandite par actions (SCA or Lux LP) with legal personality; and
  - Société en commandite special (SCSp or Lux SLP) without legal personality.
- Both have been purposely targeted at alternative investments, including private equity and venture capital, as Luxembourg continues to dominate the EU onshore market.
- The USA has both a LP and a limited liability limited partnership (LLLP).

The main features of limited partnerships are:

- Generally they are 'pass through' entities from a tax perspective, resulting in income being attributed to individual limited partners personally. This is not true of all offshore jurisdictions, however, e.g. Malta, where its LP structure is taxable as if it were a company.
- The general partner assumes responsibility for the operations of the fund and, in so doing, takes on unlimited liability.
- Limited partners have no responsibility for the operations of the fund but can make investments into the partnership and are liable only for their paid-in or committed amounts.
- As a rule, a general/limited partnership must be formed by at least two persons, comprising of one general partner (GP) and one LP, but can have multiple GPs and many LPs.

Figure 3.5: Basic limited partnership structure

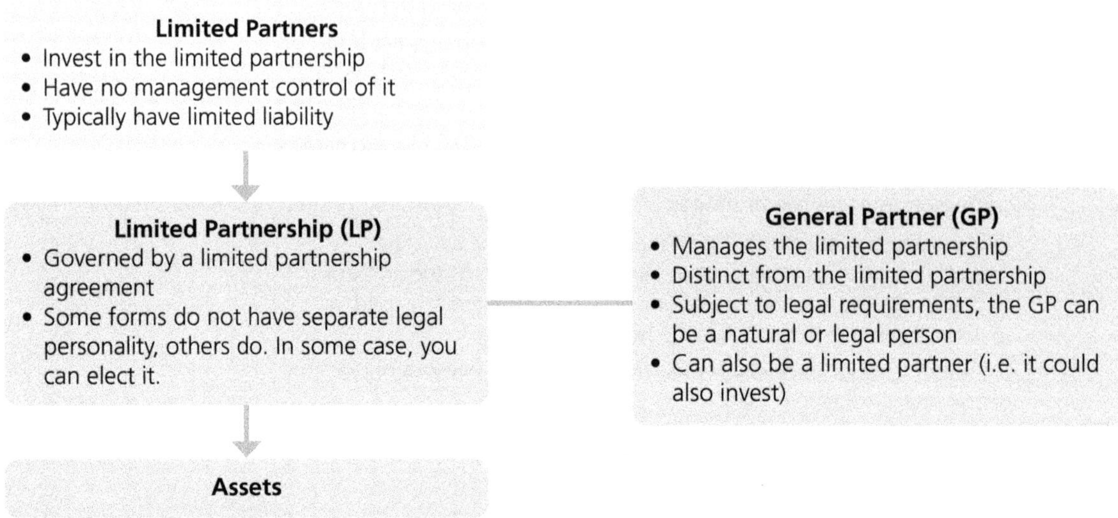

Limited liability partnerships

LLPs are a newer form of partnership aiming to take the best bits of both companies and limited partnerships to form a hybrid structure.

Whilst the UK and the US have utilised LLP structures for some time, it is taking offshore jurisdictions longer to adopt similar structures and indeed some, such as Malta, do not have an equivalent structure at all at this point in time.

LLP structures are not particularly common in fund structures and it remains to be seen whether this position will change.

4.4 Trusts

Unit trusts have long been utilised in fund structuring, due to their simplicity and the flexibility of the structure. As the name implies, a unit trust is a trust and so requires a trustee to be appointed. That trustee will have responsibility for the management of the unit trust and for the ownership of the trust's assets.

Investors in a unit trust structure typically receive units and thus become unitholders. Their rights as unitholders will derive from the trust deed, to which they adhere through an adherence agreement, and the application form, which binds them to the scheme particulars.

Figure 3.6: Basic unit trust structure

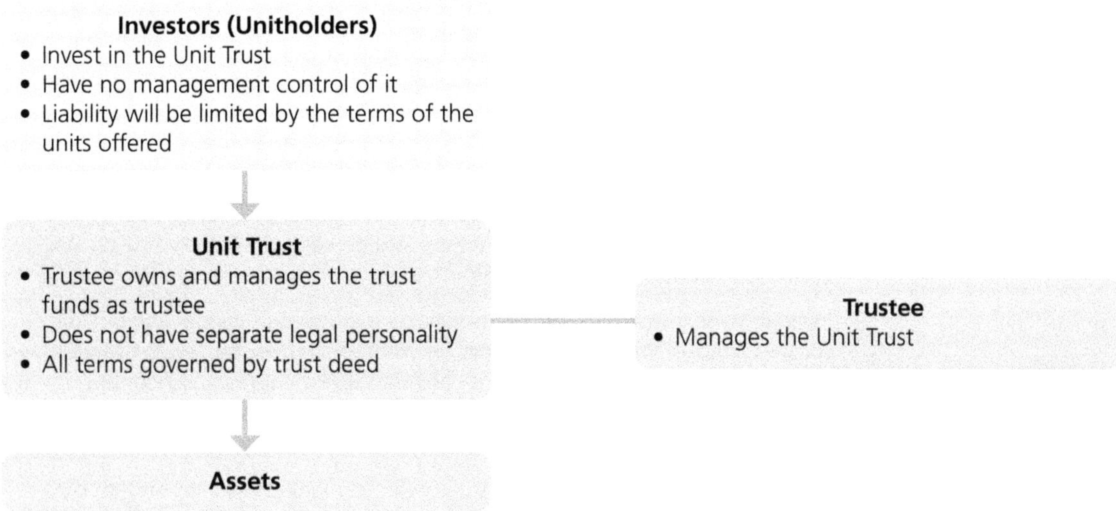

Like a cellular corporate structure, the trustee may establish sub-funds within a single unit trust by issuing units in the name of the specific sub-fund. In order to prevent the assets of one sub-fund being used to discharge the outstanding liabilities of another, the trust deed and the subscription agreement will ensure their legal segregation by the inclusion of non-recourse language. However, as the basis of non-recourse is one between the trustee and its unitholders, rather than being enshrined in law (as for PCCs and ICCs), the trustee will need to take care when contracting with third parties to ensure that specific non-recourse provisions are included to preserve the integrity of each sub-fund as distinct from one another.

4.5 Choice of legal structure

Far from stemming from any scientific process, the choice of legal structure will often be determined by its familiarity to targeted investors and, essentially, its familiarity to those charged with putting it together (e.g. lawyers, tax advisers).

4.6 Taxation considerations

Tax structuring is key when targeting an investment fund at a certain type of locality of investor, as investors are keen to find as tax neutral a structure as possible. This does not mean that investors are looking to evade paying tax, just that the structure should not unnecessarily erode returns by incurring unnecessary double-taxation or other unfavourable tax treatment. Key in structuring funds, therefore, is researching where tax treaties exist and the tax treatment of each potential legal structure amongst others.

The way in which taxation occurs is an ever-changing landscape for investors and for fund managers. For this reason, good tax structuring does not seek to exploit tax loopholes but to provide levels of certainty about how various elements of the fund will be treated for tax in the countries it touches, whether through its investors or investments, so that investors may base decisions upon such treatment.

5. By return of capital and/or income

Understanding the needs of the investor will be key, whether that be capital appreciation and/or regular income.

Invariably the investor's source jurisdiction's treatment of capital and income for tax purposes will have an impact on whether an investor favours capital appreciation over income yield. But capital requirements versus income requirements will also be driven by the type of investor involved, the term of investment and market perception.

Capital appreciation models may suit longer-term investors investing to 'buy-and-hold' for some time, as the investments may not naturally tend towards regular income throughout their lifespan (e.g. the construction of assets with a view to immediate sale) or the investor may not be in need of regular income for some time (e.g. pensions). Many private equity funds historically based their investment premise on long-term capital appreciation, i.e. through the purchase and improvement of assets for later sale. In more recent times, however, private equity investors have also looked for income return.

Income models may suit shorter-term investors or those looking for a regular yield, e.g. to fund certain expenses or to be utilised to diversify their own investment pool. Institutional investors have looked much more for income return in recent years as a way of delivering consistent value to investors less willing to tie-in capital long-term without return.

Some fund models are established to provide both income and capital returns, seeking to return income throughout the lifespan of the fund but also to return capital periodically, e.g. upon the sale of assets. Infrastructure funds, in particular, saw a great level of success in the wake of the financial crisis with investors favouring the return of stable, frequent income whilst still retaining the possibility of capital returns through opportunistic disposals of assets.

6. By equity or debt interests

Funds may issue both equity and debt to its investors. This may drive capital/income returns and also dictate the seniority of investors.

Equity investments result in the holder owning a piece of the fund, whether that be a share in a company, a unit in a unit trust or a limited partnership interest in a LP. With that ownership, the holder acquires certain rights such as the right to vote in investor meetings and the right to share in the profits.

Differing rights may be offered in various classes of equity investment through the constitutive documents of the relevant legal entity. In the case of companies, for example, investors may be offered the chance to invest in differing equity classes.

6.1 Class

- Investment may be based upon various classes of share or units being offered, each with their own terms and entitlements.
- The starting point for equity issues is the ordinary share, which entitles holders to receipt of income, to vote at general meetings and to share in the capital upon winding up.
- However, funds may be structured to allow or disallow certain rights from being attached to the issue.

6.2 Preference

- Shares or units may be issued with preferential rights to dividends and a preferential right to the assets of the company in making up their capital return.
- Preference shareholders typically do not have the right to vote at general meetings.

6.3 Participation

- Shareholders have the right to share in the assets of the fund following repayment of other creditors along with ordinary shareholders.

6.4 Debt interests

Debt investments, on the other hand, do not convey ownership of an entity to the debt provider but instead create a legal obligation on the fund to pay back money within a certain timeframe and based on certain parameters, such as the rate of interest to be paid. In providing debt financing, the holder of the loan or promissory note may also be provided with collateral providing an element of guarantee for the loan in the event of default and may be offered seniority over some or all of the equity holders.

The terms and preference given to debt holders will be dependent upon the terms of the documentation creating that debt rather than being enshrined in the entity's constitutive documents.

7. Upfront or commitment basis

Upon acceptance as an investor into a fund, that investor will agree to invest a maximum amount of money. This money may be invested upfront, i.e. the fund receives all of the investment monies from the date of acceptance into the fund, or may be invested on a commitment basis, meaning that the fund may call monies from an investor when required up to a maximum commitment.

Private equity structures have typically favoured a commitment basis, requiring investors to fund investments at the time of their acquisition rather than retaining surplus funds available for investment. However, for publicly listed private equity funds, the commitment basis of investing is not an option, and so interests will be purchased and traded on an upfront basis.

The commitment basis way of funding provides the advantage that a fund is not laboured with cash drag, i.e. the dilutive effect on profits of having cash sitting uninvested. However, the risk of the commitment basis is that investors may be late funding commitments when required or may default, causing delays to time-sensitive acquisitions or even the loss of them.

For funds funded on an upfront basis, the challenge becomes one of effectively discharging funds available for investment. In order for the manager to perform in respect of its investment premise, it must be putting as much of the fund's money to good use as possible at any one time. A fund with too much cash on hand will result in dilution to profit unless the cash can be put to good use, e.g. through further investments or through cash investments, e.g. in term deposits or cash funds.

8. Open- or closed-ended

The terms open- or closed-ended relate to the manner in which investor capital may be both invested and redeemed.

8.1 Open-ended

- Funds run on regular cycles of cash inflows and outflows, with shares/units issued (created) to meet inflows and redeemed (removed) to meet outflows. In this way, the size of the fund is dependent upon the monies invested (AUM) rather than any maximum limit being applied.
- Open-ended funds may invite daily, weekly, monthly etc periods for this purpose, with applications received by the fund being pooled until the next dealing/redemption period.
- Because investors have more freedom to invest and exit the fund at permitted intervals, open-ended funds tend to be created for less defined terms than closed-ended funds, with their lifespans based more on the manager's ability to continue to invest funds in accordance with the fund's stated objectives.
- Investors will invest and redeem upon the prevailing net asset value of the fund.
- Open-ended funds must balance the inflows and outflows of investor capital. The manager will need to retain cash reserves to meet redemptions, which may include allocating a specific cash reserve or having the ability to quickly liquidate assets to meet outflows.

8.2 Closed-ended

- Funds operate on the basis of defined periods in which to invest and in which rights to redemption exist.
- Typically a closed-ended fund will have an initial subscription period, which may last a day or for a longer period, dependent upon the method by which subscription is offered. During that 'open period', subscriptions may be received and shares/units issued.
- At the end of the open period, the right to subscribe will cease and the fund will be barred to new subscriptions.
- Closed-ended fund investors typically do not have a right to redemption that they may exercise but are instead subject to compulsory redemptions during specific periods, most commonly at the cessation of the fund, i.e. to distribute final proceeds and close down the fund. Funds may create extraordinary redemption periods or may seek to close out investors by other methods, such as tender offers or share buybacks. But for the compulsory redemption period at the cessation of the fund, other redemption periods will be at the discretion of those managing the fund (e.g. the board, trustee or general partner).
- Because investors do not have the right to exit the fund at will but are instead committing to a period of investment, closed-ended funds will be created for defined periods of time to create certainty as to the longest term of retention of that investment.
- The scheme particulars may permit investors to approve extensions to those periods, for the purpose of orderly disposal of fund assets, but will otherwise expect their holding in the fund to come to an end upon the expiry of the defined fund period.
- Investors will invest at a fixed price at the launch of the fund. Any open periods subsequent will be offered at a common price based upon the prevailing net asset value of the fund and taking into account any other rights attaching to the shares to be issued or any equalisation that may be required to bring those shares to a par with those already in existence.
- Shares may be sold outside of specified redemption periods on the secondary market. This may be through a listing (utilising a stock exchange or other trading platform) for public funds or by other means, such as a matched-trades basis on a private market.

9. Closed-ended fund raising

Closed-ended capital raisings may be given various names, but generally fall into two categories.

9.1 Private placement

Investment is offered to a targeted group of potential investors, who agree to participate and to take up shares in a private fund.

9.2 Public offerings (including IPO, secondary capital raisings, tap issues)

- As the name suggests, shares or units are offered to the public through their admission to a stock exchange or other approved trading platform (e.g. the Alternative Investment Market).
- At initial fundraise, an initial public offering will be conducted, typically seeking to raise funds based either upon a minimum capital raise or an accepted range between a minimum and maximum number.
- Subsequent shares can be offered through various methods, including a secondary capital raising, typically where significant amounts of capital are being raised, and a tap issue, typically where top-up funds are sought.

10. Leveraged or unleveraged

Investment funds may be given the power to borrow money. This may be attractive where the size of the assets sought exceeds the capital raised or where the opportunities available in the market exceed the capital that has been raised or which may be raised in time to take advantage of those opportunities.

As borrowing money brings with it its own cost (i.e. in the form of interest charged and, potentially, in administrative and usage costs), fund managers must ensure that the cost of leverage does not exceed the benefits to be derived from this access to greater financial resources or that the ratio of leverage employed is too great for the fund to service.

Leveraging a fund will, invariably, bring with it a greater level of risk and volatility than an unleveraged fund, as the fund may have a substantial creditor to discharge. However, the advantages of leveraging are that a fund may access a wider more diversified pool of assets and/or may target a higher value of assets because of its greater firepower, thus making the funds invested go further.

Leverage may be achieved through various routes including:

- Bank financing through traditional lending bank routes. Banks providing debt financing will seek a high level of certainty of return, including collateralising fund assets and only providing senior ranking debt (i.e. debt that gets repaid first in line before any other debt, investors or creditors).
- Through the issue of loan or promissory notes as an investment type (see above).
- Through financing by private parties, such as private equity financers, venture funders and other privately available sources of funding, e.g. debt funds. Such debt providers will set their own terms for the provision of financing based upon relevant risk parameters and the general availability of debt financing by other sources (i.e. supply/demand).

11. Private or public funds

11.1 Private funds

The default position for funds is that they are privately offered vehicles, meaning that they are offered only to targeted investors through private placement or similar methods. Funds may be privately offered where an investor base already exists, meaning that there is no need to market the fund in a more general sense, and such investors do not require the fund to be publicly quoted to be eligible to hold investments in them.

The effect of remaining as a private fund is that the price of the fund is based upon its net asset valuation rather than any external market factors. However liquidity can be limited in the case of private, closed-ended funds where the opportunities to exit the fund will be limited either to discretion of those managing the fund or the possibility of finding an eligible purchaser.

Private funds are typically subject to fewer continuing obligations, as those investing in them are more sophisticated and so have a greater understanding of both the mechanics of the fund and inherent risks. Indeed, in some jurisdictions a private fund may have very few regulatory requirements imposed on them.

Additionally, private funds are under no obligation to make proprietary information public, as they are able to limit distribution of information to its investors and some limited third parties, such as a regulator.

11.2 Publicly quoted funds

A fund may be publicly quoted in order to:

- Allow certain investors access to the fund, because their own make-up may create limitations on investments into unquoted products.
- Create liquidity in the fund's own stock; this is particularly pertinent for closed-ended funds, where rights to exit are limited and so holders must look to secondary markets to find buyers in the event they wish to exit their holdings. Stock markets provide access to buyers and sellers.
- To access a wider pool of investors.

The effect of a public quotation will be greater volatility in the price of the stock, with pricing matched against supply and demand rather than being matched against the net asset valuation of the fund itself.

In addition, the scrutiny placed on public markets means that listing authorities must be prescriptive as to the types of stock to be admitted on public markets and the obligations imposed on them. As a result, listed funds are subject to a number of conditions for listing and continuing obligations surrounding, in particular, the levels of delivery of and transparency in information provided to investors and to prospective investors.

12. Scrutiny and investor protection

12.1 Regulatory bodies

Regulated funds

Because of the scrutiny placed on those involved in managing and administering the assets of others, funds worldwide are dominated by regulation designed to ensure that those running and managing funds treat investors fairly based upon both the collective group and knowledge of the individual investor types within the fund (i.e. retail, institutional etc). This regulation brings about requirements to:

- produce scheme particulars relating to the fund, which shall include:
  - investment objectives, parameters and restrictions, including the ability to leverage the fund within certain limits;
  - the level of authority placed upon the key parties to the fund, such as the board, fund manager and investors (i.e. through voting rights, entitlements, discretion to act etc);
  - fees payable to key parties, such as the fund manager and administrator, including management fees, performance fees and any commissions payable;
  - fund pricing and how that relates to subscription and redemption prices;
  - investor warnings, including risk statements confirming that investors understand that there are no guarantees as to performance;
  - categories of investor that are eligible to invest in the fund, including minimum levels of subscription and routes to invest to demonstrate such eligibility; and
  - key terms of the substantive documents underpinning the fund structure, such as the Articles of Association or the Limited Partnership Agreement.
- produce supplemental scheme particulars where the terms and rights attaching to a series or class of investor unit differs to another in issue;
- produce audited accounts on a periodic basis, which must be shared with investors; and
- produce key information for investors within set timeframes, including contract notes.

Those managing funds will be subject to their own levels of regulation, including:

- fit and proper requirements, to ensure that those charged with executive responsibility are appropriately qualified and experienced and carry out their affairs with integrity and independence of judgment;
- capital requirements, to ensure that they run their own business in a solvent manner at all times;

- requirements to have proper procedures in place, to ensure that all working on fund matters carry out tasks in a compliant and consistent manner; and
- staff screening requirements, to ensure that those employed to carry out fund tasks are appropriate in relation to their level of seniority and that they act with probity, integrity and skill befitting their role and seniority.

12.2 Unregulated funds

Certain jurisdictions recognise forms of unregulated or near-unregulated funds (so-called light-touch regulation):

- A Jersey unregulated fund is a Jersey domiciled fund which is either to be offered to certain eligible investors only or is listed on an approved exchange or market and opts out of regulation as a fund in Jersey. There are two types of unregulated funds: unregulated eligible investor funds (UEIF) and unregulated exchange traded funds (UETF).
- The UEIF is only open to eligible investors, meaning:
  - an investor who makes an initial minimum investment equivalent to $1 million;
  - a person or entity (or an employee, director or shareholder thereof, or consultant thereto) whose ordinary business or professional activity includes acquiring, managing or giving advice on investments;
  - a functionary or an associate of a functionary to the unregulated fund;
  - an employee, director or shareholder of, or consultant to, such functionary or associate who is acquiring the interest in the fund as remuneration or reward for any trust established by them; or
  - an individual whose property has a total market value of not less than $10 million.
- There is no restriction on the number or type of investors in an UETF.
- In both cases, an offer document must be published and must include the fact that the fund is unregulated, which must be acknowledged by investors in writing. In large this is due to the fact that an investor takes on the risk of the fund being unregulated, which includes the fact that the promoter does not have to establish a track record.
- Guernsey's funds offering does not recognise a particular definition of a fund and instead adopts a set of characteristics that, if present, will ordinarily result in regulation being required as a collective investment scheme.
- These characteristics are as follows:
  - **Pooling of contributions of investors** – This means that a group of people, ordinarily unrelated to one another in any way, pool their contributions into one fund.

   - **Third party management of the portfolio assets** – Meaning that a third party is appointed who selects and manages a group of assets.
   - **Spread of risk** – The fund invests in more than one asset, such as a number of properties or a diversified portfolio of equities.
- For those entities outside of these characteristics (i.e. a single investment only or a small group of related parties), the Guernsey Financial Services Commission will ordinarily regard the structure as falling outside of the scope of a regulated fund. In these situations, a fiduciary licensee may, instead, administer the structure but it will not be recognised as a fund.
- Ultimately, Guernsey does not have any form of wholly unregulated fund.
- Malta has introduced the notified alternative investment fund (NAIF), an unregulated fund structure designed to provide alternative investment fund managers (AIFMs) with a solution to market alternative investment funds (AIFs) within the EU as early as ten working days from the date of filing a completed notification pack.
- The Malta NAIF is only available in limited circumstances in accordance with the Investement Services Acts (List of Notified AIFS) Regulations, where:
   - the fund is managed by an external AIFM (i.e. a manager regulated pursuant to the Alternative Investment Fund Managers Directive (AIFMD));
   - the fund is only available to professional and/or qualifying investors;
   - it is not a debt fund (specific prescribed categories); and
   - the fund invests in financial assets.
- The Malta NAIF is a direct response to Luxembourg's own fund offering, the Luxembourg Reserved Alternative Investment Fund (RAIF), another form of fund available within the EU providing a solution to AIFMD, as the RAIF must be managed by an AIFM.
- Cayman offers unregulated funds largely through exemption under the Mutual Funds Law. Key examples would be funds:
   - offered to sophisticated and high net worth persons; and
   - those not incorporated in Cayman but offering subscription in Cayman through an appropriately licensed person and the interests are listed on an approved stock exchange or are regulated by an approved overseas regulatory authority.
- Additionally, a fund may be exempted from obtaining a licence and registered with the Cayman Islands Monetary Authority where the fund is held by not more than fifteen investors, the majority of whom are capable of removing or appointing the operator of the fund. In which case, Cayman will treat the fund as a Private Fund.
- In Bermuda, private funds (no more than 20 investors and closely-held) and closed-ended funds are excluded from the scope of the Investment Funds Act 2006 and are, thus, unregulated. In addition, Bermuda has two classes of exempted funds, being Class A and Class B.

- Class A Exempt Funds are those whose interests are offered only to qualified purchasers and are managed by eligible investment managers. Class A funds must have a local administrator, registrar, auditor and custodian/prime broker. Otherwise, such funds may be classed as Class B Exempt Funds.
- The BVI utilises the terms Professional Fund and Private Fund to denote those funds with the lightest touch regulation, however both must register under the Securities and Investment Business Act (SIBA).
- Mauritius does not recognise a form of fully unregulated fund, however the nature and extent of regulation applied will depend upon the type of investor permitted to invest in it.

Test yourself 3.2

Identify the three main characteristics of an investment fund.

12.3 Light-touch regulation

In nearly all instances of unregulated fund, there can be found a layer of regulation, hence why many jurisdictions choose to adopt light-touch regulatory models rather than declaring them unregulated structures.

Both the Malta NAIF and Luxembourg RAIF will be indirectly regulated through the AIFM, which must comply with the terms of AIFMD when managing and marketing AIFs in Europe. Similarly, the Jersey UETF will be subject to the listings rules of its approved markets, which are designed with some form of investor protection in mind.

In addition, Jersey has added a specific form of light-touch regulated fund, the Very Private Fund, which does not require the full form of regulation but need only gain consent under Jersey's Control of Borrowing Ordinance (COBO), bringing it within the scope of a lighter form of regulation.

In May 2016 Guernsey announced its own lighter-touch fund product, named the Manager Led Product (MLP). Like the NAIF and the RAIF, the MLP regulates the investment manager rather than the underlying fund. This is a departure for Guernsey fund regulation, which traditionally has regulated both the manager and the fund itself.

The MLP allows one investment manager to absorb all the incidence of conduct of business and capital adequacy rules, while permitting multiple fund structures to exist under its regulatory obligations. That investment manager must adhere to Guernsey's AIFMD Rules 2013 in order to be eligible and is designed to allow those managers to demonstrate to the EU competent authorities that they intend to be compliant with AIFMD.

The thought processes and benefits behind lighter-touch regulation are to bring fund products to investors that:

- remove regulatory duplication;
- create a more efficient path to market; and
- reduce administration fees (in respect of those vehicles no longer subject to various rules).

13. Custodians

Certain regulatory models will require that a custodian or prime broker is appointed. The requirement to appoint a custodian will depend upon the jurisdiction of the fund and the category of fund selected.

A custodian is a financial institution that holds customers' securities for safekeeping to minimise the risk of their theft or loss. A custodian also ensures that those assets are only dealt with in a manner allowed by the fund offering documents. Since they are responsible for the safety of assets and securities that may be worth hundreds of millions or even billions of dollars, custodians generally tend to be large and reputable firms.

Custodians are generally subject to regulatory obligations themselves, whether under applicable banking and/or investment regulation, to ensure that their duties are aligned with general investor protection rules.

13.1 Types of fees

As considered above, when structuring a fund, management fee structuring is key. But there are also other service providers to consider, all demanding fees for their services. All fees must be transparent to ensure that an investor understands what proportion of funds invested or profits generated will be utilised towards paying fund principals, such as the fund manager, administrator and custodian.

13.2 Fund administration fees

Administration duties will typically divide into:

Net asset valuation and other administration tasks
The administrator will be charged with maintaining records of all financial transactions by the fund and using them to calculate the NAV in accordance with the terms of the offering documents.

Accounting
Funds will generally be required to provide financial information to investors and other stakeholders, such as the regulator, in accordance with approved accounting principles, typically IFRS or GAAP. The administrator will typically be charged with compiling this information into the funds accounts.

Corporate secretarial
As the focus on corporate governance increases, so too do the requirements for a strong corporate secretarial service to ensure that the fund remains in good standing, according to its legal composition, and to ensure that key decisions,

policies and other requirements, such as record keeping, are adequately discharged.

Share dealing

A fund must understand its investor base at all times, including contact details and the number of shares/units that investor holds, through the maintenance of investor registers.

In addition, the share dealing function will ensure that applicable anti-money laundering (AML) and countering financing of terrorism (CFT) policies are adhered to by collating and reviewing customer due diligence (CDD), which will include the receipt of an application form relevant to the fund in question and verification documentation in relation to the investor.

Alternatively these services may be performed by an external registrar/transfer agent.

Compliance

A compliance function is necessary to ensure that regulatory obligations are adhered to at all times.

For these services, the administrator will command a fee, which may be:

- ad valorem, meaning based upon a percentage of the NAV from time to time;
- a fixed fee;
- time spent, dependent upon the amount of work the administrator performs; or
- a combination of the three.

Administration fees are typically market-led by jurisdiction as administrators compete in a competitive market.

13.3 Custodian fees

Custodian fees will be market-led by jurisdiction, however a common pricing model is ad valorem for these services.

14. Key documents

With the asset class, investment objectives, targeted investors and primary fund structure identified, the fund manager will need to compile a set of key documents that will both establish and underpin that structure.

14.1 Offering document

Often referred to as scheme particulars or the prospectus, the offering document is both the key marketing document when marketing the fund and the basis of the legally binding contract between the fund and its investors upon receipt and acceptance of a fully signed application form.

The offering document lays out the key terms of the fund offering, including:

- **The investment parameters** – This is a detailed summary of what the fund may invest in and how it will utilise those investments to generate investor returns. This section will set out the rules the fund manager must comply with in carrying out the investment objectives, such as restrictions as to the type of investment and concentration limits to ensure a diversified spread of investments and risk.
- **Key principals** – This section will lay out who will manage the fund on a day-to-day basis, such as the board of directors or the key parties behind the general partner, as well as setting out who the fund manager is and pertinent background information, such as past performance figures.
- **Cost** – This section will detail how expensive the cost of the fund will be to an investor, including fees payable to all key principals, in particular the way in which the management and performance fees are calculated and paid, including any detail of prospective clawback.
- **Valuation methodology** – This section will detail how the value of the fund and thus the value of an investor's holding will be calculated and shared from time to time.
- **Investor warnings and guidance** – This section will include a list of prospective pitfalls investors ought to be aware of according to their investor type, jurisdiction of origin and their attitude towards risk.
- **Statutory provisions relating to the form of entity utilised** – This section will detail the legal detail of how the fund mechanics work as to the rights of each investor.

The offering document will also contain further detail required by regulation and, in the case of listed funds, by the applicable listing rules. Typically these will include the frequency of production of financial information and their provision to investors and warnings relating to the risks inherent in financial products.

The purpose of the offering document is, therefore, to serve as the terms and conditions applicable both to the investor in choosing to invest but also the fund and those parties that make up the fund as to their obligations and responsibilities.

14.2 Statutory document

Dependent upon the legal form the fund adopts, the articles of association, trust deed or limited partnership agreement must be provided to the investor as it forms the legal mechanism through which an investor may acknowledge and exercise his rights.

14.3 Application/subscription form

Each investor will complete an application form in order to be accepted as an investor. In addition to legally binding the investor to the offering document and other fund documents, this is the mechanism through which the regulatory obligations relating to AML and CFT are discharged. The form will create an obligation for investors to furnish the fund (through its administrator, typically) with client due diligence for identification and screening purposes and an acknowledgement that no investment may be accepted until such obligations are exhausted.

14.4 Adherence agreement

In respect of LPs and unit trusts, each investor must also become a party to the overarching entity agreement, either the limited partnership agreement or the trust deed. This will be achieved through the execution of a deed of adherence, through which the investor agrees to be bound by the terms of the overarching legal agreement.

14.5 Investment management agreement/investment advisory agreement

Any agreements with investment professionals will be scrutinised by the regulator and any listing authority as well as by the investors, who will wish to understand the terms against which the fund manager will act. As a material document, pertinent terms of the agreement will be replicated in the offering document, however the full agreement may also be made available to investors whether on demand or through the availability of inspection at given premises.

14.6 Custodian agreement

Where a custodian is appointed, pertinent terms of that agreement will be replicated within the offering document, typically those relating to the exact nature of the responsibility assumed and how the custodian will be remunerated for it.

14.7 Administration agreement

Due to the significant cost and responsibility incumbent on the administrator, key terms of this agreement will be made available to investors.

Whilst unlikely to be disclosed, a service level agreement (SLA) may also be entered into with the administrator to ensure that key tasks are completed within acceptable timeframes and within acceptable margins of error.

- It is essential that the administrator performs certain of its functions within acceptable timeframes. For instance, where the NAV is critical to the completion of financial statements or the pricing of further issues or redemptions of shares/units in the fund, it is imperative that they are completed within a set timeline or those processes reliant upon the NAV may be unreasonably delayed. The effect of delays could be disastrous.
- Other functions may be less time critical, however the fund principals may wish for them to be completed within certain timeframes to assist in the orderly management of the fund. One example is the timeliness with which board information should be made available to board members (i.e. boardpacks and minutes), which is essential in the interests of good governance.

- Acceptable margins of error should be documented in order to assist in appraising the performance of the administrator from time to time. Delays and errors will occur, as that is human nature, but the administrator must be clear as to when such delays and errors will cease to be acceptable, whether by their scale or the frequency with which they occur. For example, one error when calculating a NAV may have an impact on the pricing of the fund and may result in the fund needing to recompense certain investors. As an isolated event, that may be manageable but persistent errors could result in financial loss and reputational loss, either of which could be catastrophic.

Test yourself 3.3

Name the key documents investors sign up to when they invest in a fund.

15. Consolidated structures

Fund structuring extends beyond the vehicle investors will invest into and will include the mechanics for investors to get into the fund and the holding structure utilised at an asset level.

Structures may also include vehicles through which the fund manager may invest or otherwise derive certain elements of their fees.

15.1 Investor access

Whilst a fund may be established with only one method of investment available to all investors, i.e. common and direct investment, certain fund structures may need to consider other methods of accepting investors.

Co-investment/side-by-side vehicles

The purpose of such vehicles is generally to secure significant investment into the fund but on differing terms to those applicable to investors entering through the fund vehicle.

For example, such investors may wish to pay discounted management and performance fees in recognition of their greater contribution to the fund. Within the fund itself, this would be prohibited under the general requirement to treat investors fairly, meaning that preferential rates should not be available to some investors and not to all. Instead a separate legal entity may be created that invests on a side-by-side basis with the fund, taking a pro-rata share of all or some of the fund's investments, dependent upon the investment parameters of the separate vehicle.

Co-investment models may also be created utilising cellular structures, whereby various cells can be created with differing Offering Documents offering differing terms based upon certain eligibility criteria.

These co-investment vehicles may be funds in themselves or may be private vehicles.

Figure 3.7: Simple co-investment/side-by-side structure

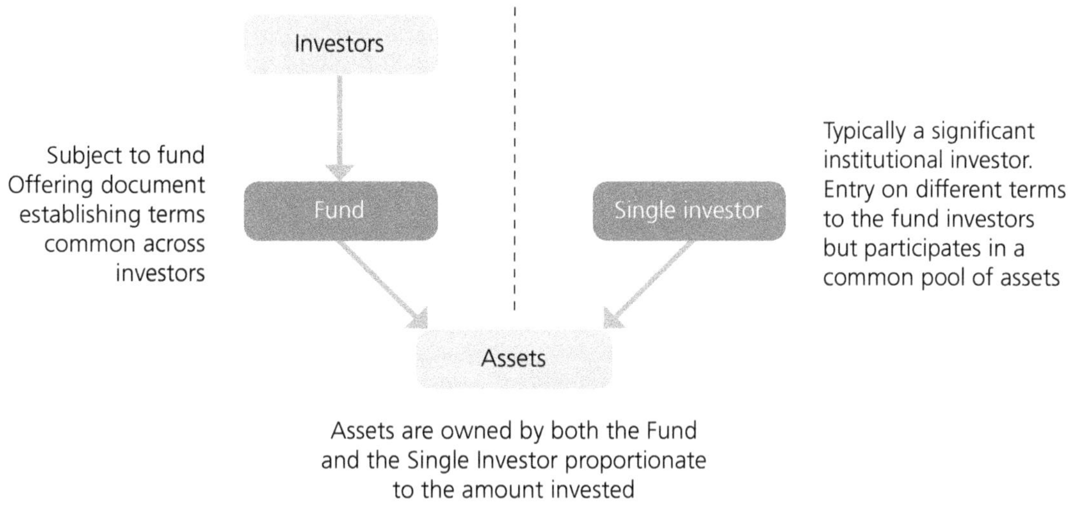

Parallel vehicles

Parallel vehicles are similar to co-investment vehicles, as they are established to invest in the same pool of assets alongside another participant. A key use of parallel vehicles can allow differing investor types to be treated differently whilst still investing into the cumulative pool of assets. An example of this is an EU AIF investing in parallel with a non-EU fund. This may be desirable where the fund's investment objectives mean that, but for the EU investors into it, the fund would have no presence in the EU. In this way, those investors outside of the EU are not subjected to EU regulation unnecessarily whilst a fund structure is established to ensure EU compliance for those investors that bring the fund in scope of AIFMD.

The use of parallel vehicles may also allow for listed funds to invest alongside private funds, giving a wide range of eligible investor types access to the fund.

Figure 3.8: Simple parallel fund structure

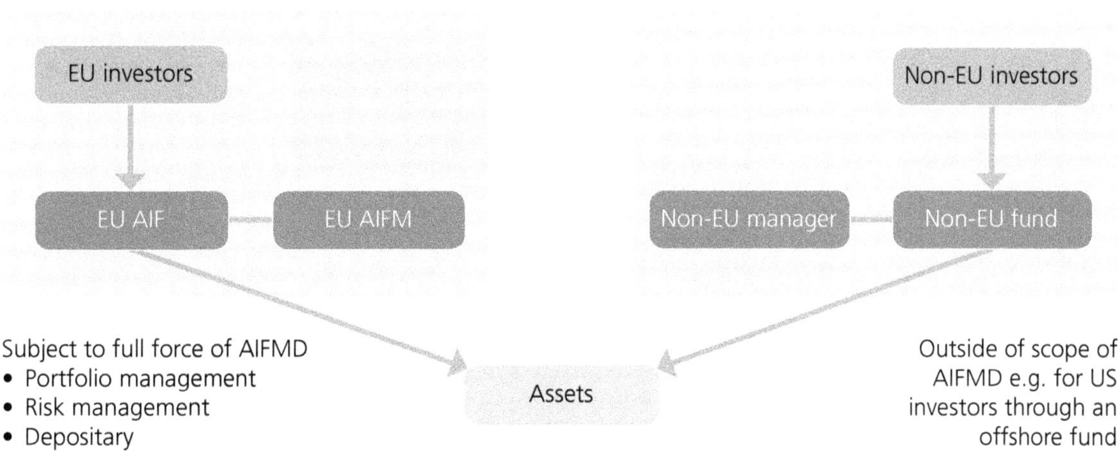

Master/feeders

A fund established to invest directly into and manage the assets may be classified as one where the master fund above it is established a separate fund (the feeder) designed to accept investor subscriptions for the purpose of investing (feeding investment) into the master fund.

Figure 3.9: Simple feeder structure

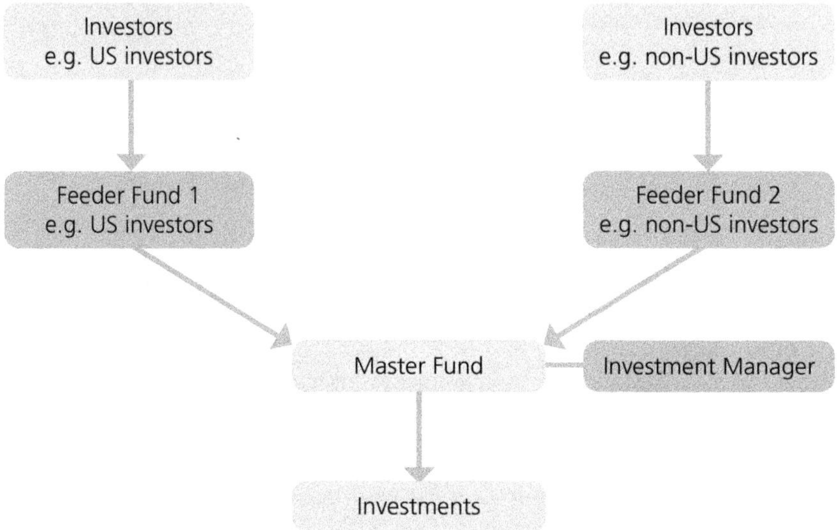

Figure 3.10: Simple fund of funds structure

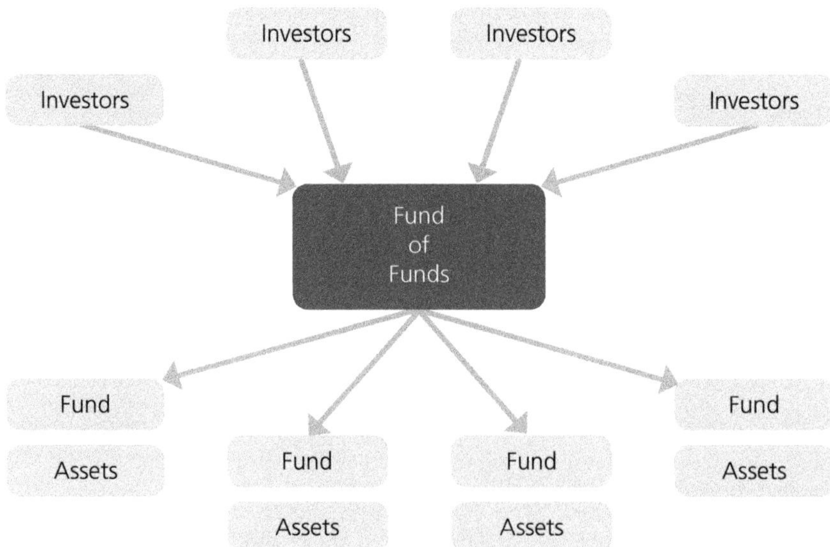

Fund of funds
A fund may be established with the sole purpose of investing into a range of underlying funds. In this way, the fund manager doesn't manage the investments but instead oversees their performance and makes recommendations as to acquisitions and disposals of other funds.

Series/vintages
Essentially series or vintage funds means a family of funds that share similar characteristics, such as a common investment manager or investment premise etc. Series of funds can allow for these similarities but also leaves room for differences, such as different fee structures or differing maturity dates.

15.2 Management vehicles

Through the separation of the fund vehicle and management vehicles, investor rights over the manager are restricted. Investors accept these restrictions because certain features common in most investment funds make these restrictions efficient, such as investor exit rights, economies of scale and assumption only of the risks of investment assets.

Whilst the fund manager may be an established onshore firm, separate entities may be formed for the purpose of assuming various management responsibilities.

General partner vehicles
Limited Partnerships are required to have a general partner responsible for the management of the LP. In fund structuring, a limited company will typically be formed for this purpose to allow the appointment of a board of directors to manage the fund.

In certain structures, most commonly seen in private equity funds, the general partner may be formed as a limited partnership, itself with a limited company to serve as its general partner, the so-called GP LP structure.

Investment adviser/manager
A separate entity may be created to separate the investment management and advisory responsibilities of the fund.

Within Europe, the separation of functions has become essential, as AIFMD requires investment management and risk management to be separated.

Carry vehicles
Typical in private equity structures, separate carry vehicles may be established for the purpose of the fund management team receiving the carry from investments.

Carried interest or carry, in finance, specifically in alternative investments (i.e., private equity and hedge funds), is a share of the profits of an investment or investment fund that is paid to the investment manager in excess of the amount that the manager contributes to the partnership.

Figure 3.11: Introducing management vehicles into the structure

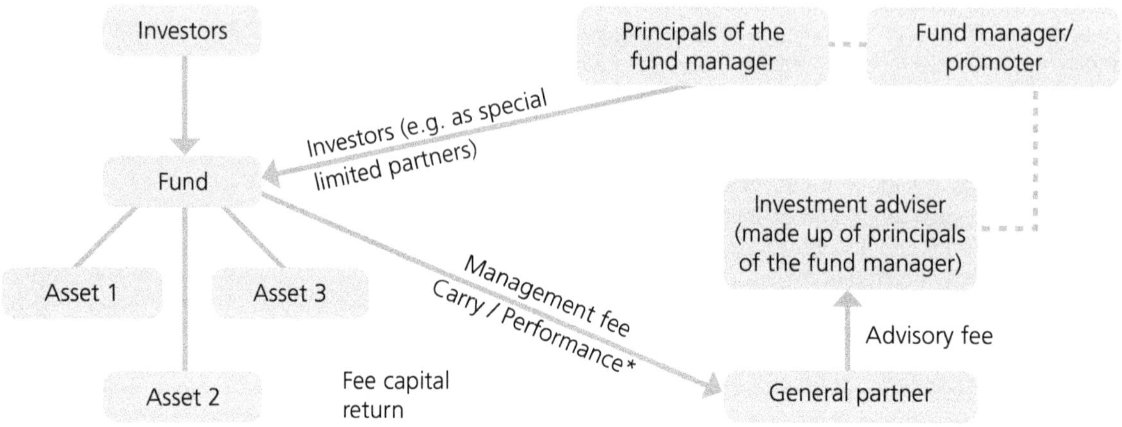

* A separate carry vehicle may be established for the purpose of receiving the carried interest (i.e. performance element).

16. Competing with onshore jurisdictions

16.1 EU

In the wake of the financial crisis, the EU has put significant pieces of legislation in place to provide greater levels of investor protection than were in place historically. Whilst investor protection measures have increased, another effect of the legislation is a protective one, as the EU aims to create a level playing field for all EU Member States to make it easier for investors to invest within the EU. As a result, third countries, i.e. those outside of the EU, have found themselves in weaker positions when trying to market within the EU.

AIFMD

AIFMD was a game-changer in the funds space as it created a new level of regulation for funds being marketed to EU investors. AIFMD was designed to create a secure and stable financial system where all significant financial market actors are subject to appropriate regulation and supervision, particularly in the wake of the global economic crisis. In this context, it is essential that the risks that AIFMs pose to their investors, the financial markets and the companies in which they invest are rigorously monitored and controlled. The crisis exposed a number of deficiencies in this regard, notably a lack of transparency, deficiencies in risk management and asset-safekeeping arrangements, and weaknesses in due diligence.

The overarching objective of the AIFMD was to create, for the first time, a comprehensive and secure framework for the supervision and prudential oversight of AIFMs in the EU. Since AIFMD entered into force, all AIFMs are required to obtain authorisation and are subject to ongoing regulation and supervision. In this way, the AIFMD:

- increases the transparency of AIFMs towards investors, supervisors and the employees of the companies in which they invest;
- equips national supervisors, the European Securities Markets Agency (ESMA) and the European Systemic Risk Board (ESRB) with the information and tools necessary to monitor and respond to risks to the stability of the financial system that could be caused or amplified by AIFM activity;
- introduces a common and robust approach to the protection of investors in these funds;
- strengthens and deepens the single market, thereby creating the conditions for increased investor choice and competition in the EU, subject always to high and consistent regulatory standards; and
- increases the accountability of AIFMs holding controlling stakes in companies (private equity) towards employees and the public at large.

This regulation established a single market for those investment managers within the EU and differing conditions to entry for third country (non-EU) investment managers:

- Fund managers established in the EU may be regulated as AIFMs, under which authority they may register, market and manage funds offered within the EU.
- Fund managers established outside of the EU can not presently be regulated as AIFMs and must, instead, market alternative investment funds through National Private Placement Regimes, which are established by each Member State. Because the application of NPPRs is at the discretion of each Member State, significant barriers to entry have been created for non-EU managers and, in certain circumstances, a total prohibition.

Non-EU countries remain optimistic that these barriers to entry will not always exist, as AIFMD allows for certain jurisdictions to be granted equivalence through third country passporting rights. ESMA has been responsible for assessing third countries, of which the offshore jurisdictions generally form a part (Malta is an obvious exception), and for determining whether they are eligible to be granted third country passporting rights under AIFMD. If granted, passporting rights will allow certain third countries to market alternative investment funds into Europe in much the same way as EU AIFMs can at present.

As at 19 July 2016, ESMA had assessed 12 third countries in this respect, including Guernsey, Jersey, Bermuda, Cayman Islands, Hong Kong, Isle of Man and Singapore to assess whether they should be eligible for third country passporting rights. Whilst no decision has yet been made, ESMA's recommendation includes that:

- there was no significant obstacles to Guernsey, Jersey, Singapore and Hong Kong;

- there was no definitive advice in relation to Bermuda and the Cayman Islands, both of which were implementing new regulatory regimes; and
- that it was difficult to assess the Isle of Man, as there is no AIFMD-like regime making it difficult to assess whether investor protection criteria are met.

Undertakings for collective investment in transferable securities
The EU created a form of collective investment scheme known as undertakings for collective investment in transferable securities (UCITS) capable of operating freely throughout the EU on the basis of a single authorisation from one Member State. Whilst UCITS have been in existence since 1985, the current form was adopted in 2014 and is known as UCITS V. UCITS run in parallel to AIFMD, which applies to hedge funds and alternative investments.

Depositaries
Both AIFMD and UCITS create a requirement for AIFs and UCITS to have a depositary appointed, whose responsibility is to act as a custodian of the fund assets. This requirement is wholly borne out of the EU's desire to increase investor protection measures and ensures that an independent party is in place to monitor the safekeeping of fund assets.

16.2 Light-touch regulation – Lux RAIF

As both AIFMD and UCITS evolve, EU Member States are enacting lighter-touch versions of these regulated structures focusing on the prudential regulation of the fund manager, which must already be regulated under AIFMD.

These lighter-touch versions result in a speedier route to market as regulators look to the regulation of the manager to preserve the protection of investors.

16.3 Malta

In recent years, Malta has established itself as a growing and significant player in the alternative investment space. Its obvious advantage is that it is a member of the EU, so is afforded the access to other EU states that all Member States presently enjoy, giving it an advantage other non-EU offshore jurisdictions until the results and granting of passporting rights are known.

16.4 United Kingdom

The United Kingdom has long been a dominant figure in fund structuring and servicing. How that position is affected by Brexit remains to be seen, however.

Currently, as a Member State of the EU, both AIFs and UCITS are available fund brands, which gives the UK an edge when marketing funds within the EU, a market many of the offshore jurisdictions, particularly those geographically closer to the EU, depend upon.

16.5 FCA 'Sandbox'

Like other jurisdictions globally, the FCA has demonstrated its willingness to innovate in the creation of new fund types. The sandbox is an opportunity for managers with little to no track record to establish a track record through an FCA lighter-touch regulated product.

The FCA states that the sandbox is a 'safe space' in which businesses can test innovative products, services, business models and delivery mechanisms while ensuring that consumers are 'appropriately protected'.

To be eligible, sandbox participants must agree to limited scope as to who may invest and the amount of investment capital that may be raised amongst other considerations.

16.6 US

Offshore jurisdictions face competition from the US in various ways, most significantly the prevalence of Delaware as a low tax, cheap and administratively light jurisdiction for the formation of fund structures on home soil but also its desirability as an offshore centre. However, those offshore jurisdictions sited close to the US, such as the Cayman Islands, do enjoy success as jurisdictions often favoured by US participants.

A significant barrier for offshore funds marketing into the US is the US's protective measures designed to keep US money within the US, resulting in restrictive and burdensome laws controlling US holdings in non-US entities. Another is the unfavourable tax treatment of US investment outside of the US, another protective measure designed to encourage US investors to invest within the US.

16.7 Asia

Singapore and Hong Kong have emerged as significant offshore centres in recent years, providing routes into Asian and out of Asian markets that many traditional offshore jurisdictions have not been able to reach either owing to country restrictions, linguistic or cultural issues or merely the lack of geographic proximity.

17. Challenges to structure

17.1 Legal environment

Changes in the legal environment will impact upon fund structuring to a greater or lesser degree and create challenges for offshore jurisdictions to innovate to remain attractive, to compete with onshore jurisdictions and to build structures rigid enough to bear legal change or flexible enough to change with it.

Legal change can be seen in the changing laws applicable to entity types globally, e.g. regular changes to or the overhauling of company legislation in multiple jurisdictions to increase flexibility and to focus on the maintenance of solvency rather than strict capital retention. It can also be seen in a regulatory context, as regulators adopt lighter-touch approaches to the regulation of key fund types to retain competitiveness on a global stage.

17.2 Tax environment

Whilst tax evasion legislation is arguably focused on large multinationals such as Amazon, Google and Starbucks, the effects and consequences of legal changes in this area will be far reaching.

Base Erosion Profit Shifting (BEPS) legislation is currently in progress, designed to ensure that profits generated in one jurisdiction are kept within that jurisdiction and taxed accordingly rather than being shifted into a low-tax jurisdiction through accounting treatments. Whilst this may not impact upon the funds themselves, the effect on fund managers remains to be fully quantified, especially for offshore funds managed by managers outside of the jurisdiction. In these instances, the question will be where is the profit generated? Once that is established, further questions as to who and how to tax those profits will be answered and could potentially impact upon the desirability of a fund manager establishing a fund offshore rather than onshore.

At an individual level, the Foreign Account Tax Compliance Act (FATCA) and Common Reporting Standard (CRS) have already become part of everyday language, requiring financial institutions to report on every account for eligible account holders for their local tax authority to share with all other tax authorities signed up to the reporting mechanisms. Its impact on offshore jurisdictions is unlikely to be the discovery of tax evaders but instead is the increasing cost of administering funds, as another layer of investor scrutiny and anti-money laundering requirements has been set in place.

Additionally, countries worldwide are considering other forms of anti-evasion legislation akin to existing bribery and corruption legislation, designed to punish those who ought to have reasonably suspected that tax evasion was taking place or being attempted. This puts a further burden on offshore jurisdictions, such as the cost of training staff to understand their increasing responsibilities.

The greatest impact on offshore jurisdictions is not so much the enactment of these provisions, as onshore jurisdictions will be equally culpable and burdened under them, but it is the disproportionate level of work offshore jurisdictions have to do to prove that they are in compliance with them due to the negative sentiments many hold towards offshore finance centres.

17.3 Perception

Perhaps the biggest challenge of all to offshore centres is the perception of others globally, including governments, the media and the general public.

For a long time, offshore centres have been labelled as tax havens, where little or no tax is due. For this reason, offshore centres are often treated as encouraging and promoting tax evasion.

Offshore jurisdictions, therefore, have a tough job of demonstrating that they have in place robust systems of control, including regulatory, legal and fiscal controls, to counter and forestall the use of funds products for anti-money laundering, tax evasion or the financing of terrorist activities.

Because of this negative perception, failings of offshore centres are amplified, including:

- Weavering in Cayman, which is oft cited as the example of poor governance and control by a board, which was rubber-stamping the activities of the manager rather than scrutinising them for themselves.
- The Sark Lark in the Bailiwick of Guernsey, for reasons similar to the above.
- Arch Cru failing in Guernsey, where the fund and administrator were situated.

17.4 Tax havens/blacklists

Both the OECD and the EU are in the process of establishing objective criteria to identify non-cooperative jurisdictions with respect to tax transparency. These will result in new forms of blacklist against different criteria to those previously in place.

The OECD's criteria are:

- If the country gets a rating of 'largely compliant' or better from the OECD's Global Forum, as regards the 'exchange of information on request' standard of transparency.
- The country commits to adopting CRS, and to begin exchanges by 2018 at the latest.
- The country has signed the 'Multilateral Convention on Mutual Administrative Assistance in Tax Matters (MCMAA),' or if it has what the OECD considers a sufficiently broad exchange network providing for exchange of information on request and automatic exchange of information.

A tax haven is a jurisdiction where particular taxes, such as an inheritance tax or income tax, are levied at a low rate or not at all. Even if offshore jurisdictions do not feature on a blacklist, their common labelling as blacklists is sufficient for them to be regarded as such. Each of Jersey, Isle of Man, Bermuda, BVI, Cayman, Guernsey etc have frequently been referred to as tax havens.

Administrators must be cognisant of and understand the legal structures utilised and the contractual structures interwoven into it. Whilst the nature of the tasks they may perform may be similar from fund to fund, the subtle nuances caused by the use of a limited partnership instead of a company or the existence of an Investment Advisory Agreement rather than Investment Management Agreement can have far-reaching consequences if they are ignored. The following are illustrative of some of the questions an administrator should ask themselves.

- Should dividends/distributions be paid gross or net of tax?
- Is a structure transparent or opaque for certain taxation purposes?
- What specific rights do the investors have according to the type of investment they hold (e.g. debt or equity)?

Figure 3.12: Key relationship components

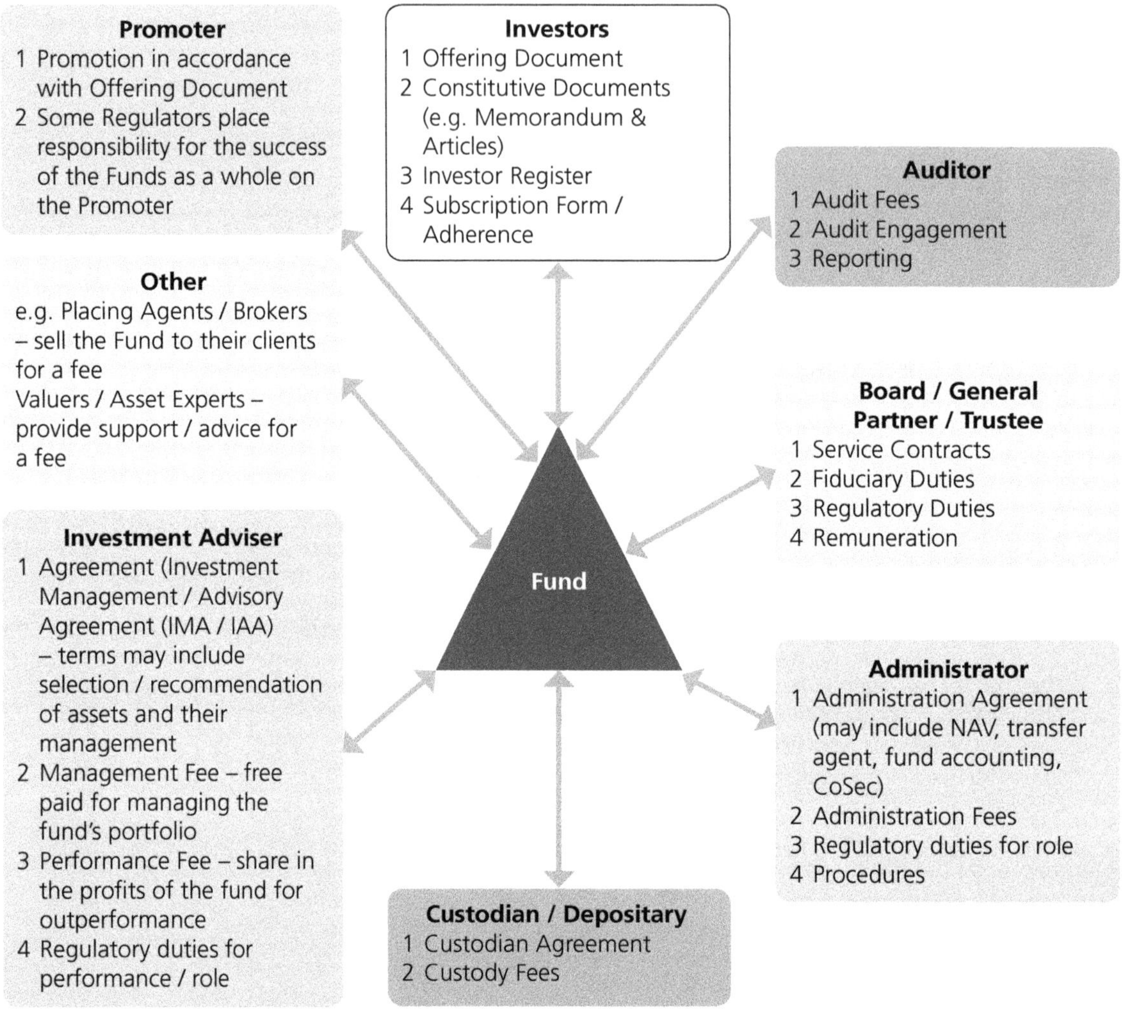

- Does the NAV need to be made publicly available (is the fund listed or not)?
- What deadlines exist for the submission of key information to third parties, such as the regulator?
- What reporting may be required and to whom? (Investors? Regulators? External regulators, e.g. relevant Member States for AIFMD purposes?)

Worked example 3.1

A structure diagram is a key tool for the administrator. Often another party will provide one, but sometimes the administrator is required to do this or may find it useful to build their own as part of its understanding of the structure. Based on the following information, compose a simple structure diagram.

- Structure Fund PCC Limited is being formed in Guernsey.
- At launch, Property Cell 1 Fund will be created. It will issue Participating Preference Shares of £1.00 each to a total value of £30,000,000.
- Also at launch, Investment Cell 2 Fund will also be created. It will issue Participating Preference Shares of $1.50 each to a total capital raise of $45,000,000 (assume this is equivalent to £30,000,000).
- Property Cell 1 Fund will own 50% of a joint venture company called In Parallel Limited, with Investment Cell 2 Fund to own the other 50%. In Parallel will issue 10,000 Ordinary Shares of £1.00 each for a total price of £10,000,000 (equivalent to $15,000,000).
- Property Cell 1 Fund will utilise all remaining funds to purchase The Very Big Building, Ipswich.
- Investment Cell 2 Fund will invest all remaining funds in the Strategy Master Fund LP.
- Property Cell 1 Fund will appoint Big Idea PM Limited as its property manager.
- Investment Cell 2 Fund will appoint Great Things IM LLC as its investment adviser.
- New Administrator Limited will be appointed as administrator to the PCC and all of its cells under a global agreement.

Chapter summary

- The structure of the fund is the culmination of a series of decisions designed to result in a structure that allows:
  - Investors to make an informed investment decision by understanding the basis on which their investment monies will be utilised and how returns are intended to be generated but also the risks inherent in making such an investment.
  - Investor rights of entry and exit to be understood and exercised.
  - Investor protection, to ensure that the most vulnerable members of society are not duped into making investments far outside of their risk appetite or tolerance.
  - Investor access to a diversified range of investments they could not access alone.

- Investor access to professional fund managers with the know-how and resources they do not themselves possess.
- Efficient methods of utilising global investor monies to invest in a wide range of investment opportunities worldwide.
- Responsibility for the proper management of the fund to be delegated to an identified group of people, with legal and regulatory ramifications in the event that they should fail.
- Conflicts of interest to be managed to ensure that the interests of the fund manager, if not aligned with those of investors, can be managed.

Chapter four

The roles of the fund manager, fund administrator and fund's governing body

List of topics

1. The fund manager
2. The fund administrator
3. The fund's governing body
4. Governance
5. Interrelationship of the three parties

Introduction

Is this chapter we will look at the roles of the governing body, fund manager and fund administrator. The fund manager is an investment professional who oversees the investments within a portfolio. The chapter explains exactly what that means and considers the component parts of the role of the fund manager in fulfilling this definition. It also addresses the position of the fund administrator. This professional performs a pivotal role in the life cycle of a fund, so much so that regulatory authorities require that the functionary is appropriately regulated. We will explore the concept of the governing body, which has the ultimate responsibility for the performance of the investment fund. This investigation is contextualised within the framework of **corporate governance**.

corporate governance
Refers to the mechanisms, processes and relations by which corporations are controlled and directed.

1. The fund manager

1.1 Introduction

A general definition will tell you that the fund manager is an investment professional who oversees the investments within a portfolio, or words to that effect. This chapter explores exactly what that means and considers the component parts of the role of the fund manager in fulfilling this definition. In so doing, we will consider primarily that the fund manager will be identifiable by the two major roles it plays:

- attracting investment capital from investors; and
- managing the investments of the fund.

We will look at the interaction between the fund manager and the fund administrator.

Finally we will consider how the manager derives its fees from the fund and how that impacts upon investor protection considerations.

1.2 Attracting investor capital

Fund managers can be likened to branded goods, with the best fund managers' brands attracting prestige and premium. At a simple level, investors will be more attracted to the premium brands, managers with good performance track records, than they will to lesser or unknown brands, e.g. managers with a history of losses or managers without an established history.

In the context of offshore funds, the identity of the fund manager will have much greater importance to institutional investors and professional and sophisticated investors, i.e. those with significant capital to invest, than it will to individual, retail investors.

As a retail investor, individuals are less likely to have studied the performance of the fund manager primarily because the choice to invest in the offshore fund usually isn't theirs to take. Instead it rests in the hands of the investment professionals and the products through which they invest. At a retail investor level, most are reliant on professional firms who manage their investments through pensions, insurances and other packages and such investors will select their investment profiles based upon the recommendations of regulated professionals, i.e. on risk and term profiling, rather than on an individual manager or product basis.

However, studies suggest that this is changing. With millenials (generally those born between the early 1980s and the early 2000s) taking much more control over their own investment portfolios, as access to online and digital platforms for direct investing become more prevalent, even the smallest of investors are likely to take a significant interest in the identity of the fund manager.

Investment professionals investing on behalf of their retail customers will take an interest in who the fund manager is, amongst other factors. This is because their ability to attract customers, and thus generate fees, will be based upon their own performance results in selecting the right stocks and products. Such professionals range from independent financial advisers, selecting investments on behalf of their clients, to institutional investors, who collectively invest their own clients' monies to generate returns.

High net worth individuals, generally seen to be sophisticated or professional investors due to access to investment advice and their ability to bear financial losses, will look to who the fund manager is as a key component of their assessment of the investment prospect.

1.3 Key considerations

Whatever bracket of investor concerned, an element of questioning will arise when determining where to place your money for investment, including asking who is managing the potential for your investment returns.

Whilst every fund manager will caution an investor that the value of investments may go down as well as up and that there is no guarantee that profits will be generated at all, no investor goes into an investment hoping to lose money. Therefore finding a fund manager to whom you are willing to entrust your own or your clients' capital is key and must not be entered into lightly.

The best fund managers are those that, quite simply, do what they promise. And so the investment parameters are the first point of research for assessing the fund manager; what is it they say they can do with your money to generate returns?

Investment funds are required to issue offering documents, where these investment parameters must be laid out in a clear and transparent fashion with the intention of answering the following questions.

What will investor money be invested in?

When considering the investment objectives, investors will need to consider just what it is the fund intends to do. In so doing, a reasonableness test must be considered. Whilst this will be easier for funds with tried-and-tested investment objectives, and thus a readily available source of information against which to compare, a more esoteric asset class or set of investment objectives, where there is generally less published information for comparison, may require different thinking in order to become comfortable with the proposition. This becomes a matter of an investor asking themselves, does it make sense? Is there a purpose for this? Is there a need for it? Is there a demand for it?

What is the offering document intending to deliver?

The next important conclusion to arrive at is that the anticipated result of delivering the investment objective seems reasonable in all the circumstances. This really boils down to an investor asking themselves, does it look reasonable or does it look too good to be true?

Independent research (by the investor or a suitable adviser) should be conducted to gauge average returns not only for the type of investment involved but also those generally being generated in the wider context of investments. For instance, if investments are generally bringing about returns of 5% p.a., an investment offering 10% p.a. might warrant greater scrutiny before either becoming comfortable with it or otherwise determining that it is too risky or that it may be otherwise unsuitable (e.g. potential fraudulent activity).

Who is responsible for that delivery and what is their track record?

This information may be more difficult to obtain, as private funds or other investments will not generally have published information on them outside of their own investors and related parties. One source of information will be to review what is available publicly, whether through online research or requesting information from other sources.

As an investor's own fire power grows, so does its ability to obtain information on fund managers, even where it would ordinarily be kept private. Such investors will be invited to road shows or private meetings, where the fund manager will go into some detail as to their experience and the performance of previous ventures, whether on a collective or individual basis. For the largest investors, fund managers will entertain far-reaching questions about past performance and other.

As in all industries, some emerge as rock-stars and attract investment easily whilst others have to work harder to gain critical mass or recognition. Investors should not be drawn to rock-stars before they have done their homework. Many of these reputed fund managers deserve their reputations, but there will always be those who abuse their positions. In recent years, some massive failures for investment funds have arisen as a result of backing unscrupulous fund managers.

What incentives or, conversely, red flags exist in respect of the fund manager?

No fund manager is managing investor money for altruistic means. The goal for every fund manager is to make money by managing the money of others fruitfully, for which they may claim both management and performance fees.

Management fees may be viewed by most to be generous, typically somewhere between 0.5–2% of the fund's AUM per annum, and therefore a lucrative form of revenue in its own right. However the true value potential for the fund manager comes from the performance fees that may be earned.

As a performance fee is paid when the investment fund outperforms its investment targets, investors must consider that this creates a potential incentive for the fund manager to take risks to achieve the highest returns possible. Whilst certain levels of risk-taking are expected, investors must consider whether the levels of risk are reasonable or excessive in the circumstances.

What fail-safes or other measures are in place to monitor how that delivery is brought about?

Larger investors will have in place numerous fail-safes of their own, most generally through the ability to lose money on some investments as they form part of a widely diversified portfolio. For this reason, a certain amount of losses can be comfortably borne whilst still generating a positive return in aggregate. However, smaller investors do not have this luxury. The smaller the investor, the larger the likely detrimental impact of an investment fund returning losses or significant under-performance. For this reason, law and regulation has been and is continually being enacted to deliver protection to the most vulnerable of investors in the market.

At the investment fund level, regulation requires that key information on an investment fund is available through the Offering Document and through regular reporting, e.g. through financial statements. But some regulators will also require more subtle forms of investor protection, including:

- The requirement to separate investment management from the risk element of the fund. This is becoming more prevalent, with AIFMD being a primary example of how risk management and portfolio management have been separated as a matter of law.
- A more traditional model for investment funds is to have the fund board largely separate, and thus independent of, the fund manager. This ensures that the investors have a collection of fund principals legally obliged to put their interests at heart, in acknowledgement of the fact that the fund manager is much more conflicted.
- The appointment of a custodian is another form of investor protection. Custodians are a regulatory requirement of many offshore investment funds and are engaged to safeguard the assets of the investment fund, typically by taking on the legal ownership or safekeeping of them in order to prove their existence. The custodian will also monitor the conduct of other key parties to the fund (e.g. in the way they generate the fund's valuation) and the way in which they deal with investors (e.g. through the presentation of financial information and at the point of subscribing or redeeming).

1.4 Managing the fund investments

Much study has been completed over the years aimed at investigating the link between the quality of the fund manager and the performance of assets managed by them. In terms of management, the fund manager's role will typically involve:

Identifying and investigating viable investment opportunities and recommendations as to disposals

Offshore funds are typically established by onshore fund managers to take advantage of expertise (e.g. administrators, lawyers and accountants) in the offshore jurisdiction selected but also to take advantage of efficiencies (e.g. bilateral tax treaties) and routes to investors that may not otherwise be available in their own jurisdiction.

This creates not only a legal segregation between the fund and its manager but also creates a segregation of jurisdiction. In order to maintain both the legal and jurisdictional segregation, the fund must establish that its mind and management exists in one jurisdiction whilst the role of the fund manager is carried out in another, i.e. that the two are not commingled nor that the manager is the de facto controller of the fund.

As a result, funds typically engage with their onshore fund manager through a series of contractual terms. Fund managers will be responsible for bringing potential investment opportunities to the fund for consideration but are not responsible for deciding whether or not to invest. Instead they will prepare an investment proposal, documenting all the relevant detail the fund's board will require in order to enter into an investment decision.

Such recommendations must be in line with the fund's offering documents and other constitutive documentation.

This applies equally to opportunities for new investments as it does for recommendations as to the optimal time to exit an investment.

Assistance in the acquisition and/or disposal of investments

Once the fund has reached a decision to proceed, the fund manager will ordinarily liaise with the fund's lawyers and key parties to the transaction to manage the process, calling upon the fund to consider and approve transactional documentation as part of that management.

Maintaining the investment

Whatever asset, the manager will assume the role of managing the performance of that investment whilst it is owned by the fund, e.g. for listed shares, daily statistics and reports will be conducted to track performance and consider whether a hold, sell or buy recommendation should be made, whereas for property funds the role may include project managing the construction of assets, managing the sale or lease of property and/or providing facilities management expertise to the upkeep of property.

During the lifetime of an investment, the fund manager will provide reports to the fund charting progress, as well as providing performance and valuation data.

1.5 The relationship between the fund manager and the fund

Offshore investment funds are the responsibility of their boards of directors and those boards will have all of the responsibility for managing the assets of the funds in accordance with the Offering Documents, law and regulation.

administration
Providing any administrative, secretarial or clerical services in relation to an investment.

Fund boards are often made up of specialists in various areas of investment funds, including corporate governance, accounting and **administration** and will frequently have someone recognised in a relevant field appointed as chairman. This means that their blend of skill and experience is appropriate for the fund but may not necessarily allow for successful growth of the investment portfolio. Whilst they possess the skills to manage offshore funds in accordance with law and regulation and will have a sufficient level of knowledge, collectively, to understand the investment parameters, the fund itself does not have either the experience or the staff to perform its own fund management and so is not adequately resourced to manage the fund's investments.

For this reason, the fund's board will contract with the fund manager to provide those skills, whether as investment manager or adviser, and adequate resourcing to support the investment objectives and, in so doing, will grant varying levels of discretion and powers in respect of investment-making decisions.

Not only does the fund manager have the resourcing and the skill to manage the fund's investments but it will also be the party most likely to be able to pursue investment opportunities and also to generate them because the fund manager will be part of a network that the fund itself is not.

In this way, the relationship between the fund and the fund manager is both strange and unique and creates a dichotomy that must be carefully managed.

Some offshore jurisdictions have tried to recognise and manage the dichotomy through the naming convention of various parties to the fund, most frequently appointing the principals in charge of the fund as the manager in some guise. However, the same issues arise. This manager does not employ staff of its own and so does not have the resources to identify and manage fund investments. As a result, it will need to engage with a third party to provide these services. Invariably, that investment manager or adviser appointed will be the party the outside world recognises as the fund manager.

In terms of the fund itself, the fund manager's obligations lie within the form of contract it has in place with the fund but is not responsible for the fund itself. Responsibility for the fund lies with those responsible for its management, i.e. the directors, trustee or general partner, who are directly responsible in law and in regulatory terms. And yet the fund does not exist without a fund manager.

The fund may select its own investments but this selection will, in reality, be limited in scope to the investment objectives, set by the fund manager at the outset, and the investment opportunities the fund manager is able to source.

The Investment Management Agreement (IMA)

The form of contract between the fund and its fund manager is known as the IMA and it governs the relationship between the fund and the fund manager. It is a key document in any investment fund and, as such, will always be identified in an offering document as a material contract and its key terms disclosed through that offering document.

Key terms of the IMA will:

- Establish the key tasks the manager must perform, such as–
  - identifying and researching suitable investment opportunities;
  - conducting due diligence on investment opportunities;
  - seeking opportunities for improvement or disposal of investments.
- Establish the extent of the manager's authority–
  - a manager may be granted a discretionary mandate, whether on an absolute basis or within set boundaries (e.g. investment acquisitions up to a certain value or percentage of AUM), meaning that the manager has absolute power over investment choices, subject only to the monitoring and oversight of the governing body;
  - disposal of assets, requiring the manager to present detailed recommendations in order to authorise a transaction;
  - the manager's authority to manage the assets and, to what extent, the fund's governing body will retain certain powers to intervene in their management.
- Establish how much the manager will be paid–
  - **management fees** – the fees for the services it provides, typically expressed as a percentage of NAV or AUM at set points in time.

Management fees tend to be set at 1–2% per annum against NAV, though the level of fees agreed will be dependent upon the relative bargaining power of both the manager and the investors the fund is targeting.

- **performance fees** – that fee the manager will receive once the investment fund's performance exceeds a set benchmark or other criteria.
- **any provision for clawback** – Investors and those charged with their protection, such as regulators, are keen to ensure that managers are only being enriched by those fees they are entitled to take. As an example, performance fees are ordinarily calculated on a periodic basis and claimed by the manager as soon as the end of the first period during which the set indicator has been exceeded. However, it may happen that in the following period the fund underperforms so drastically that any previous performance is wiped out. In these instances, many are keen to see that the manager remains responsible and so the investment fund may recoup (clawback) some of the performance paid to its manager.

2. The fund administrator

2.1 Introduction

A fund administrator performs a pivotal role in the life cycle of a fund, so much so that regulatory authorities require that the functionary is appropriately regulated.

2.2 The role of the fund administrator

Fund administration is the set of activities carried out in support of the process of running an investment fund. Whatever its name and whatever its structure, the basic components of the role remain the same, including:

- **Calculation of the net asset value**

  This is the process by which the value of the fund is determined on a periodic basis and for varying purposes. For example, the NAV determines the price at which units/shares in the fund may be redeemed or purchased.

- **Maintenance of financial books and records**

  It is vital that transactional records are kept at all times, whether physical movement of cash, in-specie movements or adjustments to account for fluctuations in valuations etc. The fund administrator will maintain and reconcile all applicable records.

- **Preparation of financial statements**

  Financial statements provide a key method of communicating with the shareholders, as well as other stakeholders, such as regulators. For this reason, it is vital they are compiled in a fair and transparent way.

- **Payment of fund expenses**

  The fund administrator will typically control the fund's bank accounts, from which all expenses will be paid in accordance with supporting contracts etc.

- **Settlement of fund investments, including any receipts of income/ dividends etc**

  Though the administrator may not always physically store a fund's assets, it will typically be involved in ensuring that their purchase and disposal are properly completed.

- **Filing the scheme particulars**

  The scheme particulars remain the responsibility of those charged with managing the fund (e.g. the board or general partner), however the administrator will typically hold the definitive version and ensure that it is filed with applicable regulatory authorities and available to other necessary parties.

- **Filing regulatory returns and notifications**

  Whilst some jurisdictions allow for unregulated funds and so regulatory filing obligations will be minimal, most funds will have to complete certain filings to satisfy the regulator as to their ongoing suitability, including financial statements and accompanying audit reports and letters.

- **Calculation of management fees and performance fees**

  The form of calculation will be laid out within the scheme particulars but the fund administrator may produce the computation in order for the fund to agree and pay the fees.

- **Monitoring compliance with investment parameters particularly and the offering document more generally**

  The offering document establishes the rules by which the fund must be operated, including what it may or may not invest in and associated limits. The fund administrator must ensure that all its tasks are completed in compliance with the offering document but will also be given responsibility to ensure that investments remain in line with them.

The fund administrator may provide additional services to those considered above, however those services will always fall outside of fund promotion (the process of attracting investors to the fund) and asset management (the process of securing and managing the fund's investments), which will rest with other parties.

By way of examples, it is also common for the fund administrator to provide corporate secretarial and regulatory compliance services as part of its overall package of services.

The fund administrator may also provide transfer agent (**registration**) functions, that is to say maintenance of the investor registers of the funds at any one time.

registration
Is comprised of two components: (a) recording particulars of a specified investor; (b) issuing a certificate or policy to a specified investor or bearer.

2.3 Regulatory expectations

Regulatory requirements are placed on those wishing to undertake fund administration duties, such as:

- In the BVI, all administrators of mutual funds carrying out their activities in or from within the BVI must be licensed by the BVI Financial Services Commission pursuant to the BVI Mutual Funds Act.
- In Guernsey, licensing is carried out pursuant to the Protection of Investors (Bailiwick of Guernsey) Law, 1987.
- Any person carrying out financial services in Mauritius must be licensed to do so pursuant to the Financial Services Act.
- Jersey administrators must be licensed under the Financial Services (Jersey) Law 1998.

The development of local laws and regulation in the interests of protecting the public in financial services have resulted in most fund administration tasks being subject to regulatory oversight. The following is taken from Guernsey's law but will be common to most offshore jurisdictions.

subscription
In relation to regulatory requirements, receiving funds or assets for the purposes of investment.

Subscription, that is to say receiving funds or assets for the purposes of investment.

Administration, that is to say providing any administrative, secretarial or clerical services in relation to an investment, including:

- the provision of general accountancy and bookkeeping services, but not the audit of accounts; and
- the provision of valuation services on a continuing basis in connection with any dealing in an investment.

Registration, that is to say:

- recording particulars of a specified investor; and
- issuing a certificate or policy to a specified investor or bearer.

The purpose of the regulation is to ensure that those carrying out those services are suitable, including that all directors, controllers, partners and managers of the licensee:

- act with probity;
- demonstrate competence;
- have the experience and soundness of judgment to fulfil their responsibilities;
- act with diligence;
- keep the interests of the clients/investors and of the reputation of the relevant financial centre in such a way that no detriment to reputation may be incurred;
- have and continue to demonstrate relevant education and professional qualifications;

- fully understand their legal and professional obligations; and
- have sufficient policies, procedures and controls in place to ensure that their duties are carried out with regard to all legal and regulatory requirements, including anti-money laundering and financial crime.

When considering the above, the regulator will have regard to whether any party:

- has committed a relevant offence, generally those involving fraud, dishonesty or violence;
- has contravened any regulatory law or those relating to AML and CFT; and
- has engaged in or been associated with business practices that may cast doubt on his competence and soundness of judgment.

All of the above forms the regulatory test, known as the 'fit and proper' test, which tests the integrity and skill of the key parties of the licensee in the manner in which they fulfil their duties.

A significant element of the test centres around financial and operational controls designed to ensure a licensee maintains:

- A sufficient capital base and insurance cover to meet the requirements and risks of conducting business. In order to assess whether these elements are adequate, the licensee must consider the risks inherent in its operations in the context of their nature and scale.
- Sufficient records to record both its financial status and all other aspects of operations.
- Sufficient controls in respect of both its records and its operations.
- Staff of adequate number, skills, knowledge and experience.
- Its complaints history.

3. The fund's governing body

3.1 Introduction

In law and regulation there must always be a body with ultimate responsibility for the performance of the investment fund. In examining what this body is, this section will identify who these people are, the duties they owe to investors and how those duties originate.

3.2 Identifying the governing body

The governing body is that person or group of people ultimately charged with managing the fund. Where the fund is a company, that company will take on those duties through its board of directors. Where the fund is a limited partnership, the role will be assumed by its general partner and a trust will be governed by its trustee. Typically all of these structural lines will arrive back at a board of directors and so this chapter will consider the responsibilities of those directors and how they may seek to perform them.

3.3 Responsibilities

Fund directors, howsoever that role is established within the fund structure, will generally consider their responsibilities through various categories:

- **Fiduciary duties** – Most, if not all, of the major offshore centres recognise that these functionaries owe fiduciary duties to the fund and its investors. The most common of these duties are those to act in the interests of the fund and to act with skill, care and diligence. These duties would ultimately fall to be judged by a court of law as they are enshrined in law, whether included through statute or resting within the common law, but many regulators will consider their application when considering whether any regulatory laws or rules have been broken.
- **Statutory duties** – These are contained within the relevant statutes underpinning the legal structuring of the fund. In recent years, fiduciary duties have been expressly inserted into various statutes, formally codifying what was best practice formerly. In addition to fiduciary duties, functionaries will be granted, amongst others, the responsibility to take care of assets, to avoid conflicts of interest, to communicate with investors and to seek permissions from investors in certain circumstances. A breach of any of these obligations can result in the functionaries being found guilty, in civil and/or criminal law, which may result in prohibitions, fines, custody and/or other financial penalties (such as restitution).
- **Regulatory duties** – Although enshrined in financial services legislation, rules and other regulatory codes may create additional responsibilities surrounding the format and provision of information to investors.
- **Contractual duties** – When an investor subscribes to the fund it enters into a legally binding arrangement with the fund, and thus its governing body. In so doing, the governing body agrees to invest those monies in accordance with the terms of the fund's governing documents, i.e. the offering document and other constitutive documents (e.g. its memorandum and articles of association).

Wherever the duty lies, the standard utilised to determine whether the duty has been met or whether it has been breached will remain broadly the same. Typically that standard is a blend of both objective and subjective considerations. This means that not only will a functionary be judged based upon what a reasonable man would have expected of someone in that position but they will also be judged upon their own experiences and skills.

For example, whilst all the directors may reasonably be seen to have been remiss in the misstatement of a fund's financial statements and guilty of a breach of duty, where one of those directors was also an accountant, the scale of fault found on his part may be somewhat greater than that of a director whose personal experience lay elsewhere.

Fault will generally be established upon the following criteria, which rest in law:

Civil considerations

- **Negligence** – Conduct that falls below the standards of behaviour established by law for the protection of others against unreasonable risk of harm. A person has acted negligently if he or she has departed from the conduct expected of a reasonably prudent person acting under similar circumstances.
- **Default** – An omission or failure to do that which is anticipated, expected or required in a given situation. It is distinguishable from negligence in that it does not involve carelessness or imprudence with respect to the discharge of a duty or obligation but rather the intentional omission or non-performance of a duty.
- **Breach of duty** – Any act which is in violation of the duties established in law or through fiduciary duties owed (which are generally now enshrined in law) to the investors (shareholders/unitholders).
- **Breach of trust** – Any act which is in violation of the duties to act in the terms specified in agreements, such as the offering documents and other constitutive documents in addition to law and rule.

Criminal considerations:

- **Fraud** – A false representation of a matter of fact—whether by words or by conduct, by false or misleading allegations, or by concealment of what should have been disclosed—that deceives and is intended to deceive another so that the individual will act upon it to her or his legal injury.

4. Governance

4.1 The Governing body and governance

Corporate governance broadly refers to the mechanisms, processes and relations by which corporations are controlled and directed. Governance structures and principles identify the distribution of rights and responsibilities among different participants in the corporation (such as the board of directors, managers, shareholders, creditors, auditors, regulators and other stakeholders) and includes the rules and procedures for making decisions in corporate affairs.

Governance has evolved over the last decade or so, creating an obligation on various stakeholders but none more so than the governing body of an investment fund. A number of offshore jurisdictions have enacted specific corporate governance codes, designed to capture these responsibilities in a formal matrix in respect of which governing bodies must find ways to comply or explain their non-compliance.

At the heart of governance is transparency, which is achieved through various broad categories of consideration, such as:

- the balance and composition of the board;
- how the board determines powers reserved for itself and those delegated to management etc;

- the directors and how they meet their legislative and regulatory duties;
- performance evaluations;
- training and development;
- conflicts of interests;
- conduct and ethics;
- accountability;
- risk management;
- disclosure;
- remuneration; and
- shareholder relations.

How corporate governance is best evidenced is not a matter of one size fits all and the governing body will need to consider the nature of the fund, including the ease with which units can be redeemed, whether the fund is private or public and the varying rights of the investors, to name a few. However, corporate governance, in particular governance failings, are shaping the way in which governance is developing.

In Guernsey, the abolition of the Sark Lark in 1999 spelled a leap forward for governance. The Sark Lark arose due to a twist that saw tax liability removed if director's meetings were held outside of Jersey and Guernsey. As a consequence, thousands of Guernsey and Jersey companies appointed Sark resident directors, each director of hundreds of companies, if not more. This practice came under criticism as Sark had no company or financial services law but, more importantly, because of the 'rubber-stamping' approach that was developed by the Sark resident directors. In the intervening years since 1999, both Guernsey and Jersey have adapted their financial services and corporate laws, introducing robust measures to engender good governance practice.

Case study 4.1

Weavering case

In more recent times, the *Weavering* case has been a well-documented instance of fund directors not meeting their duties to the required standard. Whilst many of the elements of that case were over turned at appeal, the Court of Appeal did not invalidate the findings of the court of first instance as to the requirements applicable to the directors of funds but clarified that a failure to meet them did not, alone, mean that there was a clear intention by a director to not perform their role.

Mr Justice Jones in that case said that 'a director must exercise his powers independently, without subordinating those powers to the will of others, except to the extent that they have properly delegated their powers.' The guidelines set down in that case suggested that directors should:

- apply their minds and exercise independent justice;
- conduct independent review in an inquisitorial manner and make appropriate enquiries of those involved (e.g. the financial statements);
- satisfy themselves as to the terms of the offering document, including legal compliance, shareholder rights and the information given to prospective investors (upon which they would base their decision);
- ensure that the investment strategy is fairly described in the offering document and that the investment manager complies with the criteria and restrictions adopted by the fund;
- ensure that there is appropriate division between the roles of the manager and the administrator;
- ensure that agendas and records of meetings are full and demonstrate consideration of appropriate matters, such as investment matters, NAV matters including changes, problems and compliance matters;
- have a full picture of the financial condition of the fund;
- ensure that fund decisions are properly documented and summarise the basis of the decisions made; and
- ensure that the frequency of meetings is sufficient in the context of the activity of the fund and the market in which it operates.

Ultimately the decision in *Weavering* confirmed to directors that their duties do not conclude with signing documents and allowing matters to proceed. Directors must be vigilant and take an active role.

The recent matter of Bordeaux and its directors, concluded in Guernsey's Court of Appeal in 2016, is another example of the way in which directors' duties are being interpreted in a judicial setting. In that matter, the directors were found not to have applied their mind sufficiently to various matters and so their conduct fell short of that considered acceptable of directors in the circumstances.

Europe's approach to governance is proving to be somewhat different. Traditionally, whilst certain fund legislation requires the presence of an independent custodian, the roles of risk and asset management have not been split and so have been capable of being performed by one party. AIFMD requires a division of those tasks. Perhaps most commonly this is achieved by the fund manager taking on asset management responsibilities and a separate fund board taking on those of risk management. Howsoever achieved, all parties must demonstrate that they are applying their minds fully to the performance of their respective roles and that they are not mere 'letterbox' entities designed to create an illusion of substance where none exists. For offshore finance centres wishing to market funds to EU citizens, those funds and their principles must adapt to the European approach, which is having, and will continue to have, some effect on both legislation and regulation in non-EU centres.

4.2 The role of the administrator in fund governance

The role of the fund administrator has been and continues to steadily grow. As worldwide focus on investor protection increases in the wake of recent crises and scandal, it is not so much the practical elements of the role that have changed but the manner in which they must be carried out, the accountability of the parties and the administrator's oversight of the entire fund.

5. Interrelationship of the three parties

5.1 The relationship between the fund manager and the governing body

This relationship is perhaps the most critical of all within a fund's structure. As considered above, the fund manager is the entity the investors buy into, as it is at that level that the investment thesis may be brought to life through previous experience, access to opportunities and the know-how to manage investments fruitfully.

However, the investors and thus, by extension, the regulator, will look to the governing body to ensure that the actions taken by the fund manager are reasonable and in the best interests of the fund and its investors.

In theory the governing body is responsible for monitoring the performance of the fund manager and determining whether they remain fit for purpose or whether an alternative arrangement might yield better results for the fund. In reality, however, it is very rare that a governing body will find itself in a position where it could feasibly consider sacking its fund manager.

In the main, replacement fund managers would be nearly impossible to find, as each has its own unique qualities that cannot easily be replicated. Moving to a new fund manager without achieving an exact fit could have serious ramifications for the performance of the fund.

Instead, the governing body's role is best served through scrutiny and challenge of the fund manager's decisions, recommendations and actions. It must also carefully consider the level of fees the fund manager earns or stands to earn and must ensure that the fund manager is only remunerated where it deserves to be and that any remuneration paid is exactly in line with the expectations created by the fund's offering document.

Balancing the more theoretical duties with those achievable in reality creates a fine line upon which the governing body must tread. Too heavy-handed an approach may result in investment opportunities being removed or the loss of critical skill and expertise that may render the investment thesis too difficult to achieve.

Additionally, investors may seek to exit a fund if the fund manager is removed from position, with many investors following the fund manager.

In the world of offshore investment funds, this balance may be best achieved through the addition of two key members of the governing body:

- The first is the chairman, which will be a person with significant skill and experience in a relevant field and with sufficient gravitas to add useful input into fund discussions but also to take the fund manager to task when necessary. As a result, the chairman must be independent of the fund manager in every way.
- The second is a board member selected from the fund manager. This is a difficult role for the incumbent, as that person will have many conflicts to manage as a result of the fact that he is remunerated by the fund manager for the returns made and will owe significant duties to the fund and its investors to act in their best interests.

The remainder of the board positions should be occupied by robust people with relevant experience and independence of mind and expression.

5.2 The relationship between the governing body and the fund administrator

The fund will contract with the fund administrator through a legally binding services agreement and thus the relationship becomes a contractual one. However the fund's governing body will rely upon the fact that the fund administrator is a licensed financial services business and that, as a result, numerous obligations are imposed upon it, designed to preserve the integrity of the fund and the investment opportunity it is offering. For instance, the fund administrator will ensure that investments bought and sold remain in line with the fund's investment objectives and also within relevant limits and restrictions. As part of this, the administrator will consider concentration levels to ensure that the levels of diversification required are maintained.

Because the fund and its governing body generally will not have staff or other resources to complete tasks in support of the fund, the role the fund administrator plays is essential, and thus it is equally essential that the relationship between the two is strong and engenders open and honest communication at all times.

5.3 The company secretary

As the fund administrator is also typically engaged to provide corporate secretarial services, often acting as the named company secretary, the administrator will also play a role in assisting the board to meet governance requirements and best practice through record-taking and retention, maintaining the legal entity in good standing and helping to ensure that investor engagement is carried out in an acceptable way.

The role of the company secretary is an important one in the context of investment funds, which must be able to demonstrate that the governing body took reasonable and measured steps to best preserve the rights and protection of the investors at all times and certainly at all operative moments (transactions, dealings with the fund manager, communications etc). The company secretary performs this pivotal role by:

- retaining corporate records–
  - Board minutes;
  - Committee minutes;
  - Investor meeting minutes (e.g. general meetings, limited partner meetings etc);
- ensuring that these documents are meaningful, and complete and accurate records of the key discussions and key outcomes of each respective meeting are captured;
- Facilitating transparent communications with investors and regulators;
- Assisting the governing body's board through the formulation of board and investor communication agendas; and
- Assisting the governing body's board through compliance with law, regulation and other applicable rules (in Guernsey, for example, this requirement is established by law for companies).

5.4 The relationship between the fund manager and the fund administrator

The two terms are frequently intertwined, with administrators often referring to themselves as fund managers. However, the two roles are significantly different from one another and so should not be confused.

The fund manager may appoint its own staff to complete the administrative functions but, even where the fund manager and the administrator are, ultimately, the same party, the fund, being a legal entity in its own right, will need to contract with both the fund manager and the fund administrator owing to the very different tasks each performs. A requirement for independence in the performance of the respective tasks is also required, given the great potential for conflicts of interest to arise and, more importantly, detriment the investors in the fund if not handled correctly and prudently.

In recent years, the role of the fund administrator has been seen as another layer of investor protection removed from the fund manager. This is because the fund administrator assumes responsibility for the production of the net asset valuation of the fund and for the production of the fund's financial statements, independently of the fund manager.

Quite often, the fund manager will take back some of the responsibility for NAV production or for the financial statements, however fund regulation in most offshore jurisdictions will not allow the fund administrator to abdicate its responsibility for these items, meaning that they remain responsible for the work of the fund manager through an outsourcing arrangement.

Thus, most fund administrators will find that their touchpoints with the fund manager occur where:

- Asset valuations are required, whether for net asset valuation purposes on an ongoing basis or for the purpose of the financial statements; and

- Investment recommendations are to be approved or put in action, as typically the fund administrator will take control of the fund's bank accounts and so be responsible for releasing monies to fund investments or to receive monies for disposals.

Test yourself 4.1

Consider the following roles and responsibilities and determine who may be responsible for them between the fund manager, the fund administrator and the fund governing body.

Description	Manager	Administrator	Governing Body
Prospective investments			
Acquisition/disposal of investments			
Monitoring/ensuring investments remain in line with the terms of the offering document			
Management of investments			
Obtaining investment valuations			
Preparation of the NAV of the fund			
Calculation of management fees			
Calculation of performance fees			
Scrutinising all fees payable to the manager for reasonableness			
Approval of management/ performance fees			

Chapter summary

- Each fund requires the presence of parties charged with its governance, investment management and administration.
- Each component part will be subject to its own respective obligations, whether owed through regulation, legislation or contract terms.
- Without a fund manager, the fund does not exist as it is the fund manager that investors ultimately buy into. However, as considered above, the fund manager performs its functions in the expectation of generating significant management and performance fees. This means that a significant conflict exists in respect of the fund manager between the prospective financial rewards and preserving the interests of investors. This conflict must be carefully managed to ensure that fees are proportionate, earned for good performance in the context of the offering documents and do not encourage excessive risk taking or unscrupulous practice.
- The roles of the governing body and the administrator protect against the fund manager's conflicts crystallising and harming the rights of investors, for example through excessive risk taking or through flawed or fraudulent practice. In this way, the governing body and the administrator are equally as important to the fund as the fund manager.
- It is worth considering the role of the regulatory bodies. Their only interest lies in preserving the reputations of their respective finance centres. They achieve this through putting in place measures to protect the public utilising those finance centres and by having powers to oversee relevant financial services businesses and, where necessary, to penalise them for failings.

Chapter five

Introduction to offshore fund administration

List of topics

1. Fund administration in context
2. Offshore funds
3. Fund administrators in action

Introduction

In this text we will consider the components that make up investment funds, key parties to the fund and the administrator's role in their operation. The role of the fund administrator has evolved significantly over time, with layers of complexity and responsibility existing now that simply would have been unheard of forty or so years ago when most of the world's major offshore finance centres were taking their first significant steps into the world of investment fund administration. This chapter will describe offshore fund administration in detail.

1. Fund administration in context

From the more simplistic role of compiling fund valuations and completing the various tasks surrounding that function, such as bookkeeping and tracking of inflows and outflows, has emerged a world of responsibility requiring thought and reasoning at every level.

At the heart of it all is the increased and increasing focus on protecting the most vulnerable members of our society, to ensure that those without the means to weather financial storms, failures and losses are not duped into risking it all in the hands of unscrupulous people intent only on lining their own pockets.

Around the world, you will see that fund regulators sprung from the existence of fund administration sectors. The earliest pioneers in fund administration did so in the backdrop of little to no regulation. Steadily regulation emerged and, as a consequence of every fund failure and of every major economic crisis, that regulation has been ramped up again and again. We certainly have not seen the last of it.

Test yourself 5.1

Is the trend for increased regulation likely to decrease in the future? Explain your reasoning.

2. Offshore funds

fund sectors
Specific locations associated with highly developed fund infrastructures.

The fundamental question, therefore, is why have **fund sectors** grown up all over the world in offshore locations?

Many will point at tax as the only consideration and label offshore finance sectors as tax havens designed only to assist people to avoid paying taxes in their own countries or in the country where economic activity occurs. Whilst it is true that tax efficiency will always factor in fund structuring, offshore fund sectors thrive for varying reasons and certainly for more reasons than tax.

At the heart of this industry is the infrastructure offshore centres have built up over a considerable amount of time. Funds industries attract key professional services, including world-class law firms and lawyers, accountants and tax experts. Off the back of that, whole groups of people have been educated in fund accounting, fund administration, corporate governance and a raft of complementary skills. In short, offshore finance centres present themselves as one-stop shops for fund managers, able to call upon structuring experts, legal advice and those proficient at looking after the fund structure throughout its lifetime, all within very small spaces.

What drives fund managers to offshore centres may well include tax efficiency, as fund structures are designed to take advantage of tax treaties in a bid to avoid double-paying or overpaying tax. But it is more complex than that. Offshore finance centres have garnered relationships with placement agents, brokers, fund managers and major fund lawyers. As finance centres have proved that they could do the job, those key parties have kept them in mind and referred their clients towards finance centres and, off the back of those successful relationships, finance centres have garnered ever growing relationships. Like fund managers, finance centres succeed or fail on their track-records.

With increasing regulation and scrutiny on inflows and outflows of cash worldwide, including investor protection, tax erosion and other measures, the offshore finance centres have demonstrated not only their resilience but also their robustness through the creation of world-leading regulatory frameworks, strong corporate governance regimes and a requirement for true substance to be demonstrated by all of their key players.

Test yourself 5.2

Besides tax considerations, what is another reason that fund sectors have grown up in offshore locations?

3. Fund administrators in action

What this means in the modern world of high finance is that an offshore fund administrator cannot be a passive entity, merely going through the motions in order to earn a fee. Fund administrators have to be so much more and anybody embarking upon a career in fund administration, whether accounting, pure administration, corporate secretarial or complementary skills, such as registration and transfer agency, must be prepared to understand the cause and effect not only of their own actions but also those of the fund manager, fund promoter, auditor and other parties, such as property or other investment managers (if not the fund manager).

For fund administrators wishing to administer funds established in Europe or selling into Europe, this role is becoming much more codified with the jurisdiction's suitability resting in the opinion of European bodies, including Moneyval, ESMA and the European Commission. Regulatory regimes must be designed with these European influences in mind and so must be targeted at ensuring that only competent parties are allowed to perform relevant tasks.

Fund administrators must also have a much greater understanding of where the money is coming from and where it is going:

- In the wake of the G20's desire to combat tax evasion on a global scale, global legislation has been created to identify where money is earned (such as FATCA and CRS) and seeking to prevent businesses from shifting profits elsewhere to exploit lower taxes or even to negate them (such as BEPS).
- At the heart of this understanding, of course, is a global desire to reduce the threat and opportunity for money laundering and for the use of finance products to fund, aid or hide criminal activity.

Administrators must also play their part in mind and management, by knowing when to challenge, when to question and when to defer to those in charge, e.g. the fund board. The latest legal decisions in Guernsey are pointing to a greater requirement for the fund administrator to be active not only in the production of valuations and other traditional administration tasks, but also in the investment parameters of the fund. Administrators, whilst not expected to become investment specialists, are expected to have an understanding of what does and does not make sense, of what should and should not work and of what is and is not permitted.

Fund administrators have a significant role to play in corporate governance. Many offshore investment funds do not have a whole staff dedicated to it and so must instead outsource functions and, in so doing, look to the general staff of the fund administrator. Specialists in corporate secretarial and corporate governance can provide invaluable services to the fund manager and fund board by providing useful advice, by understanding the rules and by helping the fund adhere to them in a pragmatic manner. Ultimately, the success of the fund administrator is as important as the success of all the other component parts. Funds that perform well in a risk-measured and reasonable way are good for the economy and good for investors. Funds that deviate from this path risk ruining the reputations of finance centres, individual parties and finance sector regulators as well as risking the personal finances of those who invest. Where any party to a fund is delinquent, regulators can, must and will step in to punish the worst offenders.

Chapter summary

- Before it became a complex responsibility requiring thought and reasoning at every level, fund administration used to be a simplistic duty to compile fund valuations and complete various tasks surrounding that function, such as bookkeeping and tracking of inflows and outflows.
- The infrastructure of offshore centres have built up over a considerable amount of time, and include key professional services, including world-class law firms and lawyers, accountants and tax experts.
- In the modern world of high finance, an offshore fund administrator cannot be a passive entity, merely going through the motions in order to earn a fee.

Chapter six
Fund accounting

List of topics

1. What is fund accounting?
2. Types of funds
3. The role of the fund accountant vs the fund administrator
4. Fund accounting specifics
5. IT systems
6. Production of fund accounts
7. Recent developments in UK accounting standards and the implications for fund accounting (850)

Introduction

This chapter will look at the field of fund accounting. It will provide an overview of what fund accounting is, moving on to looking at what types of funds we refer to when talking about fund accounting, the differences between a fund accountant and a fund administrator, how they interact together and how the administrator role is crucial in order to enable to accountant to carry out their duties.

The chapter will then move on to discuss specific activities involved in carrying out the accounting function for different types of funds, also looking at the process involved in the production of fund accounts.

Finally, we will look at the recent developments in accounting principles and standards and the impact of these changes on fund accounting.

1. What is fund accounting?

Fund accounting is a broad term used to define the process of accounting for different portfolios of investments. Generally speaking, fund accountants will be employed by managers or administrators of investment funds, however, it is also not uncommon for fund managers and administrators to outsource the accounting function to third party accountants or accounting firms.

The fund accountant will be responsible for not only producing financial statements annually, or more frequently as required, but for providing analysis of the financial data such as trends and movements from the previous period in order to enable the directors or other senior management to make decisions and review the performance of the fund. Often the role of analysis falls to more senior fund accountants.

Fund accounting involves not only accounting for the day-to-day transactions within a fund, covering general income and expenses, but calculating the often daily NAV of the fund, carrying out periodic reconciliations and investigating discrepancies. NAV will be discussed further in the next chapter.

The accounts of a fund are a key document for providing crucial information for current and potential investors as well as a number of other stakeholders such as lenders, regulators, shareholders and tax authorities. Fund accounting is therefore a vital service for most funds.

2. Types of funds

There are several different types of investment funds we refer to when talking about fund accounting, the most common of which are expanded upon below, however many other types do exist such as ethical funds which exist solely to invest in companies and organisations that are deemed to be ethical and socially responsible.

mutual funds
These pool together the funds of several investors in order to invest these funds in specific markets.

hedge fund
A hedge fund, whilst still pooling investor funds together is targeted more towards sophisticated investors with substantial sums available to invest.

private equity funds
Investment schemes funded through substantial amounts of pooled capital obtained from institutional investors such as pension funds, insurance companies and also high net worth individuals.

equity funds
Can be broken down further into several different types of equity funds but of the purpose of this chapter we will focus on the most common and straight forward type of equity fund.

2.1 Investment funds

Investment funds can be broken down broadly into **mutual funds**, equity (stocks), fixed income (bonds) and money market, **hedge funds**, **private equity funds** and real estate funds.

2.2 Mutual funds

These pool together the funds of several investors in order to invest these funds in specific markets. They can be either open-ended (the investor can join the fund at any time, thus new shares can be issued at any time) or closed-ended (there are a fixed number of shares from the outset and investors cannot simply redeem their shares – they must be traded with other investors).

2.3 Equity funds

These can again be broken down further into several different types of **equity funds** but for the purpose of this chapter we will focus on the most common and straight-forward type of equity fund. These funds invest in equities (shares of businesses) commonly through the purchasing of company stocks which are publicly traded on an exchange such as the London Stock Exchange (LSE) or the New York Stock Exchange.

2.4 Fixed income funds

Fixed income funds, also known as bond funds, invest in corporations or governments by way of loan, for which they receive an agreed amount of interest on regularly agreed dates for a set period of time. This is referred to as the 'coupon'. The income earned on these funds is guaranteed and therefore tends to generate lower returns than say equity funds. Governments issue what are known as 'treasury bills' in return for monies received, which detail the coupon rate of interest payable and the duration. Companies issue 'corporate bonds' and banks issue 'certificates of deposit'.

fixed income funds
Also known as bond funds, invest in corporations or governments by way of loan, for which they receive an agreed amount of interest on regularly agreed dates for a set period of time.

2.5 Money market funds

Money market funds are a type of fixed income fund. They are open-ended funds that invest solely in short-term securities, primarily treasury bills and certificates of deposit.

money market funds
A type of fixed income fund that is open-ended and invests solely in short-term securities, primarily treasury bills and certificates of deposit.

2.6 Hedge fund

A hedge fund, whilst still pooling investor funds together is targeted more towards sophisticated investors with substantial sums available to invest.

In contrast to mutual funds, hedge funds focus on investing in less conventional and arguably riskier products, often referred to as alternative investments. Hedge funds have diversified portfolios and flexible investment strategies with the aim of generating high returns for the investors. Hedge fund investors tend to be high net worth individuals or institutional investors.

2.7 Private equity funds

These are investment schemes funded through substantial amounts of pooled capital obtained from institutional investors such as pension funds, insurance companies and also high net worth individuals.

Funds remain active for set periods of time in order to generate returns for the investor, commonly referred to as the internal rate of return (IRR).

Classically, private equity funds exist in order to identify specific business opportunities which will increase their investment portfolio, generate high yields for the investors and obtain strategic business advantage. The most common ways of doing this are through buyouts or acquisitions of privately owned companies, restructuring or mergers.

The assets of private equity funds tend to be considerable extending often to nine or ten figures.

2.8 Property funds

Property funds invest in commercial and corporate buildings. These investments can be held for the purpose of generating a regular income by way of rent.

Other types of property funds invest in development properties with the aim of eventually selling the properties for a significant profit.

3. The role of the fund accountant vs the fund administrator

The main roles and responsibilities of the fund accountant have been touched upon in Section 1. For many types of funds, the fund administrator plays a significant role in the chain of events before the accountant steps in.

Many investment funds have a substantial amount of daily processing that is required in order to run a fund, frequently these roles are outsourced to external administration companies. Top administration companies of multi-managed funds with regards to assets under management in accordance with Hedge Fund Alert as at April 2016 are listed in Table 6.1.

Table 6.1: Administration companies of multi-managed funds

Administrator
BNY Mellon
State Street
SS&C GlobeOp
Citco
SEI
MUFG
Northern Trust
Hedgeserv
Renaissance Technologies
UMB Bank

Fund administration companies are responsible for carrying out the day-to-day operations of the fund. Specifically, they would perform the following duties:

- Processing of investor subscriptions and redemptions, issuing contract notes and bookkeeping these transactions.
- Investor relations – dealing with all investor queries and keeping investors up to date with information as required.
- Sending NAV statements to investors.
- Maintenance of records with regards to investment purchases and sales and bookkeeping these transactions.
- Maintenance of the fund's books and records.

Many administration companies have in-house accountants carrying out the accounting function, although as mentioned on page 99, this can be outsourced also.

Generally, the fund accountant will rely on the information input by the administration team in order to facilitate their work.

The accountant will carry out a high-level review of the information book-kept in the system with regards to investor subscriptions and redemptions and investment purchases and sales. Any discrepancies identified will be discussed and resolved with the administrators.

The fund accountant will generally be responsible for book-keeping any movements with regards to the valuation of investment portfolios based on information provided from the investment manager.

Where the fund is a mutual fund with investments in listed securities or bonds where prices are readily available from sources such as Bloomberg, updating the investment prices and therefore values can be carried out by the investment manager, the administration team or the accountant, depending on how straight-forward the investments are.

The fund accountant will then be responsible for calculating and processing any creditors and accruals that are required. The fund accountant is often also required to attend board meetings to discuss and explain the financial information produced.

4. Fund accounting specifics

There are many specific aspects of fund accounting depending on the type of fund. We will go through each of the fund types and expand on the accounting specifics that we would expect to see.

4.1 Mutual funds

Mutual funds tend to have a significant number of transactions daily on the investor's side and the investment side.

All of the expenses of running the fund are deducted from the total assets of the fund. The individual investors of the fund are entitled to their share of the net assets of the fund, depending on what percentage of total capital they have contributed through their investment. Naturally, this is only on the winding up of the fund. The investors can receive regular returns through dividends paid out of any excess distributable profits or opt to reinvest any proposed dividends back into the fund.

From a taxation perspective, the fund accountant is only concerned with calculating any applicable corporation tax, individual tax liabilities on returns paid out to investors are the responsibility of the investors.

The accountant (or indeed the administrator or fund manager) will calculate the NAV per share of the fund, often on a daily basis by dividing the net assets of the fund by the number of shares in the fund. The NAV per share is relied upon by directors and shareholders to assess how the fund has been performing, comparing this figure over time. Also, potential investors will use this as an indicator of how one fund is performing against another, which is key when making the decision over which fund offers the best value.

Making it work 6.1

Table 6.2: Brilliant Property Fund, balance sheet

BALANCE SHEET
BRILLIANT PROPERTY FUND

Assets		**2015**	**2014**
Current Assets			
	Cash	7,521	3,253
	Pre-paid expenses	18,255	19,365
	Rent receivable		
Fixed Assets			
	11, Langton Road	210,750	195,500
	3, Park Square	365,500	355,000
	25, Garden Mews	250,000	250,000
	The Shire, Essex	1,350,000	1,245,000
	100 Shares – Equity Fundsmith	45,000	44,000
	Mercedes SLK230	50,000	50,000
TOTAL ASSETS		2,297,026	2,162,118
Liabilities			
Current liabilities			
	Insurance	25,400	21,500
	Short-term finance	15,000	14,500
	Tax payable	28,000	25,000
		68,400	61,000
Long Term Liabilities			
	Long-term debt	450,000	420,000
Shareholders' funds			
	Paid-up capital	2,500,000	2,500,000
	Retained earnings	125,000	110,000
		2,625,000	2,610,000
TOTAL LIABILITIES AND SHAREHOLDERS' FUNDS		3,143,400	3,091,000

Table 6.2 is a balance sheet of a set of financial statements for a mutual fund. We would expect to see as a minimum:

- investments (recorded at purchase cost initially and then valuation);
- cash;
- debtors;
- dividends receivable;

- accrued management and advisory fees due;
- other payables;
- dividends and distributions due;
- investor deposits (under capital contributions).

In the profit or loss account we would expect to see as a minimum:

- dividend income;
- realised gain or loss on investments;
- unrealised gain or loss on investments;
- management and advisory fees;
- administration fees.

The statement of changes in net assets would detail the movements with regards to investor contributions, redemptions and dividends/ distributions paid out to investors.

4.2 Hedge funds

Due to the riskier and more complex nature of the investments found in hedge funds it is often recommended that outsourced accounting shouldn't just be recommended but actually compulsory in order to provide a third party controls check and remove any bias. This being said, hedge funds tend to use in-house accountants. Where the accounting is carried out by an external administrator/ accountant they are deemed to be independent.

Alongside NAVs which are produced, generally once a year, investors also receive other accounting reports which give detailed information on the performance of the fund.

As with mutual funds, potential investors use NAV history as well as the additional reports referred to above to make investment decisions.

Making it work 6.2

Table 6.2 on page 104 shows a balance sheet of a set of financial statements for a hedge fund. We would expect to see as a minimum:

- investments (recorded at purchase cost initially and then valuation);
- cash;
- debtors;
- dividends receivable;
- due from broker;
- investments sold short;
- due to broker;
- management fee payable;

- other payables;
- dividends and distributions due;
- investor deposits (under capital contributions).

In the profit or loss account we would expect to see as a minimum:

- dividend income;
- realised gain or loss on investments;
- unrealised gain or loss om investments;
- management and advisory fees;
- administration fees;
- transaction costs;
- borrowing fees;
- carried interest.

The statement of changes in net assets would detail the movements with regards to investor contributions, redemptions and dividends/ distributions paid out to investors.

4.3 Private equity funds

The accounting for private equity funds is unique due to the nature of the investments within the fund, which can be extremely varied and tend to be illiquid (companies). This results in widespread, often complex, valuation techniques.

All investments should be accounted for at 'fair value' in accordance with all current accounting standards. Fair value is defined as the price received to sell an asset or paid to transfer a liability in an orderly transaction between market participants at the measurement date. Defining fair value for the investments within the portfolio of a private equity fund due to the nature would be carried out by valuation specialists rather than the fund accountant.

The structure of private equity funds typically involves general partners (GPs) who are typically the partners of the PE firm. The GPs are responsible for making the investment decisions on behalf of the fund and managing the fund. Each fund generally has one GP.

Limited partners (LPs) are the providers of capital contributions into the fund. The investments are referred to as capital commitments. One fund can have as many as a few hundred different LPs. The terms of a limited partner's investment, including the duration of the fund, extension options, management fees and how any profits of the fund will be divided, are set out in what is known as the limited partnership agreement (LPA).

Accounting for private equity funds with regards to expenses and distributions is dependent solely on the terms as agreed in the LPA. The LPA determines how these expenses and distributions are spread across the GP and LP. The terms can often be complex, having a number of specific conditions overall, as well as per investment deal.

Accounting standards (expanded upon in Section 6) define how the accounting of private equity funds should be carried out, for example how much control and equity stake the fund has over each business investment in their portfolio will impact what method of accounting should be applied. The accounting standard applied also impacts how the capital commitments are treated:

- Under International Financial Reporting Standards (IFRS) partner capital commitments are treated as debt which have a finite life.
- Under United States Generally Accepted Accounting Principles (USGAAP) partner capital commitments are treated as equity with an infinite life, unless the LPA states that they can redeem their investment at a specific point in time.

A further complication with regards to accounting for private equity funds is that some funds invest in businesses by way of a mixture of both debt and equity. These two elements will need to be separated for accounting purposes, with the interest and dividends due being accounted for accordingly.

Making it work 6.3

Table 6.2 on page 104 shows the balance sheet of a set of financial statements for a private equity fund. We would expect to see as a minimum:

- investments (recorded at purchase cost initially and then valuation);
- cash;
- other receivables;
- carried interest;
- other payables; and
- borrowings.

In the profit or loss account we would expect to see as a minimum:

- interest income;
- dividend income;
- unrealised gain or loss on investments;
- carried interest;
- administration fees;
- transaction costs; and
- interest expense.

The statement of changes in net assets would detail the movements with regards to investor contributions, redemptions and dividends/ distributions paid out to investors.

4.4 Property funds

Accounting for property funds is similar to private equity funds in that, as the underlying investments are illiquid, valuations can be more complex to ascertain, especially where the portfolio includes development properties. Therefore, they are usually carried out by property valuation experts rather than the fund accountant.

Making it work 6.4

Table 6.2 on page 104 shows the balance sheet of a set of financial statements for a property fund. We would expect to see as a minimum:

- investment property (recorded at purchase cost initially and then valuation);
- rental revenue receivable;
- cash;
- debtors;
- borrowings;
- creditors; and
- taxation payable.

In the profit or loss account we would expect to see as a minimum:

- rental income;
- property expenses;
- profit or loss on sales of investment property;
- management and advisory fees;
- administration fees;
- transaction costs; and
- taxation.

The statement of changes in net assets would detail the movements with regards to investor contributions, redemptions and dividends/ distributions paid out to investors.

Test Yourself 6.1

Look at Table 6.2 on page 104. List all of the issues you can identify with the balance sheet.

5. IT systems

Accounting for funds can be complex and the specialised nature of many funds means that most generic software will not be sufficient. Looking at private equity for example, the software required needs to be sophisticated enough to manage the data of hundreds of investors, manage company-specific valuations data, perform complex waterfall distribution calculations and manage basic day-to-day expenses.

There are many tailored systems which allow the administration and accounting of a fund to run smoothly alongside one another.

Highly automated, efficient software helps to reduce the risk associated with operational errors and delays and improves the quality of data output, producing more meaningful reports.

A sophisticated software package can assist fund accountants in the following ways:

- automated generation of accounting and financial reports;
- previewing general ledger entries before they are fixed in order to make corrections;
- combining various charts of accounts into one system;
- tailoring charts of accounts to specific clients/entities;
- enabling the accountant to define year end closing rules;
- automatic reconciliation between various ledgers; and
- providing an audit trail of who has amended postings and when.

Popular systems used in the UK include Oracle, Acufund, and Investran.

6. Production of fund accounts

This section highlights the key stages that a fund accountant would generally follow in the production of annual financial statements for a fund. These stages are not exhaustive and are for the purpose of providing a generic base only:

- The board minutes of the fund would be reviewed for the period under production and to date to gain an understanding of what had happened during the period. If the accountant was close enough to the daily activity of the fund this step may not always be carried out.
- Bank reconciliations will be reviewed to ensure they have all been completed at the period end.
- The general ledger is reviewed to ensure transactions booked by the administration team appear reasonable. This ledger is reconciled against the purchase and sales ledger and the subscriptions and redemptions ledger. Any discrepancies will be discussed with the administration team.
- Any additional creditors and debtors will be book-kept. For example, accruing for the audit fee for the period once agreed.

- The accountant will update the investment valuation in the books as necessary, assuming not already updated by the administration team. Where there are external valuation reports these will be used by the accountant to update the investment valuation.
- Any other adjustments required will be posted, such as any foreign exchange differences arising as a result of revaluing foreign currency assets and liabilities at the year end date.
- Once all adjustments have been made, the trial balance will be produced and put into the format of the financial statements.
- The notes to the financial statements will be updated as required to reflect what has happened during the period. Likewise, the disclosures in the financial statements will be updated to ensure they are in line with requirements for the accounting standards under which the financial statements are prepared.
- The director's report, investment manager's report, chairman's statement, strategic report and any other reports required (commonly referred to as the 'front-end' of the financial statements) will be collated by the accountant and included.
- Assist in the preparation of tax returns as required.
- Once a draft has been created the senior management team, directors will review the full financial statements.
- Where auditors are involved, the fund accountant will generally deal with these interactions.

7. Recent developments in UK accounting standards and the implications for fund accounting (850)

Fund accountants must prepare financial statements in accordance with a recognised accounting framework. The framework applied is usually dependent on where the fund is domiciled and referred to as Generally Accepted Accounting Practices, or GAAP – for example US GAAP, Canadian GAAP, Chinese GAAP, India GAAP, French GAAP.

A company can choose not to prepare their financial statements under their local GAAP and instead prepare their financial statements under IFRS.

The Financial Reporting Council have replaced UK GAAP with Financial Reporting Standard 102, the Financial Reporting Standard applicable in the UK and Republic of Ireland (FRS102). This change was applicable for all entities with accounting periods beginning on or after 1 January 2015.

The introduction of FRS 102 was designed to align accounting principles more closely with IFRS and has resulted in many significant changes from UK GAAP, which will impact on the fund accounting industry greatly. The main areas of impact for funds are defined in Table 6.3.

Table 6.3: Old UKGAAP v FRS 102

Topic	Under old UK GAAP	Under FRS 102
Investments in listed shares	These investments may be accounted for at either cost or fair value.	These investments in publicly traded shares must be accounted for at fair value.
Investment properties	Requires revaluation to open market value each year. The cost less depreciation model is not allowed.	In most cases, revaluation is required each year. However, if fair value cannot be measured reliably without undue cost or effort (the FRC expects this to be rare), the cost less depreciation model is used.
Goodwill and intangible assets	Maximum useful life of 20 years or less, but this can be rebutted when longer or indefinite life can be justified.	Must have a finite life, and useful life shall not exceed five years when no reliable estimate can be made. The July 2015 amendments to FRS 102 changed this to ten years. These amendments also make it clear that only in exceptional circumstances will entities be unable to make a reliable estimate of the useful economic life of goodwill and intangible assets. This change is not effective until periods beginning on or after 1 January 2016.
Recognition of intangible assets acquired in a business combination	Many intangible assets are subsumed within goodwill as they are not separable.	More intangible assets are likely to be recognised separately from goodwill.
Merger accounting, excluding group reconstructions	Merger accounting for business combinations required if certain strict conditions are met.	Merger accounting is generally not permitted, but is required for certain business combinations involving public benefit entities.
Deferred tax	Based on timing differences.	Additional deferred tax recognised on, for example, business combinations and revaluations of property, plant and equipment and investment properties.

Fund accountants preparing their first FRS 102 financial statements need to prepare comparative profit and loss account statements and balance sheets in accordance with the new requirements.

The balance sheet prepared under the previous accounting framework will form the basis of the opening balance sheet under FRS 102 – a number of adjustments will be required.

Chapter summary

- The fund accountant plays a crucial role in the world of funds.
- The administrator relies on the accountant to turn all of the data input into the system into a meaningful output such as financial statements, management reports and variance analysis reports. Neither the administrator nor the accountant can function effectively completely independent of one other.
- There is significant reliance on the outputs provided by fund accountants by several stakeholders.
- Directors, investors and potential investors make decisions based on financial performance as reported by the fund accountant. Investment managers make investment decisions factoring in the financial position of the company and the cash resources available as reported by the fund accountant.

Chapter seven
Net asset valuations

List of topics

1. The ultimate purpose of NAV
2. Basics of a NAV
3. The relationship between NAV and performance
4. Open-ended and closed-ended funds
5. NAV as a cost of the fund
6. The effect of the nature of assets on NAV
7. The purpose of NAV – putting it in context
8. Effect on NAV where a price cannot be found

Introduction

Whatever the structure or the asset class, all investment funds are fundamentally the same and the principal concepts they are built upon are all wonderfully simple and easy to understand; **net asset value** (NAV) is the product of a fund's assets less its liabilities. However, to the frustration of all fund administrators, fund managers and accountants are able to take the simplest fund building block and turn it into a dodecahedron of complexity.

net asset valuations
A fundamental element of pricing funds and also for calculating performance, but in themselves they are neither the price nor the measure of a fund's performance.

Such is the case with NAV. In its purest form NAV is the amount remaining after deducting the fund's liabilities from its assets.

1. The ultimate purpose of NAV

We should start with why anyone wants a NAV. NAVs are a fundamental element of pricing funds and also for calculating performance, but in themselves they are neither the price nor the measure of a fund's performance.

2. Basics of a NAV

At its simplest, the NAV is the result of the following:

Assets less liabilities equals NAV

My fund has only 1 asset, which is £50 cash in the bank, and it has 1 liability, it owes its fund administrator £10 in fees. Its NAV is £50 less the £10 which equals £40.

	£
Assets	50.00
Liabilities	(10.00)
NAV	**40.00**

However, as a huge proportion of the work of the fund administration industry is devoted to calculating NAVs, clearly it isn't always this easy. The NAV story is a long one and it gets more and more complex as it goes on.

2.1 Building a NAV – day one

When a fund launches, it pulls a price out of thin air to attach to its units or shares. Funds often launch at £1, £10 or £100 a share or similar round numbers in other currencies. That is the last time the price is an arbitrary one decided by the fund promoter.

Let's take a daily dealing, open-ended fund (Fund A).

Fund A launches at £10 per share and 10 investors each subscribe for 100 shares. The fund manager now has £10,000 to play with. He immediately buys a basket of investments in the sectors and in the proportions dictated by the prospectus, holding back only £1,000 to cover ongoing running expenses.

Fund A – Day 1

	£	£
Subscriptions 1000 shares at £10 each	10,000.00	
Use of funds	Retention for costs	1,000.00
	Funds utilised for investment	9,000.00

2.2 Building a NAV – asset prices and valuations

Day 2 of Fund A dawns and a new investor wants to buy 100 shares. Fund A has already issued 1,000 shares to 10 investors. How much should we charge the new investor for his 100 shares?

Let's calculate the NAV and see how much Fund A is worth. We will start with assets. £1,000 in the bank is easy. Then we see how much the investments made yesterday are worth now. Now we have a problem. We look at our price feeds and the prices of the various stocks change before our eyes. What's worse is the manager didn't only buy sterling denominated assets but he invested half the money in US Dollar denominated stock and the exchange rate is also changing by the second.

We need to freeze time. What time shall we choose? The London Stock Exchange and the New York Stock Exchange have different trading times. Luckily this was all considered before Fund A launched and the prospectus has a whole section devoted to decisions like this. Our example of Main Market exchange-traded stocks in only two currencies is about as simple as it gets and for more complex alternative investment funds the administrator needs to be well guided on cutoffs, rates and so on by the prospectus.

As a consequence, administrators pore over the pricing sections to ensure they understand them, they actually make sense and they can be done.

Fund A tells us to use the close of day prices and the current day 9am exchange rate. Both markets moved down about 10% (terrible day for the fund to make its initial investments) and the exchange rate hardly moved.

After converting the US Dollar values to sterling we calculate that the mid-market value of the stocks is £7,500. Wow, the value of our shares has gone down more than the markets. We were expecting a 10% drop of around £900 not £1,500. What has happened?

2.3 Building a NAV – interrogating the figures

The first thing is we never bought £9,000 of stocks. Costs of buying the US Dollars, bank wire charges and custodian transaction charges diluted our investment. The second thing is one of our stocks dropped nearly 20% and though a few also moved against the market by going up, it wasn't enough.

As an administrator when calculating NAV, we have checks and balances built into our systems to alert us for any contra-market movements, which not only helps verifying our price feeds but also roots out any input or other errors. A good administrator also applies a reasonableness test.

2.4 Building a NAV – liabilities

Ok, we now have £7,500 of stocks and £1,000 in the bank. Our NAV is therefore £8,500. However, this is not as simple as it first appears – we have forgotten to deduct our liabilities.

For our pure NAV calculation we have no liabilities. If our manager had leveraged his investment by borrowing money, then this is when we would've deducted the amount of the debt.

2.5 Building a NAV – the end result

Our NAV is £8,500, we have 1,000 shares in issue so each, at the snapshot moment in time, was worth £8.50 each.

	£		Day 1	Day 2
Subscriptions 1000 shares at £10 each	10,000.00			
Use of funds	Retention for costs (cash in bank)		1,000.00	1,000.00
	Funds utilised for investment/value of investments		9,000.00	7,500.00*
	Total Assets		**10,000.00**	**8,500.00**
	Liabilities		–	–
	Total Assets LESS Total Liabilities (NAV)		**10,000.00**	**8,500.00**
	NAV per share		**10.00**	**8.50**

* includes deduction of brokerage costs and diminution in value

2.6 How the NAV influences pricing

The question remains then what to charge those investors who subscribe on Day 2. It hardly seems fair to charge our new investor £10 a share because he will lose out and the other investors will each be a bit better off. If we charge £8.50 a share then no one wins and no one loses.

Unfortunately that's not quite right. Fund A has been running for a day and has incurred running costs. Also prior to launch Fund A incurred costs that can be reclaimed by the promoter as described in the prospectus.

This is the moment the NAV becomes a fundamental component of pricing. We take our £8,500 NAV and deduct from it one day's worth of contractual fees and claimable expenses as well as one day's worth of amortised setup costs. Luckily, for this example, they come to exactly £100, so our price computation is now £8,400 divided by 1,000 shares giving us a price of £8.40 per share.

	£		Day 1	Day 2
Subscriptions 1000 shares at £10 each	10,000.00			
Use of funds	Retention for costs (cash in bank)		1,000.00	1,000.00
	Funds utilised for investment/value of investments		9,000.00	7,500.00
	Total Assets		**10,000.00**	**8,500.00**
	Costs/Liabilities/Deductions		–	(100.00)*
	Total Assets LESS Total Liabilities (NAV)		**10,000.00**	**8,400.00**
	NAV per share		**10.00**	**8.40**

* Contractual fees computed at £100.00.

Because there are costs to both buying and selling investments, we think it fair that the new investor should also fairly share in them. For this reason, we have calculated the mid-price of £8.40 from which we will derive a bid and offer price by dropping the price to £8.39 (Bid) for anyone selling their shares back to Fund A and we will charge our new investor £8.41 (Offer) for each of his 100 shares. The bid and offer prices were calculated in accordance with the pricing procedure described in the prospectus, which for the sake of our simple example turned out to be a penny either way.

We have covered the basics of NAV and pricing and touched on how NAV is a component of performance reporting. There are other complications to both NAV calculation and price computation dependent on circumstances and asset types, which we will explore further below.

3. The relationship between NAV and performance

It is important to remember that NAV and price are two different things. Whilst the term NAV is often used to mean both NAV and price by the general public, a simple growth in NAV doesn't indicate the fund is performing well. Similarly a reduction in NAV doesn't mean that the fund is doing badly.

Imagine Fund A sacked the manager, who lost over 25% on day 1, and has, under new management, grown from £8,500 to £100 million. From that statement can we tell if it has performed well?

We can deduce that it has done well for the new manager taking his 1% management fee on £100 million, but we have no way of knowing if the initial investors have made any money.

Let us look at the price per share. It is £6. We know our initial investors paid £10 so if they are still in the fund does that automatically mean the performance for them has been dire? Perhaps not.

We look more closely at Fund A and note that in the period since launch it has paid dividends totalling £10. It seems that our initial investors have done well, with Fund A returning all of its initial capital to investors, meaning that the amount left in the fund is pure profit. From that can we deduce that Fund A has performed well?

Unfortunately not.

It has been 10 years since Fund A launched. In that time, inflation has averaged 20% per year and the benchmark index has grown by 250% since the fund launched.

Simple performance evaluation

	Fund A	**Comparative (benchmark index)**
Initial amount invested	£10.00	£10.00
Total return	£16.00	£25.00
Performance ratio *(w/o inflation)*	160% (or 1.6x)	250% (or 2.5x)

Inflation will have a diminution effect on the above, because the value of money itself changes over time. For example, based on US inflation from 2005 to 2015, an item that cost $5 in 2005 may now cost $6.15, demonstrating the effect of inflation; $5 then is no longer worth $5 now, but instead has a value of $4.03 in relative terms. The effect of inflation will therefore dilute the performance figures.

Performance calculation is a topic in its own right and at its most esoteric vastly out-complicates even the most complicated NAV calculation. It does however have a part to play in pricing by tracking the liabilities incurred by performance fees.

Test yourself 7.1

Why are NAV and price different?

4. Open-ended and closed-ended funds

open-ended funds
A daily dealing fund where NAV and price are directly connected, which can be good for investors because they can put money in or take it out whenever they like, and receive or be charged the value mostly dictated by the underlying NAV per share.

closed-ended funds
When NAV and the price are linked but not in the same way and not with the same absolute correlation. A closed-ended fund issues a number of shares, invests the cash and generally expects to hang onto it for the life of the fund, often seven or eight years.

Our example was that of a bog-standard **open-ended** daily dealing fund where NAV and price is directly connected (Fund A). If the NAV per share increases, the price goes up, and vice versa. When considering **closed-ended funds**, NAV and the price of them are linked but not in the same way and not with the same absolute correlation.

4.1 Open-ended fund

Fund A can create and destroy shares as needed. If people are buying, Fund A creates more shares to meet this demand and, if more are selling than buying, it destroys (redeems) them. If daily dealing, this can be great for investors because they can put money in or take it out whenever they like and receive or be charged the value mostly dictated by the underlying NAV per share.

But this can also be bad for the manager and sometimes the investor. If Fund A suddenly becomes unpopular and a huge number of sale orders are received, the manager will be forced to sell whatever he needs to raise the cash to meet the redemption requests. This may force him to sell long-term investments at a loss. Additionally, though the price is being carefully calculated to pay out a fair amount per investor, the operating costs of Fund A remain the same, only now there are fewer investors to meet those costs, meaning that each investor pays more towards these costs on a pro rata basis. Often these remaining investors are also left with the 'turkey' investments the manager is finding difficult to unload. In other words, open-ended funds can end up as a fire sale where too many investors are looking to exit the fund, as investments must be sold quickly to generate sufficient cash to meet these redemptions. Prospectuses often build in emergency measures to close the gate on (halt) redemptions to ensure an orderly exit, i.e. avoid fire sales as much as possible.

4.2 Closed-ended fund

Fund managers often prefer the security of closed-ended funds. A closed-ended fund issues a number of shares, invests the cash and generally expects to hang onto it for the life of the fund, often seven or eight years. This allows the manager some certainty that he can make long-term investments without being forced into a fire sale.

Closed-ended funds calculate NAVs but do not use them for pricing unless they issue further tranches of the same share class. Instead they are issued as one indicator to holders and those potentially looking to purchase shares as to the value proposition of the fund to them.

Over the life of an eight-year investment, investors' circumstances can change, and a secondary market exists where shares in closed-ended funds change hands. In these instances, the NAV may help to inform the price, however the price agreed will be that determined between buyer and seller and is driven by supply and demand.

If sellers outnumber buyers, then the sellers are more likely not to get the full value as indicated by the NAV but instead will be forced to deal at a discount (reduction) to NAV. Conversely if the fund is thought to have invested in the next big thing or is otherwise popular, buyers may seek out sellers and be willing to pay a premium (more than) to NAV, risking their money against the possible reward of a big future payout.

Thus, for closed-ended funds, even though the NAV is not used directly for pricing, it clearly is needed both as a component of performance calculation and as an indicator to the market when a bidding war starts.

Closed-ended funds are unlikely to calculate daily NAVs. Monthly or quarterly NAVs are very common and the frequency is driven by investor or regulatory demand rather than by the manager's desire to add to the fund's costs.

5. NAV as a cost of the fund

NAV calculations, though computerised where they can be, are very labour-intensive and in an age where fund total expense ratios are constantly under scrutiny, reducing the frequency of NAVs can make quite a saving.

A simpler but unpublished form of NAV calculation is sometimes carried out in the interim and used as a tool by the manager.

6. The effect of the nature of assets on NAV

Closed-ended funds are more likely to invest in illiquid assets (i.e. those not readily realised for sale). The manager will know he has many years to profit from the investment and can take some time to dispose of it when it has nothing more to give.

NAV calculations become more difficult when illiquid and esoteric assets are involved, as will be explained further below.

Fund A was invested in main market traded stocks. For an administrator that is a walk in the park, as various services stream the prices and they can be piped straight into the administrator's computer system as a fully automated process.

The administrator is expected to always seek two pricing sources and check one against the other. Once this meant printing a long list of investments and ticking them back to two pricing sources. One was often the *Financial Times*. This resulted in hours of tedious effort and was, of course, prone to human error. The need for double-checking also added to this incredibly labour intensive task.

Now two independent feeds can check each other and automatically alert the administrator of discrepancies or unusual fluctuations and the NAV system can monitor that investigative procedures are followed, ensuring accuracy and reducing the business risk for the administrator.

However not all assets are traded on stock exchanges and so sources of pricing can become trickier.

Source of independent pricing is a tenet of fund administration. Not only is this beneficial in ensuring accurate NAVs, but it also prevents manipulation of prices by various interested parties. Assets with prices supplied by non-independent parties, such as the fund manager, hugely increase the risk that NAVs will be inaccurate or even designed to deceive.

In the interests of investor protection, more and more regulatory pressure is being placed on investment funds to utilise pricing sources independent of the fund manager for the purposes of calculating NAV. However, this may not always be possible and the more esoteric (alternative, new, unknown, factor-dependent) the asset class, the less likely it is that independent pricing sources will be available.

6.1 An example – Derivative Alpha

Let us take an example of a highly esoteric asset we will call Derivative Alpha. Derivative Alpha has been designed by a rocket scientist who realises there is more money in the hedge fund world. He fully understands it and has a dozen whiteboards covered in mathematical hocus pocus, which he uses to explain it to anyone who is interested.

The fund administrator can easily record 1,000 units of Derivative Alpha on his NAV calculation and all that is needed is a price to multiply by to get the value:

- The manager provides the administrator with a spreadsheet which calculates the price when certain variables are entered.
- A Big Four accountancy firm has audited the spreadsheet and signed it off as OK.
- The administrator is confident that the spreadsheet cannot be tampered with and has a procedure for receiving the variables from several sources and entering them.

- The administrator has no idea if the price that comes out is correct and relies on the rocket scientist to sign off on it every time.

In this example, there really is nobody but the manager capable of providing the valuation inputs because the asset class is so specialised that data from elsewhere would be meaningless. This is where the role of the auditor becomes so critical. As part of their audit work, the auditor must test the fundamental principles of the manager's pricing models and methodology and report on its reasonableness. This will include not only understanding the numbers used but evaluating the risk parameters and other discounting factors employed.

In these scenarios, i.e. where assets are so esoteric or the potential outcomes so variable due to their very nature (such as the outcome of litigation cases, the stage at which cases are concluded, remaining routes of appeal and the effect these factors have on an award of damages), pricing models are based on probabilities rather than certainties and so the calculations and the results of them are less certain; sometimes referred to as Monte Carlo simulations. Because of this lack of certainty, a great number of discounting factors will be applied, potentially resulting in a range of prices. The price utilised for NAV purposes will often be the most heavily discounted within the range (the lowest) until a key event triggers a re-evaluation (i.e. greater certainty, comparables in the market, an essential event has occurred).

Who carries the risk for the incorrect pricing of Derivative Alpha and therefore the risk of incorrectly calculating the NAV?

6.2 The administrator's role in the pricing of assets

The administrator is aware a major weather event has hit the area of the plantation and news reports say millions of hectares of trees have been uprooted. The NAV is due to be published and the property manager is unable to be contacted, having set out to inspect the damage. The manager tells the administrator to apply the approved formula and publish the NAV. The administrator is in a quandary and turns to the fund's auditor for advice. The auditor rightly points out that the prospectus allows the formula to be applied and that there is no confirmation that the plantation has been damaged in any way.

Who knows what the outcome may be and it is always possible that the fund regulator will be brought into the loop at some time.

As the number of alternative assets grow exponentially, conversations like the above happen more frequently and NAV calculations have moved further away from being a science and closer to being an art.

As the bog-standard daily dealing fund has become more automated, and in fact has drifted to the almost fully-automated exchange-traded funds (ETFs), the hedge and private equity funds have moved further into the space where experienced fund professionals are needed in the NAV process due to the specialist skills required and the number of variables to be considered when pricing the investments.

On a more general basis, the administrator must be aware of its responsibilities for an incorrectly calculated NAV. Because the calculation of NAV is provided by the administrator under contract, there will be consequences where it gets it wrong.

- **Financial impact**

  Perhaps the most obvious impact. Because the NAV is often utilised as a basis of the fund's price (whether in pricing open-ended funds for subscriptions and redemptions or as a point of reference against which funds may be priced as public exchange traded equities), a mistake can be costly. For example, the net effect after subscriptions and redemptions of an open-ended fund on any one dealing day may be that, due to an over-valuation of the NAV, the fund has paid out too much money to redeemers and received too much money from subscribers. In the event that the fund cannot put this position right, the administrator will be looked to to make up any shortfall. This could be quite costly for an administrator and could even potentially put the administrator out of business. There may be other financial impact for the investors (as referenced above) and to the fund itself, which may find itself in a distressed position where the error cannot be put right.

- **Reputational impact**

  Errors can lead to lack of confidence in the fund and may, ultimately, see investors withdraw interest and withdraw investment. The potential effects could be devastating for the fund manager (dealing with a fund failure) and key connected parties.

  Alternatively an administrator may be sacked for persistent or significant errors. This would, most likely, be treated as a fundamental breach of the administration agreement with the investment fund able to terminate without notice.

- **Regulatory impact**

  All instances of NAV calculation error must be recorded as breaches by the administrator. Regulators will require the administrator to notify them of any significant breaches (i.e. those having a material impact on the NAV or the orderly functioning of the fund) but also of any pattern of breaches (i.e. consistently getting the NAV wrong). Such errors may result in a regulator determining to sanction the administrator through the use of fines or even removal of an administrator's license.

Even if the administrator is not penalised for the breach, the regulator may see the breach as significant or persistent enough to suspend trading in the fund. In the case of an open-ended fund, a suspension can be significant, as investors are prevented from redeeming and subscribers from purchasing shares. If this situation cannot be corrected, the fund may find itself in a distressed situation, which could lead to fire sales of assets to meet redemption requests and, ultimately, the failure of the fund.

7. The purpose of NAV – putting it in context

NAVs are only an indication and by now you will realise no one ever buys or sells at NAV.

NAVs are snap shots in time. By the time they are published, in fact even before the process of calculating it began, the world had moved on. Time, effort, experience and expensive infrastructure is all devoted to produce a largely arbitrary number which can be meaningless in a heartbeat.

But the NAV is fundamental to our industry, as one component in tracking the fund's activity, value and performance, which is why administrators strive to do them well against an ever more complicated and complex backdrop.

8. Effect on NAV where a price cannot be found

Pricing is fundamental to NAV calculations and we have seen how sourcing them ranges from the completely automatic to the highly labour-intensive processes. We have also seen that some prices are so hard to determine that an almost creative element has to be utilised. We have also seen that the oversight to ensure NAVs are correct is leading to a greater amount of senior staff time at a time when costs are being driven down generally in the industry.

What happens if a price cannot be found? Assets which cannot be priced or assets which have no present value, two different things, certainly complicate NAV calculations.

8.1 Assets with no present value

Open-ended funds have the issue that investors who leave the fund but have received no value for the unpriced assets will lose out if those assets are found to have a value in the future. Hedge funds and hedge funds of funds have often found themselves affected in this way because of their high-risk approach to investment.

The fund may find itself carrying lines of assets that once had significant value but are now marked as having none. For NAV calculation purposes care has to be taken not to fall into the trap of not looking for a price at every valuation. Valueless assets can suddenly become desirable even if at only a few pence in the pound compared to the original book cost. An unexpected decision in a foreign court, a liquidator stumbling upon a forgotten or previously stolen asset or such like, can suddenly make a difference. Usually the fund manager is best placed to determine if an asset remains unpriced and all must hope that the scheme documents set a procedure to follow in such cases.

The side pocket became a useful tool for parking assets and linking them to the original owners so no one can lose out if the assets come back to life. Although it slightly increases the workload, the benefit of cleaning valueless assets out of NAV calculations makes it worthwhile.

8.2 Unavailability or delay in the price

The asset which has value but no price or a price that is difficult to obtain is a more difficult problem. Many NAV calculations sit waiting to be signed off and published but for one missing price. This can be particularly difficult for the fund's year end NAV, which is a fundamental part of producing the annual audited financial statements.

Corporate governance, regulatory requirements and accountancy codes set incredibly high standards for every element of producing year end accounts. Obviously the NAV is very important and often an extra NAV has to be produced on the year end date even if it is only one day after the last regular NAV date.

Accounts production, audit and submission to regulators run under a very tight timetable of events and a delay in one can cause a disaster. Late submission of accounts to the regulator could cause a fund to be suspended pending investigation; this would impact the investors and all the service providers and must be avoided at all costs.

The NAV is the trigger event for the accounts. If it is delayed by weeks (not unknown), desperately searching for the final price to complete the calculation, all the other timetabled targets can be missed resulting in an untimely scramble on the last days.

Why can prices be hard to find or delivered late by the pricing source?
We have considered the requirement for the NAV to be completed timeously and based upon reliably sourced pricing inputs. But what happens where prices are received late?

It is important to understand why a price might be received late. Where prices are readily available through an independent price feed, e.g. Bloomberg or Reuters, the possibility of delays is significantly low. The possibility, however, increases as the source of pricing becomes less easy to find or more reliant on manual provision/tasks.

For example, pricing for funds of funds is reliant upon the pricing of the underlying funds being concluded and available. The best source of the price might be the fund's audited NAV, but this may not be available for a number of reasons, including a disparity in the financial year ends of the underlying fund (e.g. March) and the fund of funds (e.g. December) and slow, delayed production of figures by the underlying fund. Similar problems may exist for private equity funds, which are reliant upon the provision of information by underlying portfolio businesses.

Other delays may be caused by the fund manager, due to their own organisational issues etc.

In these instances, there may be other reliable sources of information available that may be used:

- Interim financial figures, often with a discounting or other factor applied to acknowledge potential volatility between the available figures and the upcoming audited figures (the best price indicator in this example).
- Pricing guidelines may exist to assist in settling outstanding pricing inputs. For example, private equity funds might refer to the IPEV Valuation Guidelines. IPEV provides high quality, best practice guidance for private equity and venture capital valuation and reporting purposes and are widely endorsed around the globe. The purpose of the valuations is to help arrive at fair value measurements that are compliant with financial reporting standards, fair value being equivalent to the summation of the estimated value of underlying investments as if realised on the measurement date (a hypothetical sales price for a given point in time).

There is no one reason for late delivery of prices but there are some usual suspects, such as incompetent third parties, misunderstandings between service providers, human error and very infrequently fraud.

Accurate and timely NAVs are essential for the fund industry and no slippage on price sourcing should ever be tolerated. From the first moment it becomes obvious that the price source is unreliable, action must be taken to make it reliable. The year end NAV will be published in a timely fashion if all previous NAVs were and any concerns on pricing must be resolved well before then.

Making it work 7.1

- Simple Fund Limited (SFL) is an investment fund with investments only in quoted stocks (listed equities). As at 30 September 2016, the fund's investments were priced as follows (according to independent pricing feeds):
  - Amazing Equity £1.35 per share – 1,000,000 shares held by SFL
  - Badly Behaving Equity £0.75 per share – 5,000,000 shares held by SFL
  - Just Right £1.50 per share – 10,000,000 shares held by SFL
  - Merrygoround Equity £0.95 per share – 5,000,000 shares held by SFL

If SFL has no other assets, total assets as at 30 September 2016 are:

Equity name	Price	Shares held	Asset value (£)
Amazing Equity	1.35	1,000,000	1,350,000
Badly Behaving	0.75	5,000,000	3,750,000
Just Right	1.50	10,000,000	15,000,000
Merrygoround	0.95	5,000,000	4,750,000
		TOTAL ASSETS	**24,850,000**

- The liabilities of SFL as at 30 September 2016 have been calculated as £5,000,000. The net asset value is:

  Net asset value = total assets – liabilities

  NAV = £24,850,000 – £5,000,000

  NAV = £19,850,000

SFL has issued shares totalling 15,000,000. The net asset value per share is:

NAV per share = net asset value/total outstanding shares

NAV per share = £19,850,000/15,000,000

NAV per share = £1.32 (to 2 decimal places)

SFL is itself a listed fund and is currently trading at a premium to its NAV of 3% based on its mid-market (average) price. This tells us that SFL's market price is 103% of its NAV per share. Based on a NAV of £1.32, this means that SFL's shares are trading at an average price of £1.36.

Where shares are trading at a discount to NAV, the average price will be lower than the NAV per share.

Chapter summary

- NAV production is now much more automated. However, automation creates its own issues, not least because many administrators do not actually understand the calculation or the inputs into it.
- As asset types become more alternative and esoteric in nature, the levels of complexity making up NAV calculations increase, resulting in the requirement for much more experienced oversight than ever before.
- Boards of directors of alternative products frequently get involved in NAV calculations, especially when it comes to decisions on prices where there are no independent verification sources, independent pricing guidelines available or clear guidelines in the prospectus. This is a clear shift and largely a by-product of increasing corporate governance standards, which are steadily raising the game in all areas of an investment fund's life.

Chapter eight
The role of safekeeping assets

List of topics

1. Appointment of a custodian
2. What do custodians need to do?
3. Segregation of assets
4. Physical assets
5. Oversight of a custodian – whose role is it?
6. Investor protection
7. Authorised investment funds and custodians
8. What are the differences between a custodian and a depositary?
9. Who may act as the depositary?
10. The depositary's role
11. Other responsibilities of a depositary
12. Regulatory framework
13. Segregation of client money and client assets

Introduction

This chapter will set out whose role it is to safeguard assets, the different titles used and how their responsibilities change, and the obligations and oversight that they need in place to ensure that the assets within a fund are safeguarded. It will also explore the provisions in different jurisdictions as to requirements for safeguarding assets.

Safekeeping of assets is an important concept in a fund structure. Investors placing money into a fund structure rely upon the assets into which the fund invests being safeguarded appropriately. Depending on the type or jurisdiction of the fund, the role of safekeeping can be assigned to a custodian, trustee or depositary. Howsoever called, they are the guardian or safekeeper of the assets, or of the title documents to them, to ensure that they are kept securely and that they are clearly designated as belonging to the fund.

It should be noted that not all funds need a custodian or equivalent. For example, under the Investment Funds Act in Bermuda, an exemption can be requested from the Bermuda Monetary Authority for fund property to be entrusted to a custodian. There has to be sufficient evidence that appropriate alternative arrangements are in place however.

The role and responsibilities of the custodian or similar will vary according to the asset class of the fund. Some funds will hold property for example, so a custodian will be potentially required to hold title deeds for the properties. Alternatively the administrator of the fund may also undertake the function of the custodian depending on the asset class of the fund, for example if it is investing into a single private company. Where funds hold assets which are electronically registered, they will need someone to hold those shares for them electronically in the name of the fund.

The type of institution undertaking the role may vary depending on what the class of assets in the fund are. Often, for high value private equity funds, they will use large bank-owned custodians which have significant capital on their balance sheet, whereas for a physical asset such as wine in a fund, a bespoke, smaller safeguarding company may be used.

In some instances, the entity appointed to perform the safekeeping role can also be given the power to take action in relation to the assets if required. This allows them to perform actions on behalf of the fund, such as place trades in relation to the investments that it holds on behalf of the fund on the instruction of the fund administrator, or respond in relation to corporate actions on the investments within the fund's portfolio.

1. Appointment of a custodian

The board of the fund will appoint the custodian chosen to act, and there are numerous factors they will have considered when deciding who to appoint. It will obviously vary dependent on the asset class of the fund itself, but generally speaking will include some of the following considerations.

1.1 Credit rating

In particular this is important for larger private equity funds, as financial stability and credit worthiness of the custodian is key as they are likely to hold electronic title for assets and therefore if they became insolvent this would have serious operational and potentially financial consequences for the fund. It also demonstrates a robustness which means they are more likely to be able to withstand significant market events.

1.2 Capital base

capital base
Capital within an institution that is considered in relation to the financial stability of a custodian, especially for private equity funds.

Again, especially for private equity funds, when considering the financial stability of a custodian they will look at the capital within the institution. Regulators will also insist that those undertaking the role have a significant **capital base** given the responsibility that they will have, for example in Guernsey, a custodian or trustee of an open-ended collective investment scheme is required to have net assets of £4 million to be considered for a custodian licence.

1.3 Track record

When appointing a guardian of assets, it is important to know what experience they have in already providing that service, both as a business and the key individuals involved within that business. In particular, where it is an unusual asset class for which the custodian is providing its services, demonstrating a proven track record of dealing with the asset class in question will be essential. It is easier to identify a custodian or trustee with a track record in relation to equities, rather than one who has experience in esoteric assets classes such as fine art. Therefore, for esoteric asset classes appointing a custodian can be more difficult.

1.4 Fees

The level of fees charged by the custodian will be important for the fund when ascertaining the overall level of charges that will be taken out from the fund per annum. If a custodian is going to be very expensive this will impact upon the overall management charges taken from the fund and potential returns to investors, and therefore the appeal of the fund.

1.5 Reporting and systems

The level and standard of reporting and access to information that is available for the fund administrator from the custodian will assist in determining suitability. For example, systems which enable ongoing, online reconciliation by the fund administrator or automated contract notes post a trade to be distributed will ensure ease of administration and therefore cost efficiencies for the administrator in relation to the fund, and ensure data is always as up to date as possible.

2. What do custodians need to do?

A custodian or trustee must evidence at any time that they have control of the assets and are ensuring their protection. In effect a custodian is akin to a legal guardian. They also need to show they have adequate records relating to acquisition or disposal of assets and that the title to the assets, howsoever held, is retained by them. For example, if it is a property then the name of the fund will be on the title deeds, but the custodian will be charged with holding those title deeds securely.

Whilst primarily the role of custodian is considered to have responsibility for holding the assets, there are many other facets to its role, which can be summarised in the following clauses.

2.1 Safekeeping

They must ensure that they hold physical custody of the investments, that they maintain bookkeeping and records associated with those assets, and of greatest importance, ensuring that those assets are not comingled with the custodian's own, or those of another fund. The custodian has to provide secure premises for assets, or secure systems for their registration, to ensure that theft or destruction of the assets does not occur.

2.2 Administration

They must maintain adequate records of purchases and sales of investments, including the accounting behind it, to ensure matching of trades and settlement of transactions. The minimum standards required in terms of records to be retained will ordinarily be set by the local regulator, unless the standards within the custody agreement exceed local regulatory requirements. The records will also need to be retained for a minimum retention period to be able to recreate any of the activity undertaken in relation to the fund in accordance with the local regulatory requirements.

2.3 Reporting

Provide reporting to the fund administrator and fund board, as required, regarding the custody services. This will involve summarising any breaches that have occurred in relation to the handling of the assets, including pricing or dealing errors, as well as value of assets within the fund under their custodianship. This can also extend to live data reporting such as providing a summary of assets in custody for the fund and number of units in each equity held to enable the fund administrator to reconcile to their own records. Accessibility of the information and frequency of this reporting will be agreed upon by the custodian and the fund administrator.

2.4 Corporate actions

Management of corporate actions to ensure that they are given to the fund administrator to make a decision, recording where a response is provided and then communicating that decision as necessary.

2.5 Exercise of voting rights

Where it is electronic records held, such as equities, enabling the exercise of any voting rights in a particular equity on behalf of the fund in accordance with the fund administrator's instruction.

2.6 Pricing

To verify the pricing by the fund administrator and maintain records on the fund value. This is a safety net, a second pair of independent eyes, to check that the value on which the fund pricing has been undertaken is correct and all underlying calculations to arrive at the NAV and therefore the price at which investors are dealing at is accurate. This is particularly important for funds dealing on a daily basis where incorrect pricing can have a massive impact on the value of the fund and the compensation that then may become payable because of the error.

2.7 Compliance

To check that any transactions are in accordance with the fund's constitutive documents so that any leveraging rules, asset class restrictions or similar are adhered to, called the investment restrictions are complied with. In terms of any further monitoring beyond that, it depends to a certain extent on the responsibilities placed on the custodian within their agreement for provision of services. However, best practice will often see a custodian undertake an annual site visit to the fund administrator to perform a compliance review. The review by the custodian will include checking dealing procedures used by the administrator, identifying if they provide for best execution, reviewing valuations procedures and checking the breaches register to ensure that, where the custodian should have been notified of the breach, that they have been. The custodian will also go over the details of any pricing errors that have occurred in the period since their last visit and ensure that the reasons why they occurred have been addressed sufficiently to prevent recurrence. The custodian will ordinarily issue a feedback report which is provided to both the administrator and the fund board. The custodian role therefore provides an independent oversight role of the activity of the fund administrator.

2.8 Cash management

On occasion the custodian will manage a client money account in order to facilitate investment. If doing so, they need to ensure reconciliation of that account, regular communication with the fund administrator in relation to investor records and the fund manager in relation to investing that money. They may also place foreign exchange transactions to facilitate trades being undertaken in different currencies. Client money accounts can also be managed by the fund administrator, so it will be down to how the fund has been established to operate and the contracts in place as to who has responsibility for operating them.

2.9 Risk mitigation

The aim of the custodian is to prevent risk issues arising in the first place, through a combination of measures, as outlined above, and secondly, if a risk incident does arise, ensuring the timely and effective dealing with it. This will involve liaising with the fund administrator and ensuring records are prepared recording the issue and how it has been addressed, updating records such as breaches registers where appropriate, and determining if the incident is sufficiently serious to require reporting to the local regulator.

3. Segregation of assets

The custodian does not become at any point the owner of the equities, but is a part of the ownership chain linking the fund investors to the securities.

It is very important that the custodian separates the assets from their own, as well as between other funds to which they are providing those services. The custodian ring fences each fund's assets so that, should anything happen to the custodian itself, or any of the other funds under its guardianship, the assets of the fund, and therefore the interests of the investors, are protected from claims of creditors of the custodian or other funds.

4. Physical assets

It is much easier when talking about the role of the custodian to consider examples where the fund holds electronically registered assets, especially when it comes to settlement and matching of trades, as this will often happen automatically via systems 'talking' to each other. There are a number of specific issues that have to be considered when custody of physical assets is involved, which include greater risks for the funds' investors, in particular in relation to security of that asset. Whenever moveable, physical assets are involved, the risk of theft or destruction increases.

4.1 Property funds

Title documents can be held by a custodian, however the process of settlement in relation to property can be long and drawn out. Consideration needs to be given to the conveyancing process, land registry requirements, valuations and insurance of the asset. Custodians of property funds therefore have to deal with issues over delays in settlement, issues with conveyance and being able to take title, as well as any mortgages and subsequent charges that are placed over the property. This requires a very different skill set to a custodian for equities.

4.2 Fine wine or other esoteric assets

Holding custody of a number of assets in one location and their security is highly important. The record-keeping and inventory style requirements for a fine wine fund are, again, very different to securities funds. Ensuring catalogues of assets with sufficient detail to be able to identify a single bottle, as well as the individual valuation of them whilst held in the fund are key to the NAV of the fund. Often in these scenarios, whilst there may be a recognised custodian appointed, they may delegate to a specialist sub-custodian who can provide secure storage, for example at specific temperatures for the wine, as well as appropriate reporting with sufficient detail and at a frequency that enables NAVs to be prepared in a timely manner. The custodian retains responsibility for oversight of the sub-custodian and will ensure adequate insurance is in place, as well as regular monitoring visits to check that the integrity of the wine is not compromised.

The custody of physical assets therefore carries additional risks and oversight requirements which require careful consideration when appointing a custodian. Identifying specialists in the relevant area with a proven track record is therefore critical for the success of the fund.

Test yourself 8.1

As a fund board, you are considering the appointment of a custodian for your fund which holds classic cars. What would be your key considerations in appointing a custodian?

5. Oversight of a custodian – whose role is it?

Generally, the board of the fund will be responsible for ensuring that the custodian is suitable, qualified and undertaking their role appropriately and in accordance with the agreement under which they are appointed. However, as the fund itself will not have staff or the capacity to undertake reviews or oversight, the board of the fund may request that the designated administrator of the fund undertakes some form of oversight. There are no set oversight criteria, as specific responsibility for oversight of custodians rarely exists in regulation, and is limited to contractual, company law and fiduciary duties. However, ordinarily the administrator will undertake a level of oversight in terms of ensuring the custodian remains licensed for the service that it is providing, that reporting is accurate and at the frequency required by the fund board and any issues that arise in dealing with the custodian are reported to the fund board. Ultimately the fund board retains the power under the agreement with the custodian to decide if they wish to cease using their services if their performance has not been adequate.

6. Investor protection

A professional custodian can offer enhanced protection to investors. The extent of any protection will depend on a number of factors, in particular the independence of the custodian and the scope of their responsibilities under the agreement appointing them as custodian. There is a limit however to the protection that a custodian can provide, for example, it will not prevent a failure to obtain best execution because it may be that the administrator does not pass the trade instruction on in a timely manner. In reality, the main protection offered by a custodian is preventing against securities theft and identification of settlement errors, and mispricing errors. It can also report to the fund board if it feels the fund administrator is failing in its obligations in any way.

The ability of the custodian to detect pricing errors for example is hugely important given the wide reaching ramifications a pricing error can have, such as in high volume dealing open-ended investment funds, where if the fund is priced incorrectly it can have huge implications for rectification of those dealt in at the incorrect price and any subsequent NAV issued.

7. Authorised investment funds and custodians

In relation to the Alternative Investment Fund Managers Directive (AIFMD), there is no concept of the role of a custodian; instead there is an enhanced role of a party called a depositary for each authorised investment fund. As we will discuss in Chapter 12, the AIFMD was introduced to enhance investor protection, and so the role of depositary was one of the measures introduced to ensure that was achieved.

The main aim of a depositary's role is the safekeeping of assets and ensuring that, for instance, the issue and redemption of units is carried out in accordance with applicable regulatory law and the fund's rules.

The AIFMD is very detailed and prescriptive as to the depositary's role and the associated liability it accepts for undertaking this important role. This is perhaps the biggest difference between a custodian and depositary, the extent of each party's liability. A depositary is subject to strict liability, which is far more onerous and stringent in terms of apportionment of liability. It means in practice that the depositary is responsible for any damage and/or loss caused by their acts and omissions regardless of culpability.

8. What are the differences between a custodian and a depositary?

A depositary acts as custodian as well as having the function of independent oversight or a sort of auditor function in relation to the fund. The depositary must ensure the following criteria are met:

- the fund's assets are held independently of the investment manager;
- that the fund's accounting records are reconciled on a regular basis with third-party records; and
- that each investor's entitlement is correctly calculated.

The ultimate aim of the AIFMD is to ensure that the depositary is preventing fraud, errors and omissions and conflicts of interest between the fund and its manager as part of its investor protection remit. It is truly a role of independent oversight.

9. Who may act as the depositary?

The AIFMD definition of a depositary is such that the entity has to be either a credit institution (i.e. a deposit-taking bank) or an investment firm with the regulatory permission necessary to act as custodian. The AIFMD stipulates that the fund's manager (the AIFM) cannot also act as depositary (as otherwise the key point of independence is lost) and that the fund's prime broker can only act as depositary if there is clear separation of the depositary function from the prime brokerage function (meaning, for instance, a separate branch of the same company so that there is no overlap of staff).

Looking at European countries where AIFMD applies (Germany, Italy and Luxembourg), depositaries must be banking institutions licensed to conduct deposit-taking business. In other European countries, non-bank institutions can undertake the role but in practice the role of depositary is dominated by banks, given their standing and the capital behind them, a key consideration for many when considering the appointment of a depositary because of the reassurance that significant capital and net assets provides.

10. The depositary's role

First and foremost, the role of a depositary is to act as custodian, and therefore has all of the responsibilities as set out above. This means that it holds the fund's assets, arranges settlement of transactions and administers income, proxy voting and corporate actions. Predominantly, assets are only held in custody where this is required to facilitate dealing and settlement and therefore this is mostly used in relation to securities such as listed equities.

The AIFMD draws a distinction between financial instruments that can be held in custody such as listed equities, and other assets, for which a depositary only needs to keep a record and verify ownership.

The AIFMD defines financial instruments that can be held in custody as:

- assets that are transferable securities, money market instruments or units in collective investment undertakings; and
- capable of being registered or held in an account directly or indirectly in the name of the depositary.

If assets are registered directly with the securities issuer in the name of the fund (negating the need for a depositary), the assets need not be held in custody. Examples of 'other assets' are non-financial assets such as commodities, interests in other funds where the fund is listed as the shareholder, unlisted equities and debt.

11. Other responsibilities of a depositary

A depositary's role is wider ranging than acting as custodian, because it is seen as more of a gatekeeper and risk mitigant, in order to provide the investor protection element. A depositary's functions extend to include:

- monitoring cash flows of the authorised investment fund;
- ensuring that the dealing of units is carried out in accordance with the applicable regulatory law and the fund's rules; and

- ensuring that the valuation of units is carried out in accordance with applicable regulatory law and the fund's rules (although in some jurisdictions, a custodian must also undertake this to an extent).

In some instances, there are additional functions assigned to the depositary, such as reconciliations, which also overlap with the role of the fund administrator. In this instance the depositary themselves does not need to undertake the work; instead they have to have a procedure in place to check that the fund administrator has proper and effective processes in place to deal with reconciliations, and then conduct sample testing of them on a regular basis to verify that those procedures are effective and are being applied properly.

Depositaries have specific responsibilities under the AIFMD in relation to cash flow. Specifically they must ensure that the fund's cash flows are properly monitored, in particular ensuring that all payments made by investors in relation to subscription of units have been received and that all cash has been booked in to the cash accounts in the name of the fund, manager or depositary, as appropriate. The secondary legislation under the AIFMD sets out in more detail that the depositary must also be implementing procedures to reconcile all cash flow movements and performing reconciliations on a daily basis or when cash flow movements occur and that the fund administrator must provide the depositary with information about payments made by investors on subscription of units at the close of each business day. This means that for any fund to which the depositary is appointed they will need to ensure that they are party to every instruction relating to each cash account maintained by the fund. This is one of the enhanced measures that was introduced under AIFMD to effectively have third party scrutiny of the transactional activity of authorised investment fund managers to reduce fraud, negligence and errors.

Where the authorised investment fund manager is undertaking the dealing and valuation of units, the depositary is required to verify that those activities are carried out in accordance with applicable local regulatory law and the fund's rules. In order to evidence this the depositary will have a programme of compliance testing which includes a review of the relevant policies and procedures (such as the valuation policy) and undertaking sample testing to ensure compliance.

Class Q Scheme
Registered funds in Guernsey established solely for investors who are considered to be qualifying or sophisticated investors.

eligible investor fund
A certified fund which is suitable for eligible Investors (professional or experienced investors) and which can be authorised expeditiously by the Jersey Financial Services Commission subject to certain requirements, as set out by them, being met.

12. Regulatory framework

Inside of Europe, the AIFMD is the primary piece of legislation that sets out the responsibilities of a depositary, which includes the role of custodian. This is discussed above.

In offshore centres, there are varying regulatory requirements in relation to the role of a custodian or trustee and additionally in relation to the type of fund that it is.

Table 8.1: Type of funds in offshore centres

	Type of fund	Type of institution permitted as custodian	Named	Requirements
Guernsey	**Class Q Schemes**	Any that is licensed under the Protection of Investors Law, 1987, and has a place of business in Guernsey	Custodian or trustee	Cannot have directors in common with the manager or be a subsidiary of the manager. Must have net assets of £4,000,000
Jersey	**Eligible investor fund**	Entity licensed for the purpose of custody in Jersey	Custodian or trustee, or depositary in a member state if an AIFM is appointed	Custody must be sourced from separate custodian/ trustee with a physical presence in the island, subject to certain exemptions for hedge funds
Bermuda	Mutual funds	Licensed in Bermuda or subject to similar overseas equivalent requirements	Custodian	Custodian must be independent of the directors of the mutual fund or partners of a partnership
Cayman Islands	Mutual funds	Any that is licensed for that activity, if Cayman-based may need to be regulated pursuant to the Mutual Funds Law	Custodian or trustee	Does not necessarily need to be Cayman-based
Isle of Man	Authorised collective investment scheme	Licensed by the IOM Financial Services Commission or regulated for that activity in a jurisdiction that the Isle of Man has a cooperation agreement with for collective investment schemes	Trustee or fiduciary custodian	Must undertake onsite testing of managers

The requirements within table 8.1 give examples of some of the ways in which regulators have tried to ensure the independence and oversight role of the custodian function to reduce risks in relation to fund assets. This is because of areas of risk which have been identified in relation to fund administration, where the role of the custodian is used to try and prevent their occurrence.

12.1 Mispricing

Where a fund is incorrectly priced, there is a requirement in most offshore jurisdictions to report it to the custodian, together with details of any compensation payable to the investor(s).

12.2 Fraud

The custodian acts as a guard or second pair of eyes in relation to any trading or transactions being undertaken to prevent employees of the investment manager or administrator committing fraud.

12.3 Failure to obtain best execution

Whilst the custodian may not be able to prevent it at the time, when undertaking reviews of the fund administrator, they will check the administrator's procedures and sample test some trade instructions to ensure best execution has been provided. Wherever they identify that it has not, a report will be provided to the fund board.

12.4 Settlement errors

When delivery of shares and receipt of monies, or vice versa, do not match up to each other, this creates a mismatch between units held and cash balances. The custodian records can help identify and rectify the matter to find out which part of the trade has not completed.

12.5 Failure to respond

Where the fund administrator does not respond to requests for instruction on corporate actions, the custodian will follow up to ensure a response is posted if required.

12.6 Failure to claim money owed

Where dividends or other income is declared, the custodian can ensure that it is claimed and apportioned to the correct account.

12.7 Conflicts of interest

It is clear that the greatest risk from a regulator's perspective is that which arises where a custodian and an investment manager or administrator are within the same group of companies, given the conflicts of interest and the potential for fraud which may arise from that, as discussed above. Having related parties involved means the detection of any kind of irregularity or the mismanagement of assets increases significantly, which negates the effectiveness of the custodian role.

13. Segregation of client money and client assets

13.1 Jurisdictions

Many jurisdictions have rules and requirements in place to ensure that, whenever a designated manager or administrator deals with fund monies or assets, they are segregated from those of the designated manager or administrator themselves, as well as from other funds that may be under their management. This is so that if anything happens to the designated manager or administrator themselves, the money and assets of the fund are separate and cannot be claimed against by creditors of the designated manager or administrator.

The purpose of the rules is to ensure that client money is always completely accounted for, held securely and any issues that arise in relation to client money are generally required to be reported to the regulator in the jurisdiction, given the serious implications.

13.2 Guernsey

In Guernsey, the Licensees (Conduct of Business) Rules, 2014 set out the requirements that have to be observed in relation to segregation of client money. This includes the establishment of client money accounts.

Client money bank accounts have to held at an approved bank (one which is licensed and regulated in a member state, Jersey or the Isle of Man). The approved bank has to provide an undertaking to the licensee in respect of how they will operate the client money account and confirm that they understand it is not the licensee's own money.

Adequate records have to be maintained of compliance with the rules, which includes reconciliation of the client money accounts on at least a monthly basis. This is to ensure that all transactions across the accounts agree between the bank's records and the licensee's own records, and also demonstrate that the client money rules are being complied with in terms of timeframe and timeliness in dealing with client money transactions.

It is strictly prohibited for the client money account to become overdrawn and there must not be a shortfall in client money when it comes to the reconciliation with the statement issued by the approved bank. If the licensee does breach this requirement, they have to immediately rectify the position.

If, in any case, the licensee receives interest on a client money account, then the details of to whom the interest is paid has to be declared within the scheme particulars for the fund.

13.3 Jersey

In Jersey the applicable rules are contained in the Financial Services (Investment Business (Client Assets)) (Jersey) Order, 2001.

This specifically requires that client money, money belonging to the licensee, and money held on behalf of or received from connected customers must be kept separate from one another. This extends to these three sources of money never being mixed and that individual transactions can be identified and traced as appropriate.

It is more onerous than Guernsey, as there is a requirement to evidence the balance of each client account each business day; and there is also a requirement that the client money account cannot go overdrawn. It is also specific that you cannot use money belonging to one client for the benefit of another.

If an overdraft does occur the licensee must pay in a sum of money equivalent to the deficit, and that money becomes client money and cannot be withdrawn by the licensee until the client responsible has made good the shortfall.

Client bank accounts must be sufficiently clearly designated to distinguish them from any accounts holding funds belonging to the licensee or other clients.

In addition to the Guernsey requirement to receive an undertaking from the approved bank, Jersey requires that that a copy of the undertaking is also provided to the Jersey Financial Services Commission.

If interest is to be paid on client money it must be done in accordance with any agreement made with the client, and if no interest is to be paid, the agreement must record that fact. If there is no agreement with the client, the licensee must disclose to the client concerned the amount of the interest received and where it has been paid.

Client money accounts should be reconciled with the statement issued by the approved bank not less than once a month and the reconciliations must be performed within 10 business days of the date to which the reconciliation relates. Any differences must be corrected immediately unless they have arisen because of timing differences between the accounting and settlement systems of the licensee and the approved bank, or if the Jersey Financial Services Commission is notified.

Chapter summary

- The role of custodian or depositary is designed to mitigate risks in the fund administration process.
- Despite the checks and balances that are required above, there is still the risk that things can go wrong. The asset could be destroyed, more common in relation to physical assets, or misplaced if there are a large number of funds to who custody services are being provided and comingling accidentally occurs, again in the example of physical assets.
- Using a custodian who is unconnected to any of the other parties to the fund gives an element of reassurance to investors as they are guaranteed independent oversight of the fund administrator, but ultimately, if a fund administrator always uses the same external custodian, that creates

a concentration risk, as if anything happens to that custodian, it will impact upon all of their funds using that custodian. That is not to say that a custodian within the same group ownership cannot be used by a fund administrator, but it should be a separate legal entity to the fund administrator to demonstrate independence in its role, and in particular, its oversight of the fund administrator.

- The regulatory requirements also assist in providing comfort in relation to the provision of custody services. Most jurisdictions require a sufficiently high threshold of capital to be held by an institution providing custodial services. Whilst this does not directly assist investors in the light of a fund failing for example, as the segregation of assets means that the capital of the custodian is not part of any pool against which a claim can be made, it demonstrates the robustness of the institution. It will provide reassurance that the custodian can withstand market events and remain trading.
- Any company that is providing custody services needs to demonstrate that it has robust arrangements for oversight of the fund manager and administrator, that it has adequate records and controls to identify any issues and that it is ensuring that assets are appropriately segregated both from their own assets and any other funds for which they act.

Part three

Chapter nine
Offshore private equity funds

Chapter ten
Offshore real estate funds

Chapter eleven
Bond funds

Fund products and services

Overview

In Part two, we considered the key components of the fund administrator's role. This part begins to break down individual asset classes and the nuances each brings with it. In exploring those nuances, this part explores key components as well as challenges and opportunities to assist fund administrators not only to perform the practicalities of their role but also to consider the value-added role of the fund administrator when administering different types of fund.

Learning outcomes

At the end of this part, you will be able to:

- Know what private equity funds, common structures and structure selection, popular offshore jurisdictions are
- Understand differences and similarities between popular jurisdictions, relevant laws and regulations and taxation factors

- Understand what makes a fund a real estate fund
- Understand investment strategies of real estate funds
- Consider the challenges facing real estate funds
- Consider real estate from a global perspective
- Understand the role of bond funds, the different types of bonds and why they are an attractive offering for those seeking a stable and reliable investment type.

Chapter nine
Offshore private equity funds

List of topics

1. Background – what is a private equity fund?
2. Basic structure of private equity funds
3. Offshore jurisdictions
4. Why offshore jurisdictions for private equity?
5. Sector analysis for offshore investment activity
6. Top global private equity firms
7. Financial services provided by offshore jurisdictions
8. Regulation
9. Legislation, structuring and structure selection
10. Taxation issues
11. Recent trends in private equity funds
12. Comparison of selected offshore private equity holding structures

Introduction

In this chapter, you will gain an understanding of offshore private equity funds. You will learn about what private equity funds are, common structures and structure selection, popular offshore jurisdictions, and growth in the offshore sector over recent years. The differences and similarities between popular jurisdictions, relevant laws and regulations and taxation factors will also be explored.

1. Background – what is a private equity fund?

1.1 Investment schemes

Private equity funds are investment schemes funded through pooled capital obtained from institutional investors such as pension funds and insurance companies and also high net worth individuals.

Typically, the amounts raised by private equity firms are substantial, and pooled into specific funds established by the firms. Funds remain active for set periods of time in order to generate returns for the investor, commonly referred to as the internal rate of return (IRR). When one fund is approaching its agreed close date it is generally followed by a new fund facilitated by a new period of **capital raising**.

capital raising
The stage of the lifecycle that involves sourcing institutional investors or wealthy investors to invest large sums of money into a fund.

Organised private equity, through the establishment of pooled investment vehicles and the management and advisory services provided by focused specialists, has grown from the middle of the twentieth century, originally in the form of venture capital and then as private equity from the early 1980s onwards.

The private equity sector has grown and diversified substantially since the 1980s, focusing on small, mid and large capital buyouts, turnarounds and increasingly real estate and technology investment. In response to the last boom and bust cycle (from 2003 to 2007), and the substantial reduction in sources of credit available for businesses and facilitating the growth of investment, the private equity sector has started to diversify into the provision of credit finance.

1.2 Business opportunities

Classically, private equity firms exist in order to identify specific business opportunities which will increase their investment portfolio, generate high yields for the investors and obtain strategic business advantage. The most common opportunities are as follows:

- **Buy-outs** – Private equity firms will seek out struggling privately owned companies and purchase the shareholding. In many cases where the company may have been struggling due to poor management, the private equity firm can source and implement a new skilled management team. If the management team were effective and the business was struggling due to cash flow issues, the private equity firm may retain the existing team and ease the strain by providing a cash flow injection.
- **Acquisitions for expansion** – This involves a private equity firm buying out a successful company to enhance the likelihood of the success continuing and facilitating growth through the provision of additional capital as required. Alternatively, it may simply invest in a portion of the shares of a profitable company for capital appreciation.
- **Restructuring** – This involves a private equity firm buying a struggling company and restructuring it completely to try and turn around its fortunes and bring it into profit.

- **Mergers** – Private equity firms often buy companies successfully trading or otherwise in order to merge them with companies that the firm already has in its portfolio in order to gain an advantage over competitors.

1.3 Life cycle of a private equity fund

There are four main stages in the life cycle of most private equity funds:

- **Capital raising** – This stage of the life cycle involves sourcing institutional investors or wealthy investors to invest large sums of money into a fund. The capital raising phase usually lasts anywhere between one and three years but can last longer. Once this phase has closed no new investors are permitted.
- **Sourcing investment opportunity** – Once the capital raising period has closed, the firm must then ensure that it has the right human capital in place in order to manage the investment portfolio and to identify the right business opportunities in which to invest the capital held in the fund, in order to give the fund the best chance of success. On average this phase lasts between two and five years.
- **Managing the investment portfolio** – When the fund has sufficient investments in their portfolio, these investments must be managed in accordance with the agreed strategy (see Section 1.2). This phase can span on average three to seven years.
- **Exiting** – Generally, private equity firms do not seek to hold on to investments indefinitely and look to dispose all of the investments held in a fund portfolio in order to return capital to investors plus a return and having hopefully made a profit in the process. Disposal is usually through sale or an initial public offering (IPO) on a recognised stock exchange. Often it can take a long time to liquidate the investment portfolio and close the fund. This phase often occurs simultaneously with the capital raising phase for a new fund.

The overall lifespan of a private equity fund commonly lasts anywhere between 10 and 15 years.

2. Basic structure of private equity funds

2.1 General partners

General partners (GPs) are typically the partners of the private equity firm. The GPs are responsible for making the investment decisions on behalf of the fund. Each fund generally has one GP. It is important to note that GPs have unlimited liability.

The GP receives compensation for the services provided by way of a management fee, this is usually around 2% per annum of the asset value of the fund. This fee is generally to cover the day-to-day running costs of the GP. In order to motivate the GP to strive to improve the performance of the fund, they are entitled to receive what is referred to as carried interest.

Carried interest is an agreed share of the profits of the fund. The calculations for carried interest can often be very complex but generally they amount to anywhere between 20% and 25% of the fund's annual profits. This is therefore the main source of income for the GP. Carried interest is paid out to the GP only after investors' capital has been returned along with the agreed IRR.

2.2 Limited partners

Limited partners (LPs) are the providers of the investments into the fund. The investments are referred to as capital commitments. One fund can have as many as a few hundred different LPs. LPs have limited liability, which is capped at the total of their investment. The terms of a limited partner's investment, including the duration of the fund, extension options, management fees and how any profits of the fund will be divided, are set out in what is known as the limited partnership agreement (LPA). The LP's will receive an agreed IRR (assuming the investments in the fund have performed as expected) plus the return of their capital contribution.

3. Offshore jurisdictions

Offshore funds are located in offshore jurisdictions or offshore financial centres.

The International Monetary Fund (IMF) defines an offshore financial centre as a 'country or jurisdiction that provides financial services to non-residents on a scale that is incommensurate with the size and the financing of its domestic economy'. Popular offshore jurisdictions for private equity funds include Guernsey, Jersey, Cayman Islands, Singapore, Mauritius, British Virgin Islands and Delaware.

Offshore jurisdictions have increasingly been specialising in establishing and running collective investment schemes.

Low or no taxation is often believed to be the sole reason for establishing a business or fund in an offshore jurisdiction, leading to such jurisdictions often being referred to as 'tax havens'. However, increasingly there are a multitude of other reasons that make such jurisdictions attractive, particularly for private equity funds, which will be explored in greater detail in Section 4. Generally, the private equity firms themselves will be incorporated 'onshore' whilst having a presence offshore, i.e. investment funds.

Private equity activity has long been a significant feature of the offshore mergers and acquisitions scene. The 'Offshore-I' publication prepared in November 2015 by Appleby Global found that since the start of 2014, 'on average one in five deal dollars per quarter was spent on an offshore transaction that involved a private equity sponsor. In the third quarter of 2015 private equity activity was even more significant than usual; there were 660 offshore deals altogether in the quarter, worth a total of $60.7 billion, and of those, 26 involved private equity firms either acquiring investments or exiting. With a combined worth of

$16.1 billion, private equity deals therefore represented over a quarter of total offshore activity by value in Q3 2015'.

Cayman Islands-incorporated companies were the primary target of offshore private equity investments in 2015. Cayman transactions accounted for nearly 75% ($15 billion) of total deal value spent offshore by private equity firms in the first nine months of the year.

After the Cayman Islands, Bermuda was the next busiest offshore private equity jurisdiction, with deals totalling 16% ($3.3 billion) of all deal value. The report highlighted the growth in popularity of Africa as a preferred offshore structuring jurisdiction, specifically Mauritius and the Seychelles. In 2015, with regards to offshore private equity transactions in Mauritius there were a number of lower value, high volume transactions totalling $273 million.

The private equity firms carrying out these deals during 2015 are primarily incorporated in the Cayman Islands or the United States, closely followed by Hong Kong, China, the United Kingdom and the British Virgin Islands.

4. Why offshore jurisdictions for private equity?

Many jurisdictions have unique factors which make them predominantly appealing to private equity funds.

The list below identifies some of the basic common threads between jurisdictions. These will be expanded on throughout this chapter, looking at some detailed examples together with identifying and discussing some of the unique factors of particular jurisdictions mentioned above:

- **Financial services provided by offshore jurisdictions** – Many offshore financial centres have perceived low political risk, and strong availability of financial service providers backed by skilled professionals such as accountants, administrators, lawyers and investment managers (see Section 7).
- **Regulation** – Increasingly the existence of an effective regulatory body is becoming a key factor when deciding where to establish a private equity fund or firm (see Section 8).
- **Legislation, structuring and structure selection** – One of the factors making offshore jurisdictions attractive for private equity firms is the fact that often there is favourable legislation specifically with regards to the structuring of private equity funds and the resulting benefits that brings (see Section 9).
- **Taxation** – Private equity funds can be registered and structured to minimise tax liabilities arising (see Section 10).

5. Sector analysis for offshore investment activity

Research carried out by Appleby Global in 2015 highlighted that there are three main sectors which have seen the most activity with regards to offshore investment of private equity firms.

Of the total number of deals that occurred during 2015, finance and insurance, professional activities and information and communication services accounted for nearly two thirds of deals and over 90% of the total value of all deals.

The largest of these sectors is information and communication, which in 2015 alone accounted for transactions worth $12 billion. There have been several significant transactions by private equity firms involving primarily buy-outs of several online retailers and application developers, such as mobile taxi booking business Ziaoju Kuaizhi.

Following the information and communication sector are the finance and insurance sectors, which during 2015 saw private equity investment deals worth $3.1 billion. This sector commonly sees the greatest number of offshore mergers and acquisitions, which has attracted the attention of private equity buyers. Insurance in particular has been the target of many private equity firms looking for buyouts due to the steady, predictable income streams which can greatly increase a firm's assets under management.

The third most active sector is that of professional services, encompassing a wide range of skills-based companies specialising in niche advertising markets and scientific research and development.

6. Top global private equity firms

Private Equity International have determined the top ranking private equity firms globally (based on capital raised between January 2011 and April 2016) as follows in Table 9.1.

The largest, most successful private equity firms do not necessarily give the largest returns, however they do have better investor relations, compliance, infrastructure and diversified strategies and structures.

7. Financial services provided by offshore jurisdictions

7.1 Private equity investment

As touched upon in Section 6.2, recent trends show the level of private equity investment in the corporate services sector is soaring as investors and potential investors are placing more and more value on non-financial related factors when deciding where to place their substantial funds, as they recognise the value creation opportunities associated with these factors.

Table 9.1: Top ranking global private equity firms

	Company	Headquartered	Investment portfolio includes
1	Blackstone Group	New York	Pactera, MIVISA, Optiv, Alta Resources LLC, Versace, Leica
2	KKR	New York	Arbor Pharmaceuticals, Panasonic, Pets at Home, Sonos, Toys R Us
3	Warburg Pincus	New York	Black Swan Energy, MEG Energy Corp, Nova, Reiss, Santander Asset Management
4	Advent International	Boston	New Look, DFS, FatFace, Poundland, HMV
5	The Carlyle Group	Washington	Air Cargo Inc, AMC Entertainment, Hertz Corporation, RAC Limited
6	Apollo Global Management	New York	Claire's, Countrywide plc, Oceana Cruises
7	CVC Capital Partners	London	Continental Foods, Formula One, Moto, Sky Bet
8	EnCap Investments	Houston	Fuse Energy, Sierra Oil and Gas, Cinco Oil and Gas
9	TPG	Texas	Burger King, Cirque Du Soleil, Ducati, Air bnb
10	EQT Partners	Stockholm	Kuoni Group, Sportradar, United Digital Group

A number of offshore financial centres are well established with a wealth of financial services providers, as such they are known to attract scores of young and experienced professionals alike together with branches of successful investment management companies, fund administration companies and legal firms.

7.2 Jersey

Jersey has attracted investors from the UK, Europe and indeed globally into private equity pooled investment vehicles for many years. As the private equity market grew in Europe so too did its presence in Jersey and it has increasingly been viewed as a key location to establish these vehicles. As a consequence, investment advisers based in the United Kingdom, Germany, Switzerland and Scandinavian countries have looked to Jersey in order to establish investment funds to pursue these opportunities, creating and developing value, jobs and new business in the process. Private equity firms from countries including the Czech Republic, India and South Africa have created investment vehicles in Jersey.

The increased demand for these investment structures over the years in Jersey led to the need for the development of superior specialist services.

Jersey enjoys highly respected leading administration service providers, with strong reputations globally offering both generic and bespoke services. These firms have also expanded their offerings to service structures established in other jurisdictions.

Alongside the strong tailored administration environment, Jersey also boasts a number of well-established and highly regarded service providers in the legal and accounting sectors.

Jersey has also experienced in recent years a significant increase in the talent pool in Jersey, as individuals seek out job opportunities with successful stable organisations and perhaps a change of pace in life, i.e. many individuals migrate from cities in the UK mainland and indeed other cities across the globe looking for a different pace of life.

Some of the leading businesses in private equity advisory services have established offices and regulated business in the island, resulting in an increase in the volume and skill set of the investment professionals on the island, but also a substantial increase in related industry professionals such as compliance managers, business risk consultants and governance advisers.

7.3 British Virgin Islands (BVI)

Another key offshore jurisdiction in the market is the British Virgin Islands (BVI). One of the biggest draws of the BVI is the operational flexibility afforded by the islands.

This flexibility is attractive to some as the administrative burden and costs of incorporating in the BVI are low. Like Jersey, there is strong availability of financial service providers supported by an array of skilled professionals such as accountants, administrators, lawyers and investment managers.

In 2016 there has been considerable interest by smaller private equity firms in the BVI, specifically those which invest in emerging markets. Due to the low administration costs, start-up businesses in their early stages and seed financings are increasingly using BVI entities.

7.4 Mauritius

In Mauritius, there is an abundance of large international banks and accounting firms with a number of fund administrators providing fund licensing and back office support services.

Private equity funds in Africa are attracted by the technical, legal, accounting skills and logistical support readily available in Mauritius compared to other parts of Africa. This results in a contribution of some 10% of the country's GDP by the financial services sector.

Like the BVI, costs of administering private equity funds in Mauritius is low compared to the costs in other jurisdictions.

Well-known institutions which have established funds in Mauritius include Standard Life, Goldman Sachs, Carlyle and BlackRock.

7.5 Singapore

Singapore is growing in popularity in the private equity market due to the stability of the Singapore economy and the connections to the Asian market. Some of the larger firms such as Blackstone Group and KKR have set up operation in Singapore, bolstering the already robust array of service providers found in the region.

Currently there are approximately 102 private equity fund managers who have headquarters based in Singapore and a further 144 globally who have secondary operations in Singapore.

The top three private equity firms in Singapore based on total funds raised in the last decade are L Capital Asia, Northstar Group and TAEL Partners.

8. Regulation

Prior to 2013, the UK saw a large number of private equity firms moving or preparing for a possible move offshore prior to the implementation of Europe-wide regulation Alternative Investment Fund Managers Directive (AIFMD) being introduced in 2013.

The impact of the introduction of AIFMD in very general terms has resulted in a significant increase in the regulatory reporting requirements and duties of fund managers of alternative investment funds which are marketed within the EU.

Interestingly around half of all private equity funds run by UK managers were already offshore, primarily in the Channel Islands.

Despite the introduction of AIFMD driving many private equity firms offshore, a strong regulatory industry is a contributing factor when private equity firms are looking for where to set up funds. Having well-respected regulatory bodies overseeing the activities of private equity funds in offshore jurisdictions is an invaluable selling tool when it comes to attracting wealthy and institutional investors.

Both Guernsey and Jersey have regulators who are deemed to be fully compliant with international standards and regulatory bodies such as the International Monetary Fund (IMF), an organisation of 189 countries, which seeks to 'foster global monetary cooperation, secure financial stability, facilitate international trade, promote high employment and sustainable economic growth, and reduce poverty around the world', and the Organisation for Economic Cooperation and Development (OECD), a global organisation which is focused on working to achieve economic and social well-being of individuals across the world.

Guernsey private equity funds are regulated by the Guernsey Financial Services Commission (GFSC), which has been seen to help foster a pragmatic regulatory environment. New private equity firms must be approved by the GFSC before establishing a fund in Guernsey.

Private equity funds domiciled/administered in Jersey are regulated by the Jersey Financial Services Commission.

The regulation system in Guernsey and Jersey is viewed as promoting an attractive, stable jurisdiction for private equity fund domiciliation and management.

Similarly, the BVI have applied OECD standards with regards to regulation and compliance.

Historically and currently, the Cayman Islands has one of the largest concentrations of private equity funds of all of the offshore jurisdictions. Interestingly, closed-ended funds in the Cayman Islands, of which private equity funds are, are not regulated by the Islands, regulatory body, the Cayman Islands Monetary Authority (CIMA). This is due to a section of the law which states that the equity interest issued by the partnership are not redeemable or available for repurchase at the option of the investors. It is also noted that the GP's of private equity funds do not require any form of licensing or approval in the Cayman Islands.

Looking at the Cayman Islands and the lack of regulation, this would appear to counteract the argument that investors, private equity firms and managers are attracted to jurisdictions with strong regulation, however the Cayman Islands has been one of the longest running offshore financial centres making it therefore difficult to carry out a like-for-like comparison in terms of popularity with other up-and-coming offshore jurisdictions.

9. Legislation, structuring and structure selection

9.1 Favourable legislation

As touched upon in Section 4, one of the factors making offshore jurisdictions attractive for private equity firms is the fact that often there is favourable legislation specifically with regards to the structuring of private equity funds and the resulting benefits that brings. Legislation and structure is unique depending on each offshore jurisdiction, so we will look at a selection in isolation.

The BVI has a familiar and established legal and court system based on English common law and therefore is familiar for UK-based private equity firms. It also provides a level of comfort over the stability of the country, which is important for investors.

There are four main type of vehicles used for private equity funds in the BVI. These vehicles are as follows:

International limited partnerships

International limited partnerships are established under the Partnership Act 1996 (as amended) (Partnership Act). In line with the more classic structure, a limited partnership has at least one general partner and at least one limited partner. The limited partner's liability is restricted to the maximum capital they contributed. The Partnership Act is somewhat unique in that it allows the limited partners a greater degree of involvement in the management of a limited partnership than some other jurisdictions.

Other specific advantages of a BVI limited partnership include:

- The ability to have a private equity fund with no cap on the number of limited partners allowed to invest.
- Confidentiality – there is no requirement to disclose the identity of the limited partners or their capital contributions to the public.
- There is no requirement for the limited or general partners to be resident in the BVI.

Business companies

A business company (BC) incorporated under the BVI Business Companies Act (as amended) (BC Act) is often incorporated to act as the general partner of a fund entity.

Some advantages of a BC include:

- Shares can be issued in any currency.
- Confidentiality – there is no requirement to file the register of members or register of directors in the public domain.
- A BC can be incorporated with only one shareholder and one director.
- The directors and shareholders do not need to be resident in the BVI.
- There is no requirement to appoint a company secretary.
- Exemption from all local taxes.
- There is no requirement for accounts and records of a BC do not need to be filed with the BVI authorities.

Unit trusts

A BVI unit trust works in a similar way to an English unit trust where the trustee of the BVI unit trust has legal ownership over the assets of the fund for the benefit of the investor in accordance with the terms of the deed of trust.

A BVI unit trust is not a separate legal entity. Unit trusts are not commonly used for private equity funds in the BVI unless, for example, it is preferable for an investor to hold units instead of holding shares in a company.

Segregated portfolio companies (SPC)

Only investment funds or insurance companies can be incorporated as a BVI SPC, following approval from the Financial Services Commission.

A BVI SPC is a single company that contains a number of segregated portfolios. The assets in each portfolio are ring-fenced and only the assets in each portfolio are available to meet the liabilities of the relevant portfolio. SPC's are the BVI equivalent of PCCs, protected cell companies, the concept of which was first introduced in Guernsey in 1997.

Under BVI law there are additional requirements for SPCs such as implementing satisfactory procedures that ensure that the assets of each portfolio are held separately. These additional requirements often lead to increased administration costs, however, a well-run SPC can often be a more cost-effective structure in the long run than an umbrella fund structure consisting of multiple companies.

9.2 Guernsey and Jersey law

In Guernsey, most private equity funds are classed as closed-ended investment vehicles and as a result must be registered or authorised by the GFSC under the Protection of Investors (Bailiwick of Guernsey) Law, 1987, as amended (POI Law).

Limited liability partnerships in Guernsey are also governed by the Limited Liability Partnership (Guernsey) Law 2013 with Limited Partnerships being governed by the Limited Partnership (Guernsey) Law 1995 (as amended).

Guernsey and Jersey are similar to the BVI in that they both have familiar and established legal and court systems based on English common law, the Companies (Guernsey) Law 2008 and the Companies (Jersey) Law 1991, respectively. In addition, the structures offered in relation to private equity funds are also companies, unit trusts and limited partnerships.

Figure 9.1 illustrates the most common form of private equity fund structure in Guernsey, and indeed Jersey.

Figure 9.1: Typical Guernsey private equity structure

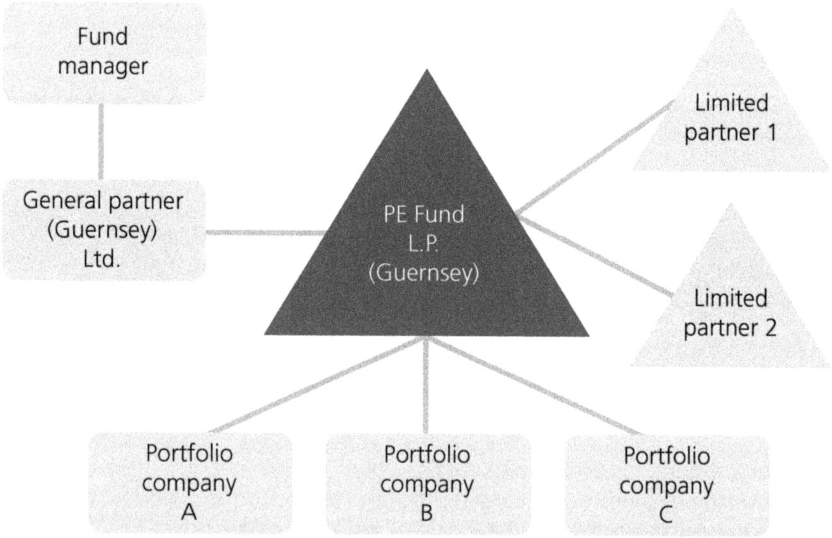

Diagram supplied courtesy of Guernsey Finance – the promotional agency for the island's finance industry internationally

9.3 Selection of investment structure

The selection of which structure to use is dependent on where the fund is being marketed and the appetite of the target investors.

Limited partnerships tend to be the most appropriate structure for investment products with high minimum investment thresholds, which private equity funds characteristically have.

While regulatory and marketing considerations are important in selecting whether to structure a fund using the company, unit trust or limited partnership form, the monetary implications for investors will generally be the deciding factor.

Overall the managers of the fund will be seeking to ensure that investors will not be disadvantaged from a taxation perspective by investing in the fund, compared to if they had invested directly in the underlying asset. This is referred to as tax neutrality.

Limited partnerships, unlike companies or unit trusts, are generally treated as being fully transparent for tax purposes and the total tax taken will be determined by the partners' individual circumstances.

Master-feeder structures are also frequently used, and enable both domestic investors and onshore investors to participate in the same investment programs. Using the United States as an example, a US taxable investor would invest directly in a limited partnership domiciled in the US. The offshore investors and US tax-exempt investors on the other hand would invest in an offshore company (or, occasionally, a limited partnership). The US investor and the offshore company, both referred to as 'feeders' will then invest all of their assets into a master fund, which is typically an offshore company that has elected to be treated as a partnership for US tax purposes.

The investment manager will then manage the portfolio at master fund level. One of the advantages of the structure is that it significantly reduces the amount of administration required as there is only investment activity at the master fund level.

9.4 Structures of private equity funds in the Cayman Islands

The available structures for private equity funds in the Cayman Islands are more straightforward. The most common structure is as an Exempted Limited Partnership (ELP) formed under the Exempted Limited Partnership Law (As Revised) (ELP Law). However as with the jurisdictions discussed above there is still the option to use a company rather than an ELP as the corporate structure for their private equity funds for a number of reasons, including onshore tax or regulatory considerations, or the investor base simply being more familiar with the concept of investing in a Cayman exempted company.

As with the limited partnership structures we have already seen, an ELP is required to have a GP, which tend to be Cayman exempted companies, however in certain circumstances, foreign partnerships established in recognised jurisdictions (e.g. the United States, United Kingdom, Hong Kong, BVI,

Singapore, Jersey, Luxembourg) outside of the Cayman Islands can act as the GP of an ELP.

Again, the GP is responsible for conducting the management of the affairs of the ELP, signing all contracts on behalf of and in the name of the ELP and is ultimately liable for all debts and obligations of the ELP to the extent that the ELP has insufficient assets.

There is no requirement for any director or shareholder of the GP to reside in the Cayman Islands. There is no upper limit on how many limited partners can invest in the ELP or requirement for them be resident in the Cayman Islands.

As mentioned earlier, the Cayman Islands remains one of the most successful offshore jurisdictions for private equity funds. This could in part be due to the similarities between the ELP Law and the Delaware Revised Uniform Limited Partnership Act.

The ELP Law adopts principles similar to those found in the Delaware Revised Uniform Limited Partnership Act, and this similarity with the Delaware model makes the ELP particularly attractive to managers and investors in the United States. However, unlike a Delaware limited partnership, an ELP does not have a legal personality of its own.

The ELP is a legal arrangement between its GP and its limited partners governed by the terms detailed in the LPA. The LPA will state that the contractual rights and equitable interests in the assets of the ELP are held on trust for the ELP by its GP(s).

With regards to participating in management style activity, limited partners are prohibited and the rules are similar to those for Guernsey, Jersey and BVI limited partnerships already discussed.

Under the previous ELP law, a GP was under an 'absolute duty to act in good faith in the interest of the ELP'. The requirement often led to conflicts of interest for the GP, particularly in the instances where it was acting as GP to more than one ELP, having to make investment decisions which may have benefited one ELP over another.

The ELP Law was revised on 2 July 2014 with the aim of enhancing and protecting the draw of the Cayman Islands as the leading offshore jurisdiction for private equity funds, which enabled the LPAs to include a clause whereby the absolute duty on the GP to act in good faith was retained subject to any express provision in the LPA to the contrary.

9.5 Mauritius

Moving on to one of the newer up-and-coming offshore jurisdictions, Mauritius offers two possible structures for private equity funds: a Category 1 Global Business Company (GBC1) or a limited partnership under the Limited Partnership Act, 2011.

The main attraction of the limited partnership as a structure in Mauritius is its tax transparency and neutrality potential. Private equity funds structured as

GBC1s are subject to tax at the maximum effective rate of 3% on its foreign sourced income.

In Singapore, Cayman Islands ELPs have historically been the preferred legal structure for private equity funds managed in Singapore. Despite Singapore having its own Limited Partnerships Act (Chapter 163B) governing the establishment of Singapore LPs, familiarity with the Cayman structure and the desire to give comfort to investors has led to private equity funds in Singapore using ELPs, even though both the Cayman and the Singapore structures are modelled based on Delaware law.

The master-feeder structure referred to in Section 9.3 is often used in Singapore, whereby a Cayman LP acts as the pooling vehicle that owns a Singapore-incorporated master fund.

Certain private equity funds in Singapore can be structured as stand-alone companies incorporated either under the Cayman's Exempted Limited Partnership Law (2001 revision) or Singapore's Limited Partnerships Act (Chapter 163B).

9.6 Classic limited partnership

Overall, across all jurisdictions, the classic limited partnership structure remains the most popular structure for offshore tax-efficient jurisdictions, such as Guernsey, Jersey, the Cayman Islands, Mauritius and Cyprus. According to Peter Furci, partner at Debevoise and Plimpton law firm in New York, limited partnerships remain the preferred model because 'they lend themselves to the basic economics and governance arrangements that are typical to private equity funds, including limiting the liability of the investors in the fund for any losses over and above their capital commitments, as well as affording flexibility in the economic terms of a given deal, unlike the fixed capital structure of a corporation'.

One of the most recent developments and challengers to the conventional fund structure is the emergence of co-investments and parallel funds.

Co-investment vehicles invest alongside the LPs but for reduced capital commitments and returns, and have greater flexibility with regards to what investments they participate in within a fund and the timing of when they can exit.

Parallel funds behave in the same way as co-investment vehicles with the exception of the fact that they are not able to pick and choose what investments they participate in and when they exit the fund.

9.7 The administrator's role in private equity funds

Though many duties of the administrator will not differ merely due to the asset class of the fund, private equity administration is typically a whole subset of administration in itself, with many administration firms set up purely to service private equity investment funds and clients. The following are the key administrative tasks particular to private equity funds:

- Investors subscribing for units in private equity funds do so on a commitment basis, meaning that they commit to invest an amount of money up to a maximum commitment. On initial subscription, the fund may require none or some of that commitment to be paid into the fund to pay initial expenses and to buy the first asset(s). To avoid cash drag, however, the fund manager will not call up any more money than is needed to meet asset and operational costs, and so the unpaid portion of that total commitment will remain available for the fund to call from time to time.
- The administrator's role in calling for payment of outstanding commitment from investors is an essential one, often requiring the completion of calculations to ensure that the amount being called is in proportion to each investor's overall percentage allocation of the fund.
- Private equity funds operate in the hope of receiving profit, whether through regular income receipt from underlying portfolio businesses or from capital appreciation (e.g. on disposal). As money is paid up from portfolio companies to the private equity fund, the fund manager will determine at what stage those monies ought to be paid to investors as distributions. Again, the administrator's role may be in calculating (or, at the very least, verifying the calculation) of monies to be paid to investors as distributions.
- It may also happen that the timing of a distribution coincides with the timing of a further capital call from investors. Here, the administrator will need to calculate the net effect of the money movement. Ultimately the investor will receive all distributions and pay all capital calls, however there is little sense in paying money to an investor only to ask them to send that amount back to the fund as a capital call.
- Many administrators will tell stories of that deal that had to be completed over Christmas or the 48 hours private equity teams put in when closing a deal. Whilst the lawyers, fund manager and general partner will be the key parties to any deal, the administrator often finds itself in a position where everything has to be dropped.
- Private equity investors require sophisticated levels of reporting, which means that administrators are challenged to find the best private equity platforms to provide the requisite levels of reporting.

10. Taxation issues

Private equity fund managers investing funds across multiple countries tend to facilitate this by using sub-advisers in those relevant countries, or via a holding company located in a bilateral treaty jurisdiction (a contract or agreement between two countries/jurisdictions).

Fund managers must take into account the potential tax liabilities for investors in order to determine the optimal tax-efficient structure for a fund.

LPs may require a manager to accommodate a wide array of tax structuring needs.

One of the most important tax considerations is permanent establishment treatment. Where private equity firms and managers are based in the same places where they invest, the onshore team's discretionary authority is often limited, with final investment decisions relegated to an investment committee based offshore, thus preventing a permanent establishment being created onshore.

In most tax jurisdictions the structure of the fund has a direct impact on the fund's tax position and whether they are seen as tax transparent or not. A limited partnership will generally be treated as being transparent for tax purposes and the total tax take will be determined by the partners' individual circumstances. In comparison, private equity funds structured as companies are generally deemed to be not transparent for tax purposes; however, it has been possible to structure companies as entities that satisfy the relevant conditions within other jurisdictions for fiscal transparency. For fiscal purposes, a unit trust has mixed tax characteristics. In certain jurisdictions it may be treated as being transparent for income and non-transparent for capital gains distributions.

As with legislation and structure options there are differences and similarities between different offshore jurisdictions. The BVI has zero-rated corporation tax, with no wealth, capital gains or estate tax for offshore entities. Likewise, in the Cayman Islands there is no capital gains, income, withholding, estate or inheritance tax.

One of the unique factors with regards for ELPs and GPs in the Cayman Islands is the treatment of future changes in taxation. The ELP can apply for an undertaking from the Cayman Islands Government that no form of taxation that may be introduced in the Cayman Islands will apply to the ELP for a period of 50 years from the undertaking being given.

The GP can also apply for (and can expect to obtain) an undertaking from the Cayman Islands Government that no form of taxation that may be introduced in the Cayman Islands will apply to the GP for a period of 20 years from the undertaking being given.

In Guernsey, private equity funds are structured so that no liability to tax will arise in Guernsey. Guernsey has its own tax regime and does not levy any capital gains, inheritance or value added taxes.

In the Cayman Islands, ELPs are generally regarded from an onshore tax perspective as being tax transparent, thus the ELP itself will not be liable to any onshore taxes, and value distributed by it will 'flow through' to the investors (and may be subject to local taxes in their hands).

In Singapore, with regards to the use of the master-feeder structure discussed in Section 9, one of the reasons for using such a structure is due to Singapore's network of double taxation treaties. Private equity funds in Singapore can benefit from employing a master-feeder structure that allows a fund to enjoy the flexibility of an LP and the tax efficiencies of a Singapore master fund.

11. Recent trends in private equity funds

Appleby Global's 2015 offshore private equity report highlighted that private equity investment activity in the offshore market continues to compare favourably with that of other world regions, ranking the region fourth globally in terms of deal value after North America, Western Europe, and the Far East and Central Asia. Dollars spent on offshore private equity transactions was worth more than that of Oceania, Africa, the Middle East and Eastern Europe combined in 2015.

Even more impressive was the high deal values experienced in these offshore jurisdictions – 41 transactions compared to 959 in the Far East and Central Asia.

This data indicates that offshore has the advantage over the rest of the world when it comes to 'big money' private equity deals. The value of deals offshore in 2015 was more than four times that of deals in the USA and more than seven times that of deals in Western Europe.

In volume terms, over 91% of transactions take place in North America, Western Europe and the Far East and Central Asia. Offshore accounts for just 1% of global private equity deal volume.

The major trends in the BVI private equity market tend to follow the trends in the global financial centres. 2015 saw a significant increase in fundraising involving BVI entities. Unlike other jurisdictions, the BVI still remains a popular jurisdiction for start-ups in emerging markets.

Guernsey has experienced over the years the net asset value of private equity funds growing dramatically to stand currently at over £80bn, an increase of 140%.

In the developing world Africa continues to attract global interest, with Mauritius fast emerging as the natural gateway for investing in Africa. Mauritius continues to offer risk mitigation and investment protection in the region through its wide network of investment promotion and protection agreements (IPPAs) and fiscal efficiency through its growing network of double taxation avoidance agreements (DTAAs), the presence of international players in the finance industry and a readily available pool of professionals.

Currently more than 50% of African private equity structures are housed in Mauritius.

12. Comparison of selected offshore private equity holding structures

Figure 9.2 provides a side-by-side comparison of the laws of the BVI, the Cayman Islands, Guernsey and Jersey, correct as at August 2015.

Figure 9.2: Comparison of offshore private equity holding structures

MOURANT OZANNES

Comparison of Offshore Private Equity Holding Structures

AUGUST 2015

This table has been prepared to provide a comparison of the laws of the British Virgin Islands (BVI), the Cayman Islands, Guernsey and Jersey as at its date of publication. It is for general information only and is not intended to, and does not, constitute legal, financial or other advice upon which you may act or rely and does not constitute an offer to provide such advice.

	BVI	Cayman	Guernsey	Jersey
Usual structure for private equity deals	A BVI, Cayman, Guernsey or Jersey holding company ("Topco", where equity will enter the structure) which owns another offshore intermediate holding company ("Midco") which in turn owns the acquisition vehicle ("Bidco"). Debt typically enters the structure at Midco level. Depending on the jurisdiction of the target asset, Midco and/or Bidco may be formed in a jurisdiction with a favourable tax treaty (eg Netherlands and Luxembourg).			
Principal legislation for companies	The BVI Business Companies Act, 2004 The BVI Business Companies Regulations 2012.	The Companies Law (2013 Revision), as amended.	The Companies (Guernsey) Law 2008, as amended.	Companies (Jersey) Law 1991, as amended.
Companies registry	The Registrar of Corporate Affairs.	The Registrar of Companies.	The Guernsey Registry.	The Companies Registry.
Incorporation	Shelf companies are not typically used. Company names can be reserved. Incorporation can take place within one day, if completed KYC is provided. The law does not distinguish between public and private companies.	Shelf companies are not typically used. Company names can be reserved. Companies can be incorporated on a same day basis if express service is used and completed KYC is provided. The law does not distinguish between public and private companies.	Shelf companies are not available. Company names can be reserved. Incorporation can take place within one day (standard), or on a 15 minute or two hour basis if fast-tracked, if completed KYC is provided. The law does not distinguish between public and private companies.	A form of shelf company is available, but is not generally used in practice. Company names can be reserved. Companies can be incorporated on a same day basis if express service is used and completed KYC is provided. Public and private companies are available. A company will be treated as public if it has more than 30 registered shareholders (excluding directors and employees).[1]
What is it?	A limited liability company ie a body corporate with separate legal personality where its shareholders benefit from limited liability.			

[1] The remainder of the table refers to Jersey private companies only. A limited number of additional requirements apply to public companies, such as the requirement to have accounts audited and for accounts to be filed. Further details are available on request.

mourantozannes.com

BVI | CAYMAN ISLANDS | GUERNSEY | HONG KONG | JERSEY | LONDON

Figure 9.2: Comparison of offshore private equity holding structures *continued*

MOURANT OZANNES

	BVI	Cayman	Guernsey	Jersey
Constitutional documents	Memorandum and articles of association. The memorandum and articles of association can be amended by a shareholder resolution. This resolution requires the approval of a simple majority (or such higher percentage as is specified in the articles of association) of shareholders who, being entitled to do so, vote in person or by proxy at a general meeting of the company. Directors also have certain rights to amend the memorandum and articles of association.	Memorandum and articles of association. The memorandum and articles of association can be amended by a special resolution. This resolution requires the approval of a two thirds majority (or such higher majority as is specified in the articles of association) of shareholders who, being entitled to do so, vote in person or by proxy at a general meeting of the company.	Memorandum and articles of incorporation. The memorandum and articles of incorporation can be amended by a special resolution. This resolution requires the approval of a 75 per cent of shareholders with voting rights (or such higher majority as is specified in the articles of incorporation)	Memorandum and articles of association. The memorandum and articles of association can be amended by a special resolution. This resolution requires the approval of a two thirds majority of shareholders with voting rights (or such higher majority as is specified in the articles of association).
Must key contracts be governed by local law?	No. The memorandum and articles of association/incorporation will be governed by local law. Other key contracts (investment and shareholders agreements, share purchase agreements, facility and bond documentation) can (and usually will) be governed by foreign law (typically English or New York law).			
Which documents are publicly available?	Certificate of incorporation, memorandum and articles of association, the date of incorporation, the identity and address of its registered agent, the address of its registered office, any public security filings, plus a few other documents that may be elected or required to be filed in specific circumstances. The registers of directors and shareholders are not required by law to be publicly filed, although a company may elect to do so.	The only information which is publicly available is the name of the Company, the date of incorporation, the address of its registered office and whether the company is active. The memorandum and articles of association and statutory registers are not matters of public record.	Memorandum and articles of incorporation, special resolutions, annual validations plus a few other documents required to be filed in specific circumstances. Confidential matters can be included in a shareholders agreement, which should not need to be filed provided it is appropriately drafted.	Memorandum and articles of association, special resolutions, annual returns plus a few other documents required to be filed in specific circumstances. Confidential matters can be included in a shareholders agreement, which should not need to be filed provided it is appropriately drafted.

mourantozannes.com BVI | CAYMAN ISLANDS | GUERNSEY | HONG KONG | JERSEY | LONDON AUGUST 20[illegible]

Figure 9.2: Comparison of offshore private equity holding structures *continued*

MOURANT OZANNES

	BVI	Cayman	Guernsey	Jersey
What other types of holding vehicle are available?	A wide variety of different types of company are available, including companies limited by guarantee, unlimited companies, restricted purpose companies and segregated portfolio companies. In addition, other types of vehicle are available, including partnerships, limited partnerships, unit trusts and trusts.	A wide variety of different types of company are available, including companies limited by guarantee, unlimited companies, limited duration companies and segregated portfolio companies. In addition, other types of vehicle are available, including partnerships, limited partnerships, unit trusts and trusts.	A number of different types of Guernsey company are available, including no par value companies, guarantee companies, unlimited companies, limited life companies, protected cell companies and incorporated cell companies. In addition other types of vehicle are available, including various types of limited partnership, limited liability partnerships, unit trusts, trusts and foundations.	A wide variety of different types of Jersey company are available, including no par value companies, guarantee companies, unlimited companies, limited life companies, protected cell companies and incorporated cell companies. In addition other types of vehicle are available, including various types of limited partnership, limited liability partnerships, unit trusts, trusts and foundations.
Registered office	Must be in the BVI.	Must be in Cayman.	Must be in Guernsey.	Must be in Jersey.
Annual returns	No annual returns. Annual government fees must be paid to the Registrar of Corporate Affairs in order to remain in good standing.	An annual return must be filed with the Registrar of Companies (together with an annual fee – see below).	Annual validations must be provided to the Guernsey Registry (together with an annual fee – see below).	An annual return must be filed with the Registrar of Companies (together with an annual fee – see below)
Government fees	Annual BVI government fees of US$350 (if authorised to issue 50,000 shares or fewer) or US$1,100 (if authorised to issue 50,000 shares or more). Additional fees may be charged in relation to applications to set up funds, carry out regulated activities etc. Additional one off incorporation fees and then annual fees will be payable to the registered agent/registered office provider, which will be subject to commercial negotiation.	Minimum incorporation fee of US$732 (scaled by reference to authorised share capital). Minimum annual fee of US$854 (scaled by reference to authorised share capital). Additional fees may be charged, depending on nature of company and set up arrangements. Annual fees will be payable to the registered agent/registered office provider, which will be subject to commercial negotiation.	Incorporation fee of £100 (24 hour incorporation service), £350 (two hour incorporation service) or £750 (15 minutes incorporation service). Annual validation fee of £250. Additional fees may be charged in relation to applications to set up funds, carry out regulated activities etc. Annual fees will be payable to the registered agent/registered office provider, which will be subject to commercial negotiation.	Incorporation fee of £200 (£400 if the expedited same day service is used). Annual return filing fee of £150. Additional fees may be charged in relation to applications to set up funds, carry out regulated activities etc. Annual fees will be payable to the registered agent/registered office provider, which will be subject to commercial negotiation.

mourantozannes.com BVI | CAYMAN ISLANDS | GUERNSEY | HONG KONG | JERSEY | LONDON AUGUST 2015

Figure 9.2: Comparison of offshore private equity holding structures *continued*

MOURANT OZANNES

	BVI	Cayman	Guernsey	Jersey
Directors and officers	Minimum of one director. No nationality restrictions or local residency requirements. Corporate directors are permitted. Directors' duties are owed to the company (though a director of a subsidiary may (if permitted by the memorandum and articles) act in the best interests of the holding company even if that is not in the interests of the subsidiary). Statutory duties are imposed requiring the director to act honestly and in good faith and in what the director believes to be in the best interests of the company. Common law fiduciary duties are equally applicable. A company secretary is permitted but not required.	Minimum of one director. No nationality restrictions or local residency requirements. Corporate directors are permitted. Directors' duties are owed to the company. Common law fiduciary duties are imposed requiring the directors to act in the best interests of the company, to avoid conflicts of interest etc. A company secretary is permitted but not required.	Minimum of one director. No nationality restrictions or local residency requirements (assuming the entity is not regulated), though local directors are available if required. Corporate directors are permitted (except for companies engaged in regulated activities). Directors' duties are owed to the company. Common law fiduciary duties are imposed requiring the director to act in the best interests of the company, to avoid conflicts of interest etc. A company secretary is permitted but not required.	Minimum of one director. No nationality restrictions or local residency requirements (assuming the entity is not regulated), though local directors are available if required. Corporate directors are permitted, but a corporate director must be regulated to act as a corporate director. Directors' duties are owed to the company. A statutory duty is imposed requiring the director to act in the best interests of the company. Common law fiduciary duties are imposed eg to avoid conflicts of interest etc. A company secretary is required.
Minimum number of shareholders	Companies must have at least one shareholder.			
Board meetings	Do not have to be held locally. Directors' resolutions can be passed in writing if permitted by the articles of association/incorporation.			

mourantozannes.com BVI | CAYMAN ISLANDS | GUERNSEY | HONG KONG | JERSEY | LONDON AUGUST 2015

Figure 9.2: Comparison of offshore private equity holding structures *continued*

MOURANT OZANNES

	BVI	Cayman	Guernsey	Jersey
Shareholder meetings	Do not have to be held in BVI. No requirement to hold annual or other periodic shareholder meetings unless they are required by the articles of association. Shareholder resolutions can be passed by written resolution if authorised by the articles of association. The majority required to pass a written resolution can be specified in the articles of association.	Do not have to be held in Cayman. No requirement to hold annual or other periodic shareholder meetings unless they are required by the articles of association. Shareholder resolutions can be passed by unanimous written resolution if authorised by the articles of association.	Do not have to be held in Guernsey. The requirement to hold an annual general meeting may be waived by members passing a waiver resolution (requiring approval of at least 90 per cent of members with voting rights and attending a meeting). Shareholder resolutions can be passed in writing. The majority required to pass a resolution in writing is the same as is required at a meeting (a simple majority for an ordinary resolution, 75 per cent for a special resolution and 90 per cent for a unanimous resolution).	Do not have to be held in Jersey. No requirement to hold annual or other periodic shareholder meetings unless they are required by the articles of association. Shareholder resolutions can be passed in writing unless prohibited by the articles of association. The majority required to pass a resolution in writing is either all shareholders with voting rights or a lower majority specified in the articles of association (though the majority can be no lower than two thirds for a special resolution).
Share capital	No concept of authorised share capital applicable to BVI companies incorporated under the BVI Business Companies Act 2004. Instead a BVI business company is authorised to issue a maximum number of shares. Bearer shares can only be issued if expressly permitted by the memorandum and articles, but are rare. Bearer shares must be 'immobilised' and held by a licensed custodian. Treasury shares are permitted. Shares can be denominated in any currency and amount and a company can have shares in different currencies and denominations.	No minimum or maximum authorised or paid up share capital. Bearer shares are permitted in some circumstances and with some restrictions but are very rare. Treasury shares are permitted. Shares can be denominated in any currency and amount and a company can have shares in different currencies and denominations. Any class of share may be issued (including ordinary, common, preference, preferred, convertible and deferred shares). The shares can have such economic, voting and other rights as are determined by the parties (with very few restrictions).	No minimum or maximum authorised or paid up share capital. Bearer shares are not permitted. Treasury shares are permitted. A maximum of 10 per cent treasury shares of the total number of issued shares in a particular class is permitted. Shares can be denominated in any currency and amount and a company can have shares in different currencies and denominations. Any class of share may be issued (including ordinary, common, preference, preferred, convertible and deferred shares). The shares can have such economic, voting and other rights as are	No minimum or maximum authorised or paid up share capital. Bearer shares are not permitted. Treasury shares are permitted. Shares can be denominated in any currency and amount and a company can have shares in different currencies and denominations. Any class of share may be issued (including ordinary, common, preference, preferred, convertible and deferred shares). The shares can have such economic, voting and other rights as are determined by the parties (with very few restrictions).

mourantozannes.com BVI \| CAYMAN ISLANDS \| GUERNSEY \| HONG KONG \| JERSEY \| LONDON AUGUST 2013

Figure 9.2: Comparison of offshore private equity holding structures *continued*

MOURANT OZANNES

	BVI	Cayman	Guernsey	Jersey
Share capital *continued...*	Any class of share may be issued (including ordinary common, preference, preferred, convertible and deferred shares). The shares can have such economic, voting and other rights as are determined by the parties (with very few restrictions)		determined by the parties (with very few restrictions).	
Employee share schemes	Companies are able to issue shares in accordance with any common form of employee share scheme. The rules of the scheme need not be governed by local law. Shares held by employees can either be held directly or indirectly via a company (often called a 'Manco') or an employee benefit trust. The company may loan money to an employee or an employee benefit trust to assist them in acquiring shares (subject to any contractual restrictions or restrictions in the articles of association/incorporation).			
Financial assistance	No statutory restrictions on financial assistance.			
How is a company funded?	The company can be funded by a variety of means including cash (where an investor will subscribe for shares using cash), assets (where an investor will contribute assets to the company in return for shares), loans and/or the provision of services			
How does a company return cash or assets to its investors?	A company can return cash or assets to its investors by a variety of means, including distributions, share redemptions and repurchases. Distributions may be paid from any source subject to satisfaction of a solvency test (both cash flow and balance sheet). Any additional requirements and/or restrictions can be built into the articles of association.	A company can return cash or assets to its investors by a variety of means, including distributions, share redemptions, repurchases and court approved reductions of capital. Distributions may be paid out of profits or share premium subject to a cash flow solvency test. Subject to satisfying the cash flow solvency test, shares may be redeemed or repurchased out of share capital, profits, the share premium account or out of the proceeds of a fresh issue of shares made for the purposes of the repurchase or redemption. Any additional requirements and/or restrictions can be built into the articles of association.	A company can return cash or assets to its investors by a variety of means, including distributions, share redemptions, share buy-backs and reductions of capital. The directors will be required to resolve that the company satisfies a cash flow and balance sheet based solvency test (other than for a court sanctioned reduction of capital), but otherwise there are limited restrictions under Guernsey law. Any requirements and/or restrictions can be built into the articles of incorporation.	A company can return cash or assets to its investors by a variety of means, including distributions, share redemptions, share buy-backs and reductions of capital. The directors will be required to make a cash flow based solvency statement (other than for a court sanctioned reduction of capital), but otherwise there are limited restrictions under Jersey law. Any requirements and/or restrictions can be built into the articles of association.

mourantozannes.com   BVI | CAYMAN ISLANDS | GUERNSEY | HONG KONG | JERSEY | LONDON   AUGUST 2013

Figure 9.2: Comparison of offshore private equity holding structures *continued*

MOURANT OZANNES

	BVI	Cayman	Guernsey	Jersey
Can it borrow, give guarantees and provide security over its assets?	Yes. Each of a BVI, Cayman, Guernsey and Jersey company has unlimited corporate capacity. Restrictions can be incorporated in its articles of association/incorporation if so desired.			
Can an investor grant security over its shares?	Yes, a shareholder can grant security over its shares in a BVI company subject to any contractual restrictions or restrictions in its articles of association. It is possible to make public filings of annotated registers of shareholders with the Registrar of Corporate Affairs.	Yes, a shareholder can grant security over its shares in a Cayman Islands company subject to any contractual restrictions or restrictions in its articles of association. There is no public register of security in the Cayman Islands.	Yes, a shareholder can grant security over its shares in a company in accordance with the Security Interests (Guernsey) Law 1993, subject to any contractual restrictions or restrictions in its articles of incorporation. There is no register of security in Guernsey.	Yes, a shareholder can grant security over its shares in a company in accordance with the Security Interests (Jersey) Law 2012, subject to any contractual restrictions or restrictions in its articles of association. Security granted under the Security Interests (Jersey) Law 2012 can be registered in Jersey.
Does it have unlimited duration?	Yes, unless its memorandum or articles of association/incorporation provide otherwise.			
Accounting and audit requirements	Companies must maintain accounting records. Such accounting records need not be made publicly available. Audited financial statements are not required unless the company is subject to regulation by the BVI Financial Services Commission.	Companies must maintain accounting records. Such accounting records need not be made publicly available. Audited financial statements are not required unless the company is subject to regulation by Cayman Islands Monetary Authority.	Companies must maintain accounting records. Such accounting records need not be made publicly available. Financial statements must be produced, covering a maximum period of 18 months. There is no requirement to file financial statements. Audited financial statements are required unless the company is exempted by a waiver resolution under section 256 of the Companies (Guernsey) Law 2008, as amended.	Companies must maintain accounting records. Such accounting records need not be made publicly available. Financial statements must be produced, covering a maximum period of 18 months. Only public companies or those subject to regulation by the Jersey Financial Services Commission (JFSC) must file accounts. Audited financial statements are not required unless the company is a public company or is regulated by the JFSC.

mourantozannes.com BVI | CAYMAN ISLANDS | GUERNSEY | HONG KONG | JERSEY | LONDON AUGUST 2013

Figure 9.2: Comparison of offshore private equity holding structures *continued*

MOURANT OZANNES

	BVI	Cayman	Guernsey	Jersey
Confidentiality	The identity of shareholders and directors is not a matter of public record, unless the company voluntarily elects to file its register of directors and/or shareholders at the BVI Registry of Corporate Affairs (which it must then keep up to date at the Registry). The BVI has entered into numerous tax information exchange agreements but it does not allow 'fishing expeditions'.	The identity of shareholders and directors is not a matter of public record. Cayman has entered into numerous tax information exchange agreements but it does not allow 'fishing expeditions'.	The identity of registered shareholders is not publicly available. A process, including a court application, may enable a person who has a proper purpose to inspect the register of members. However, the register of members holding redeemable or non-voting shares is not subject to this application process. Generally redeemable shares are used to preserve confidentiality though nominee shareholders may also be used. Guernsey has entered into numerous tax information exchange agreements but it does not allow 'fishing expeditions'.	A company's annual return will disclose details of the registered shareholders of a company as at 1 January in each year, though nominee shareholders may be used to preserve confidentiality. Jersey has entered into numerous tax information exchange agreements but it does not allow 'fishing expeditions'.
Exit options	A variety of methods are available to effect a sale, including a traditional share purchase transaction, a statutory merger, a mandatory 'squeeze out' and a scheme of arrangement. BVI, Cayman, Guernsey and Jersey companies are regularly used for IPOs and have been listed on most of the world's major stock exchanges, including the London Stock Exchange, the New York Stock Exchange, NASDAQ, the Hong Kong Stock Exchange, Euronext and the Toronto Stock Exchange.			
How is it wound up/ dissolved?	Voluntary liquidation (if the company is solvent). This process must be conducted by a voluntary liquidator.	Summary winding up (if the company is solvent). This process can be conducted by the directors or by a liquidator.	Summary winding up (if the company is solvent). This process can be conducted by the directors or by a liquidator. A voluntary strike off process is also available.	Summary winding up (if the company is solvent). This process can be conducted by the directors or by a liquidator.
Tax	The BVI has no income tax, corporation tax, capital gains tax, inheritance tax, gift tax, wealth tax or any other form of direct taxation or withholding. There are no currency exchange controls in the BVI.	Cayman has no income tax, corporation tax, capital gains tax, inheritance tax, gift tax, wealth tax or any other form of direct taxation or withholding. There are no currency exchange controls in Cayman.	Guernsey has a standard zero per cent rate of corporate tax for Guernsey tax resident companies (subject to limited exceptions not relevant to this area). Guernsey has no withholding tax, capital gains tax, inheritance tax, gift tax, or wealth tax. There are no currency exchange controls in Guernsey.	Jersey has a standard zero per cent rate of corporate tax for Jersey tax resident companies (subject to limited exceptions not relevant to this area). Jersey has no withholding tax, capital gains tax, inheritance tax, gift tax, or wealth tax. There are no currency exchange controls in Jersey.

mourantozannes.com BVI | CAYMAN ISLANDS | GUERNSEY | HONG KONG | JERSEY | LONDON AUGUST 2015

Figure 9.2: Comparison of offshore private equity holding structures *continued*

MOURANT OZANNES

	BVI	Cayman	Guernsey	Jersey
AML/CFT	BVI, Cayman, Guernsey and Jersey have strict AML/CFT regulations and high regulatory standards. Successive independent reports, including by the IMF, have recognised the BVI, Cayman, Guernsey and Jersey as leaders in the field of compliance and governance.			
FATCA compliance	In June 2014 the BVI and the US signed an intergovernmental agreement to improve international tax compliance and to implement FATCA based on the model 1(b) IGA. As a result, the withholding tax and account closure requirements will not apply, apart from in circumstances of unresolved significant non-compliance. Under the terms of the agreement, financial institutions will provide the BVI Islands International Tax Authority (BVI ITA) with the required information. The BVI ITA will then forward that information to the Competent Authority in the USA.	In November 2013 the Cayman Islands and the US signed an agreement to improve international tax compliance and to implement FATCA based on the model 1(b) IGA. As a result, the withholding tax and account closure requirements will not apply, apart from in circumstances of unresolved significant non-compliance. Under the terms of the agreement, financial institutions will provide the Cayman Islands Tax Information Authority (Cayman TIA) with the required information. The Cayman TIA will then forward that information to the Competent Authority in the USA.	In December 2013 Guernsey and the US signed an agreement to improve international tax compliance and to implement FATCA based on the model IGA. As a result, the withholding tax and account closure requirements will not apply, apart from in circumstances of unresolved significant non-compliance. Under the terms of the agreement, financial institutions will provide the Guernsey Administrator of Income Tax with the required information. The Administrator will then forward that information to the Competent Authority in the USA.	In December 2013 Jersey and the US signed an agreement to improve international tax compliance and to implement FATCA based on the model IGA. As a result, the withholding tax and account closure requirements will not apply, apart from in circumstances of unresolved significant non compliance. Under the terms of the agreement, financial institutions will provide the Jersey Comptroller of Taxes with the required information. The Comptroller will then forward that information to the Competent Authority in the USA.
Quality of legal profession, service providers and the courts	Very high. Most lawyers have practiced in London or another major international finance centre and many are dual- or multi-qualified. The local courts commonly preside over large and complex international disputes. The Judicial Committee of the Privy Council in London is the court of final appeal.			
What are the benefits of this particular jurisdiction?	The legal regimes in each of the BVI, Cayman, Guernsey and Jersey for private equity transactions are materially the same, with the result that the choice of jurisdiction is unlikely to be driven by particular laws. The choice of jurisdiction will generally come down to other factors such as: • Investor preference – investors will often prefer to invest via certain jurisdictions, due to perceptions of and/or existing relationships within certain jurisdictions (eg Asian and Russian investors will often be more familiar with BVI, US investors will often be more familiar with BVI and Cayman; European investors will often be more familiar with Jersey and Guernsey); • Sponsor preference – if the sponsor has existing operations and/or relationships in a particular jurisdiction • Sector – certain jurisdictions are more closely associated with certain sectors (such as Guernsey with gaming and Jersey with UK real estate) • Tax – each jurisdiction is tax neutral so they should all offer the same benefit in this respect.			

mourantozannes.com BVI | CAYMAN ISLANDS | GUERNSEY | HONG KONG | JERSEY | LONDON AUGUST 2015

Making it work 9.1

Though fund administrators may not need to know everything about structuring a private equity investment, it is important to understand the key detail to be considered when compiling an investment recommendation for potential selection.

An investment study must demonstrate to those charged with making a decision what the opportunity is, how it compares to similar/other opportunities in the market, how it will be funded and how it will earn money. As a result, the investment recommendation must do the following:

Consider the investment qualitatively:

- **Market** – Is this an industry that's growing? Will it grow more quickly/slowly in future years? Does the manager see positive or negative trends due to technology/regulations/competitors etc?
- **Competition** – How does this company fare against its competitors? Does it have a unique advantage that others can't replicate? Are there barriers to entry?
- **Growth Opportunities** – How quickly can the company grow in the future? Is there any 'low hanging fruit' or room to easily win more customers/revenue in the future? Do you expect it to grow faster or slower than the market as a whole?
- **Risks** – Every investment carries risks. Are the key risks here related to the market, or the economy as a whole? To the competition? To government regulations? Is there any way of mitigating these risks?
- **Other relevant information** – E.g. is anything especially notable about the management team, the products/services or other items unique to the deal?

Consider the investment quantitatively:

- **Valuation overview** – How much is this company worth? What methodologies is the manager basing it on?
- **Valuation detail** – This will depend upon the nature of the opportunity being evaluated, but will detail how the valuation overview is compiled.
- **Valuation** – The manager must always provide its indication of valuation.
- **Modelling**
- **Assumptions** – Purchase/Exit EBITDA multiples, leverage, growth, and profitability.
- **Sources and uses** – How much debt/equity will be required? How much of that is being spent on acquiring the company vs transaction fees/paying off debt?
- **Income statement/cash flow statement/debt schedule**

- **Returns and sensitivities** – Including IRR calculation and IRR over a range of purchase/exit multiples and other assumptions.

Finally, present the case summary. This is the opportunity for the manager to bring all of the above points together into an investment recommendation.

Chapter summary

- There is a growing trend for the usage of offshore jurisdictions in the establishment of private equity funds.
- Perhaps unfairly, a lot of these jurisdictions are deemed to be used by private equity firms purely for the taxation benefits enjoyed, however as covered in this chapter there is a lot more to the story than that.
- Along with the benefits with regards to taxation, there is no doubt that these jurisdictions are striving to build a name for themselves as superior financial centres with top level standards and infrastructure at their core, competing not only between themselves for global investment but with onshore structures also.

Chapter ten
Offshore real estate funds

List of topics

1. Background to real estate funds
2. Investment objectives
3. Investor considerations
4. The challenges for real estate funds
5. The role of the property manager
6. Property derivatives
7. The role of the investment manager
8. The role of the fund administrator
9. An evolution of real estate funds – government initiatives
10. A global perspective

Introduction

Real estate funds are, arguably, one of the easiest to understand from a basic conceptual context. Real estate is, at its simplest, bricks and mortar. It is the asset we can all see and, to many extents, understand even if we don't know much about the architecture and engineering that goes into it.

But within the asset class of 'real estate' there can be much variety both in terms of the activity of the fund and when considering how returns are generated. This chapter will explore:

- the varying investment objectives of real estate funds and the way in which monies are returned to investors;
- the challenges faced by fund administrators; and
- the size of the real estate asset class worldwide and on a jurisdictional basis.

Finally, this chapter will consider real estate in the context of much broader and evolving portfolios, including infrastructure funds.

1. Background to real estate funds

1.1 The need for real estate

The evolution of real estate has created ever more inventive ways of funding it and has changed the face of those who do so.

Traditionally, real estate assets would be constructed on a domestic basis, meaning that they would be built locally and to meet local needs. However, the world has shifted rapidly away from one where requirements for property and the way in which it is funded are so localised.

Gone are the days when feudal landowners owned entire towns and villages and thus were responsible for building and maintaining all of the local real estate. Gone too are the days of governments being able to afford to meet the real estate needs and demands of the people; instead we are witnessing patterns of governments seeking more and more to place social assets into the hands of individuals or consortia formed to blend public need with private funding. Coupled with the trend in the western world for people to own their own homes, this has put massive pressure on funding.

In the office sector, cities globally are competing every day to fill their skylines with more and more novel buildings that not only are architectural and engineering wonders but also provide big business with cutting edge technology in terms of comfort, communication and green credentials.

1.2 The need for funding

Building new developments, whether they be homes, offices or municipal buildings, requires significant cash injection upfront. Banks have been a traditional source of funding, with financing given in the expectation that, once built, profits will be generated, which will allow the bank financing to be paid off along with the interest due on it.

Funding may also be sought from private high-net worth investors looking to earn their own profits at the point that properties are sold or through the retention of portfolios yielding regular income.

Where government, bank or private funding is not available, an investment fund can provide another route to funding.

2. Investment objectives

Real estate investment funds will be established to do different things, not only by the type of property they invest in but also in terms of the activity they perform.

2.1 Construction of assets

Architects, developers and others may seek to fund brand new projects from the ground up. Fund managers may team up with such parties to form an investment fund proposition.

Generally investors opting to invest in funds which are constructing the fund assets should expect to invest their money for a considerable period of time. As the properties generally do not begin to perform (i.e. generate rental yield or disposal proceeds) until they are fully constructed, a period of investment from three years is not unusual.

2.2 Purchase of existing assets

Investment funds may be focused on buying real estate with a view to generating profits through its subsequent use of the property. This may include buying property simply to manage its use or could include the purchase of distressed assets, perhaps where a developer is unable to discharge the bank debt and so another source of funding is required to keep the development afloat, or the purchase of property with a view to repair and improve it, e.g. because its current owner does not have access to the funds to do so or does not wish to do it themselves.

Property may be bought at many stages, including:

- as a plot, potentially with the view to enhance its value by gaining planning permissions;
- as a plot with planning permissions attached, e.g. with a view to develop that land;
- as partially constructed assets, e.g. because a developer has gone bust or as part of a joint venture with the developer, who may sell some or all of their stake in order to gain valuable markets, knowledge etc from the fund professionals; and
- as constructed assets with a view to manage them during a life cycle.

2.3 Improvement

It may make good economic sense to purchase already existing property and enhance it to generate profits. This could include improving residential property to attract a new market of clientele (e.g. in up-and-coming locales), to subdivide it into a greater number of properties or to repurpose it (e.g. turning school buildings or commercial properties, such as mills and factories, into new residential properties or office space).

2.4 Rental

A number of rental markets exist in respect of property, including residential, commercial and office properties, with many market participants unable or unwilling to own properties outright.

An example of this includes those who are looking for office space but may not have the means or the critical mass to buy the type of office space they aspire to. This creates an attractive proposition to own office property and lease it on a sub-divisions basis. This is also an attractive model in multi-purpose properties, where some space may be leased as office space and other as retail units, gyms, hotels, etc. The fund manager can utilise their skill to manage the building and to find quality tenants for the building, enhancing the value of the overall piece by maintaining high occupancy levels (which increases demand and thus rent that may be demanded).

2.5 Management

Different types of property require different skills to ensure that they are retained in a way that is profitable and appropriate. As property needs change, more and more areas of skill are developing in order to understand those needs. In recent years, this has included new markets being created for student accommodation, where we are seeing the decline of private landlord properties in favour of serviced properties recommended to or attached to specific universities.

This also includes care homes, from supported living to specialist care homes (e.g. dementia care). As populations are ageing, the ability for the state to provide funded care for old age is dwindling. In an area with increasing law and regulation controlling it, the need for professional property managers is growing and the number of managers entering this space is increasing.

2.6 Disposal

Ultimately an investment fund must have a way of disposing of its property assets, at the every least in order to wind down the investment fund and return final monies to investors. Disposal, therefore, may be the main investment objective (e.g build to sell model) or may be in order to realise residual assets, including to realise a capital gain or even in the expectation that the asset is a wasting asset.

2.7 Real estate category

Of course, the type of property dealt with will differ from fund to fund, including:

Residential
The need for residential accommodation grows all the time. In spite of harsh market conditions, the desire in the western world to own your own home fuels the need for homes to be created.

Commercial (offices)
Office space requirements change all of the time, with top grade office space desired by all in a market of consolidation but also of business failures.

Commercial (retail)

A challenging proposition for all involved, as the trend towards online retail continues to grow. However retail property funds have been successful when involved with large shopping centre projects and trends appear to demonstrate that these large-scale projects will continue to prove successful with shoppers, as they give up the high street.

Commercial (warehouses, etc.)

Large-scale commercial property is seeing growth, as businesses must hold more stock in order to deliver instant products to clients and also cost savings.

Student accommodation

Student accommodation is a relatively new need in the general residential market. Historically universities would offer halls of residence or there would be a plethora of privately owned houses and flats to house all students. This model is changing for various reasons, including:

- The number of university students is increasing, meaning that there are more to house every year.
- The demands on housing are changing, as students demand en-suite accommodation with communal areas, security, on-site management, high-speed broadband and many more mod cons than students were previously able to access.
- Parents looking for greater levels of security for their children, including housing accredited by the university, with on-site security features.
- Private landlords are less able to make decent returns from letting their own properties, as rents, understandably, need to be low and the risk of letting to students is greater than retaining their properties for professionals.
- Council and other demand for properties to meet social housing needs means that private landlords can make better money renting to the local council than privately to students.

Care homes

Our ageing demographic is putting pressure on governments to provide sustained care and quality of life. As more and more governments are cash-strapped, investment funds are offering a solution, often offering facilities management and specific care home experience, given the increasing regulation surrounding these homes, especially in light of high-profile media coverage.

2.8 Type of return

Dependent upon the investment objectives of the fund, investors may receive returns based upon:

- Capital appreciation, e.g. from the sale of property.
- Income yield, e.g. from rental yields.
- Both, e.g. from a combination of selling and renting property.

3. Investor considerations

Who invests in real estate investment funds is important to consider and the make-up of investors will change dependent upon the type of real estate asset, the investment objective selected and the make-up of the investment fund itself.

When considering its own make-up, an investment fund may consider the following:

3.1 Open-ended or closed-ended

An open-ended fund will allow investors to redeem (exit their investment) at regular periods, whilst a closed-ended fund will provide an investor with a longer period of tie-in and fewer options for sale.

For funds focussed on the construction of assets, liquidity will present a challenge in open-ended funds. Construction of assets will utilise a lot of capital at its various stages with very little return, if any, until the assets are completed and available for sale etc. Open-ended real estate funds with assets in construction may combat this challenge by creating assets in a staged way, i.e. holding a portfolio of complete, near-complete and commencing construction to allow for the life cycles of the properties to create liquidity. This will not eliminate the early-days challenge and fund managers may have to be prepared to holdback funds to provide liquidity in these earlier days, in spite of the cash drag it may create and the impact on overall performance.

An open-ended model may better suit investment objectives where funds have operating assets, e.g. through rental yield, as the investment fund can hold a liquidity buffer through retention/availability of yield for periods of time.

3.2 Publicly quoted or private

The benefit of a public quotation (i.e. IPO) may be that liquidity for investors can be created even where a fund itself is closed-ended. However, public funds bring their own challenges, including the abundance of rules aimed at corporate governance and transparency, that the fund must pass. It will also mean a fund manager having to publish much more detail about what they do and how they do it in the public domain, which they may not want to do, especially where methods used are innovative.

Certain investors like or require investments to be publicly quoted and so a fund targeted at those investments will ordinarily opt for a public quotation in order to become eligible for investment.

4. The challenges for real estate funds

Real challenges exist for funds investing in property:

4.1 Supply and demand

For the investment proposition to be compelling, the fund manager must demonstrate that not only is there demand for it but that suitable property can be either sourced or created to satisfy that demand.

4.2 Price and pricing

The investment fund must be able to buy the property at an attractive price, a price that leaves sufficient margin for the fund to generate profit, whether that be through income yield or capital gain.

The investment fund must be able to sell or rent the property at attractive prices.

Valuation of the property, e.g. for NAV purposes, must be obtainable. Whilst pricing may be simple to obtain for certain property, i.e. because of the existence of a market establishing a range of prices, other property may not be so easily valued.

4.3 Grade/quality

Ensuring that the quality of the property matches and is sufficient for the needs of the target market is key.

4.4 Availability of financing

Financial lending for property purposes will impact upon investment funds, either because the investment fund itself requires external financing (beyond its capital ability) or because the investment fund has been established to provide financing where a bank would not.

4.5 Unpredictability

Predicting all of the above would be nigh on impossible and so it is in managing the unpredictability where the greatest challenges lie, including:

- default by tenants;
- inability to find tenants or purchasers;
- withdrawal or unavailability of financing;
- cost of financing;
- black swan events (e.g credit crunch, government u-turns);
- acts of God (fire or vandalism);
- construction delays; and
- other parties going bust.

5. The role of the property manager

Many real estate investment funds will appoint a property manager, who, as the name suggests, manages the property, whether that be the upkeep of the physical building, the sourcing and retention of tenants or the management of services within the operations of the real estate (cleaning, lift maintenance, etc.).

The property manager may be people in common with the investment manager/adviser but it may also be a wholly separate party. Largely this will depend on the expertise and resources of the investment manager. An investment manager with property management expertise to sell will sell it.

As the property manager is providing a service to the fund, the fund must execute a formal engagement agreement with the property manager, known as the property management agreement (PMA). The PMA will establish:

- The services to be provided by the property manager, e.g.–
  - **Building maintenance** – Inbuilt into the real estate assets will be a programme of maintenance to ensure that the quality of the real estate is maintained. The PMA will set out what this programme is and the quality to which assets must be maintained.
  - **Sourcing and managing tenants** – Where real estate assets are held for the purposes of earning rental income, it is important that tenancy rates remain high both in terms of rent paid and occupancy. An empty building or a building unable to attract quality, paying tenants will underperform and may result in the investment fund defaulting in respect of lending covenants (where leverage is applied) or investment objectives (e.g. where the rental income cannot support the dividend target). Therefore performing real estate is essential.
- Fees payable to the property manager.
- Property manager's obligations–
  - The investment fund will look for regular reporting from the property manager in respect of occupancy rates, rental defaults and general property issues dependent upon the nature of the real estate.
  - The fund will also look to the property manager to market available properties and to report on trends within the sector.
  - The property manager may also be best placed and qualified to value real estate for the fund based upon prevailing market conditions.

6. Property derivatives

Real estate as an asset class does not always mean investing in the bricks and mortar of real estate. Real estate investment funds may also be established with the objective of investing in property derivatives, whether as an entire strategy or as part of a blended strategy.

Investing in a portfolio of real properties can bring uncertainty and volatility. As we considered in terms of challenges above, many contributing factors can have either a positive or negative impact on the performance of any one asset.

Derivatives rely on a point of reference as to the performance of the market, in the United Kingdom this is the Investment Property Databank index and in the US these are NCREIF, S&P/Case-Shiller and Rexx. These real estate indices track the performance of the sector as a whole, which can give a real estate fund access to the entire sector rather than merely a select pool of physical assets.

Rather than investing in physical property assets, buying a derivative means that you are investing in what is commonly known as 'synthetic real estate'. The most common types of derivative are:

- **Property index notes (PIN)** – Essentially a form of bond. The PIN holder receives capital growth at redemption and income by a regular periodic coupon (income). In this way, an investor receives the total return of the commercial property market, just as they would with a physical transaction in property.
- **Total return swaps (TRS)** – A TRS is an exchange of cashflows. A purchaser buys a TRS based upon a fixed percentage set as a measure of change in the relevant index. TRS may be priced at either negative or positive percentages, indicating the amount an investor pays for it but also how much an investor receives by way of performance. Whilst a negative percentage will result in money due to an investor upon purchase, an ongoing negative percentage will result in an investor paying out in relation to performance.
- **Forwards/futures** – These contracts are agreed based upon future returns in any annual period. A contract is set and, upon its maturity, the difference between the realised (actual) total return and the traded price is exchange. These types of contract are over-the-counter derivatives requiring a counterparty (such as a bank).

In a real estate fund context, a fund may be made up of entirely property derivative contracts as its sole investment objective. This may allow funds to gain greater exposure to the market than through buying physical assets or may even allow a fund to quickly change the composition of its portfolio (e.g. between retail and industrial property) to take advantage of strong sectors in the market but also to reduce its exposure to poorly performing sectors. Another potential use of derivatives is for an investment fund to utilise them in a blended objective; in this way, an investment fund might hedge its position in order to try to minimise any effect of underperformance of its physical assets (i.e. where its assets are not performing as well as the indices are).

7. The role of the investment manager

Clearly, the role of the investment manager is to maximise yields and/or profits from the real assets held in order to, ultimately, deliver acceptable performance for investors. Not only is the investment manager taking a management fee for doing so, but it will also be aiming to make performance fees and to capitalise on its performance record when raising further funds (investors will back managers with good performance histories). The question then is how is performance determined in the case of real estate assets?

At a simple level, the assets may appear to be successful where they are rented at high occupancy and at good average rents for the sector or where their disposal values are higher than their acquisition prices and at a level either at par with or better than a comparable market. However, for investment funds, it is never that simple.

Let's take Fund A and Fund B. Both funds launched in 2010 with identical investment objectives by property type, geography, acquisition costs and, at launch, both raised a similar amount of capital. How does an investor understand which performed better over their lifetime?

One way of comparing performance is by comparing Fund A to Fund B, but that will only get us so far. If Fund A outperformed Fund B, what do we truly know? On the face of it, you may look at Fund B as a bad investment but the comparison made here gives you no indication of Fund B's performance relative to anything wider than Fund A. Fund A and Fund B may be the two highest performing funds in this area.

To truly consider this position, fund analysts, financial advisers and investors will consider individual fund performance against varying indicators, which are then used to benchmark the fund. For real estate, benchmarking can be relatively easier than for other asset classes as established property indices exist charting property prices and average sectoral yields (considered above). This allows commentators to compare a portfolio of assets and to compare their performance to the average performance of that sector of real estate over a similar period of time, even being able to drill down by geography, property grade and property type (e.g. residential, commercial) etc to ensure that any comparisons are like for like.

8. The role of the fund administrator

8.1 Servicing real estate funds

Fund administrators provide back-office services for fund managers. For real estate funds, these services will include:

- **Assisting in the papering of key events** – Although lawyers and other professional real estate parties will be engaged by the real estate fund, the fund administrator may need to handle the logistics of papering the transaction by tracking down signatories, returning paperwork to other advisers and maintaining all originals for the investment fund's records.
- **Transferring or receiving funds** – The fund administrator will typically control the bank accounts and so will need to ensure that monies are available and that payments are made on time. This may include monitoring the receipt of rents, whether direct from tenants or through a property manager, or making monies available for acquisitions of real or synthetic property assets.
- **Bookkeeping** – Ensuring that the books and records are maintained.
- **Valuation** – Real estate can be valued in different ways and at different periods, including:
  - **At cost** – Certainly in the early days of investment, valuing the property at the price purchased may be prudent. However regard will have to be had to the state of the relevant market, as this may suggest whether a valuation at cost remains appropriate or not.
  - **Desk-top valuation** – A property fund will ordinarily hire a valuer from a Royal Institute of Chartered Surveyors (RICS) qualified firm to

provide a desk-top valuation. This won't entail a full evaluation of the property but will provide an indicative value based upon the nature and scale of the property relative to others of a similar nature or class. Such valuations may be relied upon in between formal valuations (e.g. quarterly desk-tops with a full annual appraisal).

- **In construction** – Assets in construction may be valued on the basis of what they are anticipated to be worth upon completion with discounts applied to the price to allow for the timescale until completion and inherent risks, including the risk of the property never being finished or of lengthy delays and the risk of the market value of the completed project never hitting projections, whether due to the market in general or to the ultimate quality or desirability of the property.
- **Fair value** – A RICS valuer may be engaged to undertake a full fair value of the property based upon its actual condition and progress against prevailing market conditions. Fair valuations tend to be provided to support the audited financial statements/valuation of the fund, with reliance on other methods in intervening periods.

Whilst the administrator will not value the property, as that will fall to professionals, the administrator will need to lock the valuation into the overall valuation of the investment fund.

8.2 Responsible administration

In order to perform the role effectively, the fund administrator must know what the fund does by understanding the investment objectives, including any limitations or restrictions. The over-arching principles of what will be included in a fund's objectives, restrictions and limits will not change from fund to fund, however, for real estate funds, fund administrators could expect to find the following key headings:

- Nature of real estate permitted by type, geography and quality.
- Condition of real estate permitted, e.g. as a plot on which to build or an existing property to renovate.
- Concentration limits, meaning that the value of a single property will be limited to a maximum when placed in the context of the portfolio as a whole, which avoids the risk of the fund not diversifying the assets.
- Whether leveraging is permitted or not and, if so, what is the maximum loan-to-value permitted (i.e. if a property is purchased for £100m and a maximum LTV permitted is 60%, the fund may borrow no more than £60m against it).

Worked example 10.1

Investment objective and policy

You have been asked to look after the day-to-day administration of a property fund, Awesome Real Estate Fund Limited (the fund), recently taken on by your employer and, as a first task, to review and report back on whether the portfolio complies with the investment policies of the fund. The fund was established in August 2014. You read the key extracts of the scheme particulars, which state the following.

The fund has been established with the objective of providing an investment opportunity that aims to provide a total return from a combination of capital growth and an appropriate dividend policy through the acquisition and active management of Grade A office property predominantly in the City of London. Target properties are intended to be fully or partially let and provide a core income which may offer opportunities to add value through active asset management across all sectors of the property market.

Investment restrictions

It is the fund's intention to utilise proceeds to assist in the acquisition of property and in the building of a diversified portfolio of property investments with a view to spreading risk.

The fund will seek to invest (or commit to invest) in accordance with the following guidelines:-

- A maximum of 25% of the assets under management of the fund (at the time of such investment) may be allocated to any one particular investment.
- Leverage must not exceed 65% of the total acquisition costs of an investment. The board must satisfy itself that there are adequate cash flows to meet all foreseeable obligations and covenants relation to the loan for any relevant property or investment.
- Property may only be England, Wales or Scotland situs and no more than 15% of the total property portfolio at any one time shall be situated outside of the City of London.
- No more than 5% of the fund may be held in cash or near-cash. The Fund is not permitted to invest in derivatives or any financial asset.

Net asset valuation

The NAV will be calculated annually and published with the Company's annual report and statements, which will be prepared up to 31 December each year, within such time as to comply with applicable laws and regulations.

As at the current date, the Fund owns the following properties:

Date of purchase	Name	Nature	Acquisition cost	Audited value	Bank financing
September 2014	57, Cavendish Walk, City of London	Grade A office space	£95,000,000	£160,000,000	£70,000,000 over 10 years; fully drawn
February 2015	Wow Skyscraper, Canary Wharf, London	Grade A office space	£270,000,000	£300,000,000	£235,000,000 over 15 years; fully drawn
April 2015	The Truncheon Building, Kensington	Grade A office space	£39,500,000	£50,000,000	£10,000,000 over 3 years; fully drawn
December 2015	Landmark Tower, Edinburgh	Grade A office space	£103,000,000	£93,000,000	£60,000,000 over 7 years; fully drawn

The fund has cash in the bank of £45,000,000 and the latest published NAV (as at 31 December 2015) was £255,000,000. The fund has AUM of £650,000,000.

Consider the following questions:

1 Is the amount of cash held appropriate?
2 Have leverage limits been applied in all cases?
3 Is the type of property acquired appropriate in all cases?

9. An evolution of real estate funds – government initiatives

Property will always be a popular asset class, as there will always be demand for real estate assets. However, government projects have added a natural evolution and extension to this asset class.

Governments worldwide are under pressure to deliver high quality municipal services, such as schools, hospitals and transport links, but with dwindling reserves and multiple challenges on the monies available, governments are having to look to private forms of funding. From this need, infrastructure funds have grown over the last ten years as an important source of financing for these pivotal projects.

In the United Kingdom, public private partnerships (PPPs) have emerged to deliver these projects. Typically infrastructure fund managers provide management through the construction and operation of these assets based upon a timeline established with the relevant government. This hasn't been without its criticism, with governments accused of handing key contracts to expensive providers, however as the scale of projects continue to grow in size the place for infrastructure funds and other participants in this space seems to be growing.

In recent years, an evolution from schools and prisons to offshore windfarms and major sewer/water projects has emerged and the financial size of these projects seems to be ever growing.

For investors, infrastructure funds can provide an attractive proposition, with many succeeding on the basis that they have provided stable income flows with longevity attached, e.g. because government contracts to operate schools and hospitals etc have a life cycle of 10+ years. Whilst some capital return may be achieved through the sale of assets at the end of their lifecycles, investors will typically have achieved return of their own capital through regular dividends rather than through the disposal of assets.

10. A global perspective

In 2015, Ernst & Young reported that traditional 'bricks & mortar' was being disrupted by new economic and social influences:

- In the world of retail, shoppers expect giant distribution centres to provide convenient and immediate access to their products.
- In residential areas, millennials want live, work and play environments rather than the traditional idea of a home with a garden and garage.
- Investors themselves are demanding more and more access to information.

We are also seeing disruption to the roots of funding, with foreign capital entering traditional real estate markets, e.g. Asian and Russian funding of large-scale residential projects in London.

10.1 Outsourcing

Another disruptive influence is cost management, with fund managers being forced to re-evaluate what they bring to the table and focusing on that. For many fund managers their role, therefore, is becoming more and more streamlined towards the real value creation, which rests solely with them, placing a shift towards outsourcing non-core functions. Fund administrators are a beneficiary of this shift, as back and middle office functions become more natural areas for fund managers to outsource to others.

10.2 Fundraising

Despite the proliferation of large-scale real estate projects in recent years, the fundraising environment continues to prove challenging. For many, traditional sources of investors are either reducing or are not able to meet the demands of ramping up activity. Instead, third party placement advisers are being turned to in order to assist in building new investor relationships. In order for fund managers to successfully raise capital, they must demonstrate:

- a defined investment strategy;
- an experienced team;
- a demonstrable track record in this relevant field;
- strong alignment of interest with investors; and
- clear capital raising strategy.

10.3 Tax

Taxation measures have a clear effect on real estate propositions. Global tax authorities have intensified efforts to combat tax evasion leading to the BEPS (base erosion and profit shifting) programme by the OECD, which aims to ensure that businesses adhere to tax regimes where they are based. In terms of investment funds, the effect of BEPS will be one of substance, broadly meaning that there are sufficient business activities to demonstrate that those activities are occurring in a particular country (e.g. the country of the investment fund) rather than the investment fund being established in a particular country for the sole purpose of claiming tax treaty benefits (which would lean more towards an intention to evade tax).

The main challenge of this changing taxation environment is to ensure that investment is not stifled by seeking to enforce tax policies.

10.4 Deal size

In 2013, commercial property deals totalled over $1.1 trillion, the highest on record since 2007. Fund managers need only pick up a small amount of this global deal flow in order to result in viable investment funds.

Making it work 10.1

See Worked example 10.1 on page 185. The property manager leaves you a message to advise that the fund is planning to buy a further property for £130,000,000, a brand new landmark building in the final stages of construction that they are very excited to have found. Prospective tenants are 'lining up around the block' to take on this prestigious space. Heads of terms were agreed back in March 2016 and due diligence has been completed; completion is diarised for 31 October 2016 and he asks you to liaise with the bank to ensure that a £50,000,000 facility they have negotiated as part of the deal is concluded and funds made available before completion. He confirms that the board are fully on board and so

all that is needed is to ensure that £110,000,00 is available on 31 October 2016 and £20,000,000 held back until the property manager confirms completion of snagging etc.

Before reverting to the property manager, you might want to consider the following:

- The first port of call must always be the scheme particulars, in particular the rules applying to who may authorise the purchase of fund investments.
- Often, the role of the property manager will allow for evaluation of prospective investments but will stop short at granting authority to approve investment acquisitions. Acquisitions will generally rest with the board. On occasion, the board may grant the property manager a discretionary mandate to acquire investments within certain defined ranges; where this is the case, the fund administrator must understand what those defined ranges are in order to know when it may accept the authority of the property manager and where it must obtain approval from the fund board.
- Evaluate the prospective investment in the context of the investment objectives and restrictions. In this example, the property manager has given us very little detail when we need to be able to answer the following questions:
  - Where is the property located? The only detail so far is that it is a 'landmark building'.
  - Is it office space and does it meet the fund's grade specifications? We are told only that tenants are lining up, but we have no idea as to the nature of the property or these tenants.
- Would the purchase breach any investment restrictions?
  - Prior to the purchase, the fund has an AUM of £650,000,000. Assuming that the property is bought for £130,000,000, this will result in the fund having AUM of £780,000,000 upon purchase, meaning that £130,000,000 will constitute 16.67% of the AUM. This is within the 25% restriction.
  - If a property is purchased for £130,000,000 and £50,000,000 of the purchase price is met through a bank facility, then the property will be leveraged. In this cash, the leverage is 38.5%, which is within the 65% limit.
- Consider how the acquisition will be funded.
  - The fund holds £45,000,000 in cash and has obtained a £50,000,000 facility, leaving it with a maximum of £95,000,000 to purchase the property, a shortfall of at least £35,000,000. It is imperative that the fund can afford to pay for its obligations or otherwise it risks reputational ruin. In addition, the fund will always want to retain a cash buffer to meet ongoing costs and other liabilities as they arise.

- Consider how to properly seek authority for the acquisition and evidence it.
  - Approach the board with queries and concerns. The fund engages the fund administrator so it is imperative to remember that you act for the fund and not the property manager.
  - Remember that property purchases and the entry into bank facilities require numerous formalities, typically requiring specialist assistance from lawyers.

Chapter summary

- Whilst fund administrators may be benefitting from fund managers' cost management considerations, expectations placed on administrators are increasing.
- A key component of the back-office function provided by administrators is to provide reliable inputs to support the fund manager's reporting requirements to its investors.
- Administrators are becoming increasingly scrutinised in respect of their abilities to demonstrate to national regulators and courts that they remain fit and proper continuously through the period of their engagement. With regulators and courts focussing on the oversight and monitoring roles that administrators play, it is not enough for administrators to passively receive information from fund managers, valuers, auditors etc, but to have a fair understanding of these matters themselves. Most importantly, administrators must be prepared to evaluate fund matters and even to challenge them from time to time.
- Whilst an administrator is not expected to be an expert in every investment proposition, understanding the investment parameters, including objectives, limits and restrictions, has become a vital component of the administrator's role.
- Considering this in the context of real estate funds, the administrator must have regard to the timeliness and completeness of information being received but also familiarise themselves with the purpose of the fund, the nature of the real estate it will invest in and the way in which it intends to create value. It must also be prepared to police the fund to some extent by challenging, e.g. where investment limits or restrictions may be breached.

Chapter eleven
Bond funds

List of topics

1. Bond fund management
2. Interest apportionment
3. Bond duration
4. Benefits of bonds
5. Negative aspects of bonds
6. Risks to investors in bond funds

Introduction

This chapter will introduce you to an understanding of the role of bond funds, the different types of bonds and why they are an attractive offering for those seeking a stable and reliable investment type.

1. Bond fund management

Bond funds do exactly as they suggest, and invest in bonds. They ordinarily pay dividends at a regular frequency, and these can be higher than some other types of secure funds, such as money market funds which are mainly cash-based and therefore do not offer as great a **return**, and given the relatively low-level risk associated with bonds, this makes them an attractive proposition for a fund asset.

return
The potential amount back that the investor will receive back in dividends or interest, ordinarily quoted as a percentage basis.

1.1 Two types of bond issuers

There are two main types of bond issuers, as well as a number of types of bond, so there are therefore different types of bond funds to take account of this. The two main different types of bond issuer can be summarised as follows:

Government issued
Bonds can be issued by a government in order to raise capital, for any number of reasons. They are considered to be a very secure instrument, because the

United States Treasuries
Government debt instruments issued by the United States Department of the Treasury to finance the national debt of the United States. Treasury securities are often referred to simply as Treasuries. There are four types of marketable treasury securities: Treasury bills, Treasury notes, Treasury bonds, and Treasury Inflation Protected Securities.

gilts
Bonds which are issued by some national governments. The term originally referred to the debt securities issued by the Bank of England on behalf of Her Majesty's Treasury, whose paper certificates had a gilt (or gilded) edge. The UK still issue gilts.

government will always have a way to ensure that it is able to meet its debt, such as utilising quantitative easing. In the United States, they are called **United States Treasuries**, while in the UK they are called **gilts**. However, the downside to the security of them being considered a safe investment is that the return offered will not be as significant as the potential returns on, for example, equity funds.

Corporate
Bonds can be issued by companies with the purpose of raising capital for the needs of the business. All corporate bonds are guaranteed by the issuer (the company that is borrowing the money), and therefore the risk attached to the particular bond is linked to the company's ability to pay the bond back at maturity. The greater the risk attached to a particular bond issuer, then the greater the rewards or returns for that bond will be.

1.2 Government issued bonds and corporate bonds

There are different types of bond that can be issued by government or corporates which are as follows:

Straight bond
A straight bond pays interest at regular intervals, and at maturity pays back the principal that was originally invested. Straight bonds are debt instruments because they are essentially loaning money (creating debt) to an entity. The government or company promises to pay the interest on the 'debt' and at maturity pay back the original loan.

Convertible bond
A convertible bond is a type of bond that the holder can later on convert into a specified number of shares of common stock in the issuing company or cash of equal value.

Callable bonds
A callable bond is one where the issuer has the right to redeem the bond before its stated maturity date and the investor has no right of refusal. As a consequence of the prepayment, the bondholder will not receive any more above-market interest payments from the investment. Wherever prepayment occurs, it forces investors to reinvest their funds into a market where interest rates are lower than the rates they had previously been receiving from the bond that has been prepaid. Nevertheless, firms issuing callable bonds generally pay higher interest rates for the right to pay back the bond before maturity.

Term bonds
Term bonds can be redeemed at an earlier date than the other issued bonds by the same issuer at the same time. This means the issuer of the bond can redeem it at a predetermined price at specific given times before the bond reaches maturity.

Junk bonds

A junk bond can also be known as a 'high-yield bond' or 'speculative bond', and credit rated 'BB' or lower because of the high likelihood of default (see credit ratings below). Junk bonds typically offer interest rates three to four percentage points higher than safer government issues because of the increased risks that are being taken by investment in them.

Angel bonds

Angel bonds are issued by companies which are highly rated from a credit perspective so pay a lower interest rate because of that, as the risk associated with them is lower. Angel bonds are the opposite of junk bonds.

Test yourself 11.1

You are offered a five-year gilt or a three-year corporate bond issued by a Plc. Which would you take and why?

1.3 Credit rating of bonds

There are a number of terms that are associated with bond funds. One such reference is the **rating** for their return (high income) or their **duration** (short, medium or long).

rating
A bond fund can be rated from high to low credit quality.

duration
The length of time for which a bond will be live, such as ten years.

An important feature of bond funds is the reference to the credit rating of the bonds they own. A bond fund can be rated from high to low credit quality. This means that if the bonds contained within in it are for a lower credit scored companies for example, they will be given a low credit rating. The overall quality rating of a fund is the average credit rating of the bonds owned by the fund. Funds that pay higher returns will typically own lower quality bonds as the rewards have to be greater to repay investors for the increased risk that they are taking. We will discuss credit risk later in this chapter.

As with equities, the price of high-return bond funds will fluctuate due to demand, or lack of it. For example, in late 2008, the price of a number of high-return bond funds was discounted as they were not attractive to investors. However, post the financial crisis in 2008, as there were few bond defaults, confidence in the bond market recovered and therefore the price recovered.

2. Interest apportionment

2.1 Day count convention

In bonds there is a concept called the day count convention. When a bond is sold between interest payment dates, the seller is eligible to a part of the dividend payment. This convention therefore deals with how interest accrues by the number of days in between two dividend payments and calculates the amount of interest that would be owed on payment date.

Among the most common conventions to calculate the day count conversion are 30/360 or 365 and actual/actual.

2.2 30/360 or 30/365

For fixed-rate bonds interest is generally calculated on either the 30/360-day convention or 30/365. This convention stipulates the month will always be treated as having 30 days in it, and the year will consistently be treated as having either 360 or 365 days.

2.3 Actual/actual basis

US Treasuries earn interest calculated on an actual/actual basis. This means all days in a period carry equal value; it also means the length of dividend periods and the resultant payments can therefore vary.

Conventions for calculation of the interest apportionment will vary depending on the currency. Therefore, it is always important to ascertain the basis of any interest apportionment if you are considering selling a bond.

For example, Euro-denominated bonds are usually calculated on an actual/actual basis, while fixed rate non-Euro denominated bonds are often calculated on a 30/360 basis.

3. Bond duration

Given that the duration of a bond can vary, whereby the lifetime of a specific bond can be classified as short-, medium- or long-term, this means that funds can invest in different maturities of bonds as part of their overall portfolio within the fund. This affects how the fund value changes with interest rates. Funds invested in longer term bonds will experience more change. As a general rule, the rewards for longer bonds are higher as you are compensated for committing for a longer period as this gives more stability to the issuer.

The bond fund itself will also generally have a specified duration, such as five to ten years, so that investors know how long that they will be 'locked in' for. Therefore, during the lifetime of a fund, the fund manager will need to monitor the portfolio, and where appropriate, sell shorter bonds and buy longer bonds to stay within the specified lifetime of the fund. This means that the bond fund never expires, it keeps on going with new bonds added to keep the fund within its remit until such time as it is due to be wound up.

4. Benefits of bonds

Whilst some may consider that investing in a bond fund provides a significant concentration risk, given that bond funds can usually invest in a number of different bond types and classes, this provides diversification, so that whilst the investment type is specific, the bonds that may be held are varied to provide risk mitigation from a concentration perspective. It also means that if there is one particular bond in the portfolio that is underperforming, then the overall impact of that is reduced because of the others within the fund's portfolio helping to balance the performance.

From an investor perspective, there is also the additional consideration of whether the income is automatically reinvested. Investors will need to ascertain this when looking at potential bond funds as, if it is, then the value of the fund is consistently added to for further investment in bonds which can be a positive in favour of the fund, but may also mean that no dividends within the investment period are paid out to investors. It therefore will result in no ongoing income from the investment within the investment period. Investors will need to consider if they are looking for capital growth or income as part of their investment.

Bond funds can provide a particular attraction for those that wish to invest in bonds, but do not want to be tied in directly to a bond themselves. For example, they may want exposure to a particular type of bond but that the life span of it is too long for their own needs. This can be addressed through a fund as, if the fund is open-ended, you can sell your shares at any time without being affected by the bond maturity date.

5. Negative aspects of bonds

However, despite all of the positive points that can be attributed to bond funds, there are also some negative ones. These can include:

- Fees which are applied to funds by the parties involved, such as the fund administrator, which are ordinarily a percentage of the fund value, which would not be payable if you held the bonds directly yourself.
- Variable Dividends – Bond fund dividend payments may not be fixed in the same way that they would be with the interest payments of a bond that is held directly, leading to potential fluctuation of the value of dividend payments each time they are paid, linked to the type of the bonds within the portfolio.
- Variable NAV – The Net Asset Value of a bond fund may change over time, whereas this does not happen with an individual bond in which the total issue price will be returned upon maturity, so long as the bond issuer does not default.
- It should be noted that there are no guarantees when investing in a bond fund. Even if the individual bonds in the fund are guaranteed by the government, or even insured through a private insurer, the value of a bond fund investment can still rise or fall.

6. Risks to investors in bond funds

There are four types of risk associated with bond funds: interest rate risk, credit risk, inflation risk and prepayment risk.

Interest rate risk

Interest rate risk is the possibility that a bond's price will change due to a change in prevailing interest rates. Bond prices are correlated to a rise or fall in interest rates. When interest rates go up, most bond prices go down and vice versa.

In general, the longer a bond's remaining maturity then the more its price will tend to fluctuate as interest rates change. However, while longer-term bonds tend to fluctuate in value more than shorter-term bonds, they will generally also offer higher returns as a result of the additional risk that the investor is taking.

Credit risk

Credit risk refers to the creditworthiness of the bond issuer and its expected ability to be able to make interest payments on time and to pay the face value of the bond at maturity. Therefore, bond funds which contain government-backed bonds will pose less of a credit risk than those issued by private corporates. If a bond issuer is unable to repay the capital or interest on time, the bond is said to be in default. A reduction in an issuer's credit rating can cause the prices of its bonds to decline and could then also impact upon the share prices of any fund that holds that issuer's bonds so that they decline as well.

Moody's
A ratings agency which assesses the credit rating of debt instruments and securities.

Standard and Poors
Another rating agency which provides financial research and analysis on stocks, bonds and commodities.

The creditworthiness of any issuer is usually derived from a bond credit rating issued by one of the credit rating agencies. Two of the most well recognised are **Moody's** and **Standard and Poors**. If the underlying bonds have been allocated a good credit rating by the agency, then this will ensure a good credit rating of the fund, assuming all bonds within it are of a similar standing. The two agencies mentioned, provide the ratings in Table 11.1 below.

Table 11.1: Credit ratings for Moody's and Standard and Poors

Moody's	S&P	Quality rating
Aaa	AAA	Prime investment grade
Aa	AA	High investment grade
A1	A+	Upper-medium investment grade
A2	A	Upper-medium investment grade
A3	A–	Medium investment grade
Baa1	BBB+	Medium investment grade
Baa2	BBB	Lower-medium investment grade

Inflation risk

Investors can be attracted to bond funds because of their regular dividends from interest earnings. The dividends, however, can be subject to inflation risk. Inflation erodes the return of any investment. In particular, if investments pay out a fixed return of interest over a set period of time, such as bonds or certificates of deposits do, as inflation increases, investors will discover that the fixed amount that they receive back has less buying power and therefore its value is eroded.

The longer a bond's maturity, the greater its inflation risk, as over time inflation may fluctuate more significantly than can be anticipated. When calculating bond returns, issuers will often incorporate expectations of inflation so that investors are compensated for expected inflation risk. If inflation rises by more than was expected when the bond was issued, investors will find that the interest and principal returned to them will be worth less than they had anticipated.

Prepayment risk

Prepayment risk is when a bond owner has their initial capital returned back to them by the issuer before the bond's maturity date is reached. This does tend to happen when interest rates fall and the existing bond they have in issue if paying above-market rates and therefore ceases to be a cost-effective means of borrowing for the issue. In these circumstances borrowers will often issue bonds or obtain loans at the new lower interest rates and use the proceeds that they raise from that to prepay other debt with higher interest rates. For example, a company may issue bonds when there is a drop in interest rates so that they have funds available to pay off **callable** bonds at their next call date. A callable bond is one where the issuer has the right to redeem the bond before its stated maturity date and the investor has no right of refusal. As a consequence of the prepayment, the bondholder will not receive any more above-market interest payments from the investment. Wherever prepayment occurs, it forces investors to reinvest their funds into a market where interest rates are lower than the rates they had previously been receiving from the bond that has been prepaid. Nevertheless, firms issuing callable bonds generally pay higher interest rates for the right to pay back the bond before maturity.

callable
A type of bond which can be redeemed by the issuer prior to the bond term expiring.

Test yourself 11.2

What would be the most significant risk to consider for a ten-year duration bond?

Chapter summary

- A bond fund is a stable investment, and one which should ensure solid, if not significant, returns.
- For balance to be achieved in relation to duration and credit worthiness, as well as diversification between bond issuers within the portfolio, bond fund managers must ensure adequate research and vigilance when structuring the bond portfolio.

Part four

Chapter twelve
Directives

Chapter thirteen
International regulators

Fund sector regulation

Overview

This part will look at the legislative framework that is in place in relation to funds, the management and administration of them within the European Union and the effect of being outside of the EU for the marketing of funds into Europe. The role of international regulatory bodies in relation to management and oversight of financial crime, securities regulation and stability of global financial markets and the interaction between the different regulators will also be examined. This part will give you an overall understanding of the different regulatory and legislative forces that impact on the operation of funds, the parties that provide services to them and the jurisdictions in which they are based.

Learning outcomes

At the end of this part, you will be able to:

- Understand the process of implementation of a directive
- Understand the impact of the main directives that apply to the funds sector
- Analyse how they have been translated into local legislation
- Learn about the different bodies around the world which impact upon the funds sector
- Understand the specific remit of each of these bodies and how they came into being.

Chapter twelve
Directives

List of topics

1. How directives come in to being
2. Alternative Investment Fund Managers Directive
3. Application of AIFMD
4. Responsibilities of an AIFM
5. Delegation
6. Delegation of portfolio or risk management
7. Letterbox entities
8. Conflicts of interest
9. Reporting requirements
10. Remuneration Code
11. Marketing in Financial Instruments Directive
12. Undertakings in collective investment in transferable securities
13. Solvency II
14. Dodd-Frank
15. Foreign Account Tax Compliance Act

Introduction

A directive is a type of legislation issued by the **European Union** compelling member states to do a certain act or achieve a certain result. This chapter outlines how directives come into being and the effect of them. It will also examine how they are applied into local legislation and explain the impact on the funds sector of some of the key directives in recent years. This includes the Alternative Investment Fund Managers Directive (AIFMD) and the Market in Futures Instruments Directive.

European Union
Consists of 28 member states, predominantly in Europe. The aim of the European Union is to implement policies to ensure the free movement of people, goods, services, and capital within its member states.

1. How directives come in to being

Under Art.288 of the Treaty on the Functioning of the European Union (EU), the EU is given the power to issue directives. The directive is a piece of EU legislation which sets out at a high level what the **member state** needs to achieve and then the member state is permitted to determine the best way in which to implement the objective set by the directive. Whilst a directive can be issued to just one member state requiring them to comply on a single aspect of EU interest, generally directives apply to all member states equally. This is certainly the case in relation to directives involving the financial markets.

The starting point is for an area to be identified as requiring a directive. Once this has been determined then the **European Commission**, the body of the EU responsible for the operational activities of the EU, will begin drafting the directive. Once drafting is complete it is then referred on to the **European Parliament** and **European Council** for their review, and then either approval or rejection.

Once a directive has been approved, the member states will be given a deadline for the implementation of the objective of the directive. If the laws of a member state already comply with what a directive requires them to do, then the member state does not need to take any action. However, where they do not comply then the member state is required to make changes to their legislative framework before the deadline set by the directive.

If a member state fails to amend its legislation within the deadline, or if what they enact does not fully meet the requirements of the directive, the European Commission can decide to initiate legal action against the member state in the **European Court of Justice**.

Whilst directives will not apply directly to all offshore centres, and in most cases offshore centres will be classed as a **third country** for EU purposes, it is important to understand the framework under which the funds industry operates in Europe.

Member state
There are currently 28 member states of the European Union. Each member state is a party to the legal treaties which founded the European Union and thereby subject to the benefits as well as the obligations of being a member.

European Commission
The European Commission is the EU's decision-making body. It represents the interests of the European Union as a whole, rather than the interests of individual Member States.

European Parliament
The elected parliamentary institution of the EU. Together with the Council of the European Union and the European Commission, it exercises the legislative function of the EU. The Parliament is composed of 751 (previously 766) members.

European Council
The European Council is responsible for defining the EU's overall political agenda, It is made up of the heads of state or government of the Member States, along with the President of the European Council and the President of the European Commission.

European Court of Justice
Is the highest court in the EU in determining interpretation of EU legislation and ensuring its consistent application across member states.

2. Alternative Investment Fund Managers Directive

The Alternative Investment Fund Managers Directive (AIFMD) was implemented for a number of reasons, but primarily as a result of the global financial crisis of 2008. The global financial crisis resulted in the near collapse of financial markets worldwide and sparked the bail out of banks by governments around the world. There were a number of contributory factors to the global financial crisis, but the impact from a fund perspective was that asset values in certain types of funds, in particular real estate, plummeted and the liquidity within funds disappeared, giving rise to investor protection issues.

The EU therefore decided that, for all alternative investment fund managers (AIFMs) operating in Europe, they wanted to ensure greater transparency, reporting and oversight by regulators, both nationally, as well as at European level through the European Securities and Market Authority (ESMA).

third country
Reference to a jurisdiction which is outside of the EU but may wish to engage in trade with the EU. Depending on the nature of services or products, the third country can apply for equivalence to enable it to trade within the EU.

Until the implementation of the Directive there was no oversight at EU level of these activities and each member state regulator operated in its own silo with varying levels of supervisory oversight applied. With the introduction of the Directive it ensured a consistent approach to all AIFMs operating within the EU. It also introduced greater protection to investors in alternative investment funds (AIFs) which was not previously available.

The AIFMD was adopted by the European Council in 2011 and came into force on 21 July 2011. Member states had until 22 July 2013 to transpose the requirements of the AIFMD into their national law, although some had still not done so as at that date and action had to be taken.

3. Application of AIFMD

The AIFMD captures managers of all types of collective investment schemes except undertakings for collective investment in transferable securities (UCITS). This means it encompasses a broad range of funds, for example, listed investment funds to funds investing in illiquid assets (for example real estate or physical assets). It applies equally to open- and closed-ended fund vehicles and does not matter what the legal constitution of the fund is.

To be authorised as an AIFM, the fund manager will have to be authorised by its home regulator to perform the functions of portfolio management and risk management. Broadly, an entity will be captured as an AIFM where it has assets under management in any AIF above the thresholds of:

- €100 million if the AIF has any leveraging within it; or
- €500 million, if the AIF does not have any leveraging within it.

As the appointed AIFM of an AIF, the AIFM can undertake any of the activities that are set out in Annex I of the AIFMD itself, so long as it has the necessary regulatory approvals in its home jurisdiction for those activities. The AIFM may choose to delegate some of the activities to third parties rather than undertake all of the work required of them. Any third party appointed does not necessarily need to be authorised to manage an AIF, but will need to be regulated in their home country to undertake the activity that they are doing. It is important to remember that, as the appointed AIFM, whilst the activity can be delegated, the responsibility for it rests with the AIFM.

4. Responsibilities of an AIFM

Two key responsibilities of an AIFM are the portfolio management and risk management of the AIF. If the management of an AIFM decides to delegate the element of either portfolio management or risk management activities in accordance with Article 20 of the AIFMD, the AIFM must ensure:

Remuneration Guidelines
Guidelines issued by ESMA explaining how firms may comply with the Annex II Principles to the Alternative Investment Fund Managers Directive in relation to remuneration policies.

key staff
Are those staff to whom the remuneration policy of the firm should apply to and will also include staff of the firm to which portfolio management or risk management activities have been delegated by the AIFM.

general principles
As set out within the COMMISSION DELEGATED REGULATION (EU) No 231/2013 within section 8 to comply with in relation to the delegation of functions under the AIFMD.

- The entity to which portfolio management or risk management activities has been delegated is subject to regulatory requirements on remuneration that are equally as effective as those applicable under the **Remuneration Guidelines**; or
- That there are appropriate contractual arrangements with the entity in relation to the activities that have been delegated to ensure that there is no circumvention of the Remuneration Guidelines, so the contractual arrangements must cover circumstances around any payments made to the delegates' **key staff** as compensation for their role in the activities being undertaken on behalf of the AIFM.

5. Delegation

5.1 General principles

If a decision is made to delegate then the relevant **general principles** must be complied with so that the delegation does not allow for circumvention of the AIFM's responsibilities or obligations in relation to the AIF. Any contract or agreement for delegation must be documented in writing between the AIFM and the delegate. As part of the general principles, there are certain set provisions which must be covered and detailed within the written agreement to comply with the AIFMD:

- the rights and obligations of both parties, specifically the right of access to records, inspection of records and provisions relating to the ability to visit the delegate to undertake monitoring so that effective supervision of the delegate can be applied;
- requirement for the delegate to undertake proper monitoring and oversight of the activities being undertaken on behalf of the AIFM and adequately manage any risks which it identifies in undertaking that role;
- confidentiality and data protection provisions relating to data of the AIFM, the AIF itself and the investors in that AIF;
- provisions to compel the delegate to disclose to the AIFM any matter that may have a material impact on its ability to carry out the delegated functions effectively, and in compliance with applicable laws and regulatory requirements;
- a requirement for a comprehensive disaster recovery plan to be in place and to be regularly tested by the delegate; and
- notice provisions in relation to cessation of the contract and the circumstances in which it may be triggered.

5.2 Ongoing obligations

In addition to the requirements of the contract content detailed above, there are a number of ongoing obligations with which the AIFM has to comply in accordance with the general principles. These all effectively centre on the AIFM's ability to oversee the ongoing compliance of the delegate, both with the contractual agreement that is in place, and the way in which they are undertaking the delegated activities for the AIFM. As noted above, whilst the AIFM may have delegated the task, the responsibility for how it is carried out rests with the AIFM, so there has to be a robust oversight programme of the delegate, including on-site visits to that delegate, to document how the AIFM has satisfied itself as to the standard and compliance of the work that the delegate has undertaken.

6. Delegation of portfolio or risk management

If a decision is made by the AIFM to delegate, there is a requirement under AIFMD to provide sufficient rationale for the decision based on the **objective reasons**. Examples of reasons that would be suitable include:

- expertise of that delegate in a specific area which the AIFM itself does not have;
- cost savings for the AIF; or
- access of the delegate to global trading capabilities.

objective reasons
Within section 76 of the COMMISSION DELEGATED REGULATION (EU) No 231/2013. The objective reasons under which justification for delegation must be made are set out.

It will be necessary for the AIFM to provide its home regulator with a detailed description of the delegate and explanation of the applicable reason(s) for any delegation, together with supporting evidence. Ordinarily this will be done by way of a specific application form issued by the regulator which requests certain information in relation to the proposed delegation arrangements.

As with any activity subject to regulatory oversight, the AIFM has a responsibility to ensure that any delegate has sufficient resources and employs staff with the skills, knowledge and expertise to be undertaking the activity being delegated. Staff of the delegate are also required to be fit and proper; that is to say that enquiries should be made for any convictions for dishonesty or fraud or regulatory sanctions applied against them in any jurisdiction. In most cases the AIFM will put together a due diligence pack which will demonstrate the enquiries made and information that they have gathered in order to satisfy themselves as to the competency and ability of the delegate and its staff to undertake the work.

Where the delegation of the portfolio management or risk management element of the AIFM's role is to happen, the Regulation sets out the types of EU regulated entities which are deemed to be appropriately authorised for such activities. It also notes that non-EU entities authorised under the AIFMD, such as those in third countries, who hold a licence for fund management from their home regulator, can act as delegates for an AIFM if certain criteria are met. If there is a written agreement, such as a memorandum of understanding, between the home regulator of the AIFM and the regulatory authority of the delegate which covers the following, then the third country entity can be a delegate if:

- provisions exist for the AIFM's regulator to obtain information and documents from the delegate in order to satisfy themselves that requirements under the AIFMD are being met;
- the AIFM's regulator can receive information from the supervisory authority in the third country for the purpose of investigating apparent breaches of the AIFMD and Regulation as soon as possible;
- there are provisions for the cooperation between regulators in the event of enforcement action in accordance with applicable local law; and
- it enables on-site inspections on the premises of the delegate to be undertaken.

In respect of the regulatory oversight provisions, the reality is that the third country regulator will have an on-site visit regime in place to visit its regulated entities and will allow for the findings of any such visit to be shared with the AIFM's regulator in the spirit of cooperation using the provisions of the memorandum of understanding, or similar document, in place between them.

7. Letterbox entities

The phrase letterbox entity is defined as an organisation which does not have any substance or form at their given address and all activities of which are outsourced elsewhere. One of the aims of the AIFMD was to prevent such situations arising. National regulators have tried a number of ways to prevent this in the past by the application of requirements such as the four eyes principle, meaning there have to be two individuals clearly resident in the jurisdiction and directing the business activities on a day-to-day basis, together with having to give approval to the appointment of key staff with sufficient experience and skills to run the AIFM. The AIFMD sets out what it deems to constitute a letterbox entity and at what point an AIFM would no longer be considered acceptable to be the manager of the AIF if such a situation were occurring. The Regulation sets out relevant circumstances as follows:

- the AIFM no longer has sufficiently skilled or qualified staff to enable them to oversee the activities being undertaken on their behalf by the delegate;
- the AIFM no longer has access to the information or records required in order to be able to fulfil its oversight requirements; and
- the AIFM delegates so many of the activities for which it is responsible under the AIFMD that the delegate is undertaking a greater part of the work than the AIFM itself.

The responsibility of the AIFM to undertake investment management functions in relation to any AIFs to which it is appointed includes, under that description, both portfolio management and risk management, so AIFMs generally retain one of the two activities to ensure they are not in danger of outsourcing too much of their responsibility. Since implementation of the AIFMD, most AIFMs delegating any activity have retained the risk management function to ensure that they are not in danger of being deemed letterbox entities.

In summary, if any aspect of the role is delegated by an AIFM they must ensure that the delegation contract gives them sufficient ability to effectively oversee the delegate and that delegation is only in relation to a part of their responsibilities, not all of them. The AIFM will also need to ensure sufficient documentation is in place to evidence how they have concluded that they can apply their oversight measures and the suitability of the delegate for the services that they will be providing.

8. Conflicts of interest

The AIFMD will not permit delegation in circumstances where there are conflicts with the interests of the AIFM, or investors in the relevant AIF, and sets out the factors that have to be considered. It will be the responsibility of the board of the AIFM to demonstrate how any conflicts are being appropriately managed. This may include specific reference in any contract or agreement to the provisions for managing any identified conflicts, or adequate disclosures of those conflicts in the offering memorandum of the AIF. The board of the AIFM has to determine whether the conflicts can be appropriately managed by the means they propose, or if they are too significant to be effectively managed, then delegation should not be permitted.

9. Reporting requirements

On 1 October 2013 ESMA issued its final guidelines on the regulatory reporting required under AIFMD.

All AIFMs are now obliged to report to their home regulator details about the AIFs under their management, which includes, amongst other information, value of assets within the AIF, the nature of the investments, types of investors and details of any leveraging.

An AIFM is required to report after they have their relevant authorisation from their home regulator in relation to the AIF, and the first reporting period will start from the first day of the following quarter and runs until the end of the relevant reporting period. The length of the first reporting period will depend on reporting frequency, which is determined by the level of assets under management. The requirements are summarised in table 12.1.

Table 12.1: Requirements for reporting

	Assets under management	Reporting frequency	Due date
AIFM reports	<€100m	Annually	Last business day of January
	>€100m to €1 billion	Half yearly	Last business day of January and July
	>€1bn	Quarterly	Last business day of the month following quarter end
Individual AIF reports	>€500m	Quarterly	Last business day of the month following quarter end

ESMA has issued guidance in respect of fund managers that are located outside of the EU, such as those based in third countries, but that market AIFs into the EU via the national private placement regimes. Regulated fund managers will be permitted to market under private placement regimes and will have to report, but only for any AIFs that they market in the EU, not for all assets under management. However, for EU authorised AIFMs, they must report in respect of all AIFs under management, irrespective of whether they market them in the EU or not.

10. Remuneration Code

An important part of AIFMD and the investor protection element of its introduction related to controls and transparency around remuneration of key staff in AIFMs. In light of this, as part of the introduction of AIFMD, the AIFM Remuneration Code was published in July 2013. After a firm is authorised as an AIFM it must comply with the requirements of the Remuneration Code and ensure that it has sufficient evidence to demonstrate how it is doing so on an ongoing basis.

In summary, the purpose of the Remuneration Code is to prevent inappropriate remuneration being offered to key staff, as excessive remuneration can be linked to risk-taking, and disproportionate rewards for taking those risks, all of which having been identified as contributory factors to the global financial crisis of 2008. The Remuneration Code is in place to ensure a clear division between taking risks and individuals receiving personal rewards, to discourage excessive risk-taking, to promote a culture of understanding of risk issues and their management and encourage responsible behaviour by key staff within the AIFM.

11. Marketing in Financial Instruments Directive

The Marketing in Financial Instruments Directive (MiFID) regulatory framework consists of a framework Directive (Directive 2004/39/EC), an Implementing Directive (Directive 2006/73/EC) and an Implementing Regulation (Regulation No 1287/2006).

MiFID and its supporting regulation are the pieces of legislation put in place by the EU in order to regulate:

- investment intermediaries that provide services to clients trading in **financial instruments**; and
- the trading of financial instruments.

financial instruments
Section C of Annex I of the DIRECTIVE 2004/39/EC OF THE EUROPEAN PARLIAMENT AND OF THE COUNCIL lists all financial instruments.

11.1 Background

MiFID came into effect in 2008 and replaced the Investment Services Directive, which was adopted in 1993. The reasons for implementation of MiFID were to improve the competitiveness of EU financial markets by creating a single EU market and introduce a level playing field for investment services and activities, whilst also ensuring investor protection for those trading in financial instruments.

11.2 What does MiFID address?

MiFID addresses investor protection in the context of the provision of investment services. It takes into account the type of services, for instance, whether it is full financial advice or execution only, and the classification of clients according to their sophistication and knowledge in relation to investment trading, with the highest level of protection granted to retail clients who are deemed to be the least sophisticated investor category. The **MiFID Rules** also cover conduct of business requirements such as suitability assessment of the product for clients and attitude of the client to risk, together with governance requirements for the business itself such as management of conflicts of interest.

MiFID Rules
Markets in Financial Instruments Directive Rules issued pursuant to the Directive to provide more detail on compliance with certain requirements of the Directive.

MiFID has provided a more stable and integrated EU financial market. However, the global financial crisis in 2008 led to the identification of some weaknesses in MiFID, and as part of the evolution of technology there have been new mechanisms for trading come into being which are not caught by MiFID. By revising MiFID this will ensure that the legislation keeps pace with technological and financial developments.

11.3 Changes to MiFID

The changes are set to take effect from 3 January 2018, with the new legislation being known as MiFID II which will include revisions to MiFID itself, together with a new Markets in Financial Instruments Regulation (MiFIR).

The rationale for MiFID II is to establish a safer, more robust, more transparent and more accountable financial system across the EU. The main changes will be:

- Ensuring all trading, wherever MiFID is applicable, takes place on a regulated platform.
- The requirement for transparency for non-equity instruments such as bonds and derivatives will be introduced. MiFID II will extend the pre- and post-trade transparency regime to include non-equity instruments.
- There will be strengthened supervisory powers for regulators and a uniform position-limits regime for commodity derivatives to improve transparency, support orderly pricing by traders and prevent market abuse and manipulation. Regulatory authorities will be able to impose limits on positions set by ESMA. It also introduces reporting obligations per category of trader. This information will be gathered and reviewed so that it can be used to consider future improvements and identify any other weaknesses that may be within the marketplace.
- There will be rules on competition in the trading and clearing of financial instruments. This will ensure access to trade venues for all, so that no one is disadvantaged.
- There will be requirements put in place for algorithmic trading activities. Algorithmic traders will have to be regulated and to provide liquidity when pursuing a market-making strategy to mitigate risk. In addition, there will be provisions to prevent automated trading from facilitating insider dealing and market abuse to occur.
- Stronger investor protection by those subject to MiFID being subject to more detailed requirements on governance and internal controls. MiFID II will also introduce powers and conditions for ESMA to prohibit or restrict the marketing and distribution of certain financial instruments, subject to certain criteria being met.
- Enhanced regulatory sanctions for those that fail to adhere to the requirements.
- A standardised regime for granting access to EU markets for firms from third countries. This will be achieved by a process called an equivalence assessment. The equivalence assessment will analyse the regulatory regime applicable in the third country to identify whether it has in place equivalent standards and obligations placed upon entities regulated there to those in the EU to whom MiFID applies, and that the regulator has similar powers of enforcement as those in the EU to utilise where non-compliance is identified. The third country will apply to the European Commission to undertake this equivalence assessment on them. This will only be applicable to the cross-border provision of investment services and activities provided to professional and eligible counterparties. In the interim whilst assessments are being undertaken, there will be a transitional period of three years where each member state's own third country regime will continue to be applicable.

The access of third country firms to the EU markets was not consistent under MiFID. Each member state could introduce its own third country regime, provided that national provisions did not mean third countries were given more favourable treatment than those within the EU.

Once the Commission has issued an equivalence decision with respect to a specific third country, ESMA will then need to establish memorandum of understandings or another form of cooperation arrangement with the regulator of that third country. It will then be up to the firm within that third country to apply to ESMA to become registered. Once registration is granted by ESMA the third country firm will be able to provide services to professional clients and eligible counterparties in the EU.

However, this is not the case for retail clients, which is currently not covered by MiFID and nor will it be by MiFID II. The provision of services by third country firms to retail clients will still be subject to the rules of the applicable member state.

Finally, MiFID II will not apply when investment services are being provided to any client where it is the client that has made contact to request the services, often referred to as reverse solicitation. This exemption will apply only to the specific service that has been requested by the client. This would not allow, for example, the third country firm to market a different product to that client for which they have not made any enquiry.

12. Undertakings in collective investment in transferable securities

Undertakings in collective investment in transferable securities (UCITS) are investment funds regulated within the EU. The applicable directive is Directive 2014/91/EU.

The Directive lays down common rules on investment funds in the EU, which therefore means UCITS can be offered cross-border. The main aims of the directive were to offer investors a wider choice within the UCITS market in the EU, to facilitate better investor information and promote efficient funds supervision.

The Directive includes rules on provision of investor information via a standardised summary information document so that potential investors find it easier to understand the product, a European passport regime for UCITS management companies, marketing of UCITS in other countries through simplified agreed common procedures, and stronger supervisory oversight of UCITS and of the companies that manage them by ensuring cooperation between the financial services supervisors of member states.

The substance of the UCITS V Directive needed to be implemented by member states into national law by 18 March 2016. The driver for the implementation of UCITS V was following the Madoff fraud and the default of Lehman Brothers which saw significant global financial unrest. It also sought to align requirements between AIFMD and UCITS and therefore there is commonality of some requirements relating to the depositary function, remuneration of personnel and regulatory sanctions that can be imposed.

12.1 Depositary function

Like AIFMD, there is a requirement that the assets of a UCITS are held by a depositary for safekeeping, and specific requirements in place relating to the eligibility to act as a depositary and the depositary's material relationships with the manager and its delegates.

12.2 Eligibility to act as a depositary

Under UCITS V the following may act as a UCITS depositary:

- national central banks;
- credit institutions; and
- other legal entities authorised by their relevant member state regulatory authority to carry out depositary activities in accordance with UCITS V. To be eligible they must be subject to minimum capital adequacy requirements, ongoing supervision and certain minimum requirements (including adequate internal policies and procedures, and robust governance processes).

A UCITS must have a single depositary, and that company cannot be appointed to act as both the management company as well as the depositary. The appointment of the depositary has to be evidenced by written contract, and must set out the minimum level of information to be provided to the depositary to enable it to perform its functions.

12.3 Duties of a UCTIS depositary

A depositary must act honestly, fairly, professionally, independently and solely in the interest of the UCITS and the investors of the UCITS at all times. The depositary must also have procedures in place to identify and manage conflicts of interest which it identifies during it fulfilling its functions.

12.4 The depositary function

UCITS V specifically sets out three principal functions that a depositary must undertake:

- the cash monitoring function;
- the safekeeping function; and
- the oversight function.

12.5 Cash monitoring function

The depositary has to have oversight of the cash movement of the UCITS and have arrangements in place to oversee and monitor those movements. That includes:

- Ensuring investors' subscription amounts and all monies belonging to the UCITS are paid into a bank account with a credit institution, central bank or third country bank, which is in the name of the UCITS, or in the name of its management company, or the name of the depositary on behalf of the UCITS.

- For bank accounts that are opened in the name of the depositary on behalf of the UCITS, ensuring that the bank accounts are not used or mixed with the depositary's own funds.
- The depositary must be aware of all bank accounts opened for or on behalf of the UCITS.

12.6 Safekeeping function

Another significant part of the depositary is the role for safekeeping. In the predecessor regulation to UCITS V it did not set out specific duties for the role of custodianship. Under UCITS V however, there are now detailed provisions in respect of both financial instruments and other assets.

12.7 Oversight duties

There are numerous responsibilities in relation to monitoring the operational activities of a UCITS, including:

- making sure any transaction in its units is undertaken in accordance with the relevant legislation;
- carrying out the instructions of the UCITS manager or investments adviser unless the instructions contravene legislation or the fund documentation;
- ensuring that for any transaction involving the assets of the UCITS, monies are remitted within the correct time limits;
- ensuring the valuation of units is calculated in accordance with applicable national laws and the fund documents; and
- ensuring income is applied appropriately.

12.8 Delegation of depositary's duties

The only function a depositary is permitted to delegate is its safekeeping function. If a decision is made to delegate this then there has to be legitimate reason for doing so. The depositary has to demonstrate that they are exercising due skill, care and diligence in the selection and appointment of any sub-custodian, as well as having in place a suitable and sufficient periodic review programme of the performance of the delegate. There also has to be ongoing monitoring to ensure the delegate satisfies the requirement to segregate the assets of the UCITS from their own assets and from the other assets of the depositary so that the assets can be, at any time, clearly identified as belonging to the UCITS.

UCITS V also places a strict liability on depositaries to be liable to investors in the UCITS for:

- The loss of any financial instrument held in custody by the depositary or a sub-custodian, unless the depositary can prove that the loss arose as a result of an external event beyond its control.

- All other losses suffered by the UCITS as a result of the depositary's negligence or intentional failure to properly fulfil its obligations, including failing in its oversight of the sub-custodian.

The UCITS V depositary liability provisions are similar to those of AIFMD, and it is not possible for the depositary to transfer its liability onto the sub-custodian. The liability of the depositary is not reduced in any way by any delegation to a sub-custodian and cannot be excluded or limited by any written agreement.

12.9 Remuneration of personnel

UCITS V introduces requirements relating to the remuneration of key personnel involved in the management and operation of UCITS. The key aspects of the UCITS remuneration regime are similar to that of AIFMD in terms of applicability to key personnel and discouraging excessive risk taking by those individuals.

13. Solvency II

Solvency II is a piece of EU legislation to provide a harmonised EU insurance regulatory regime. It replaced 14 EU insurance directives that were previously in force.

13.1 Key objectives

The key objectives of Solvency II were as follows:

- **Improved consumer protection** – To provide a uniform level of policyholder protection across the EU.
- **Regulatory consistency** – Regulatory requirements will be harmonised between national regulators within each Member State.
- **Regulatory change** – Emphasis is now on evaluating insurers' risk profiles and the quality of their risk management and governance systems as part of the oversight process.
- **Increased international competitiveness of EU insurers** – Solvency II is such a comprehensive programme of regulatory requirements for insurers that confidence is provided in the EU insurance market and how robust it is.

13.2 The three pillars to Solvency II

Pillar 1
Contains details on the calculations, models and capital requirements that must be adhered to. This includes the solvency capital requirement (SCR) which is a risk-responsive capital measure to ensure that each insurer can meet its ongoing obligations for the next 12 months. If for any reason this level of capital is not achieved, then it can result in regulatory action. The minimum capital requirement (MCR) is the minimum amount of capital the insurer needs to cover its risks. If an insurer's risk capital falls below the MCR then they are not able to write any further business.

Pillar 2
Provides details of the own risk and solvency assessment (ORSA). The ORSA is 'all processes and procedures employed to identify, assess, monitor, manage, and report the short- and long-term risks a reinsurance undertaking faces or may face and to determine their own funds necessary to ensure that overall solvency needs are met at all times'. This is how a company demonstrates set out in all aspects of its business how its SCR will continue to be met on an ongoing basis. The methodology of it will vary.

Pillar 3
The final pillar is about supervisory oversight, disclosure and transparency requirements like the solvency and financial condition report (SFCR) and quantitative report template (QRT).

14. Dodd-Frank

Dodd-Frank was introduced in the US in response to a number of different economic and regulatory drivers, primarily as a result of the financial crisis in 2008, where weaknesses in the overall US financial system were identified.

Increased ability to oversee financial markets trading
To do this, the Financial Stability Oversight Council was introduced to look out for risks that affect the entire financial industry in the US. It also oversees non-bank financial firms like hedge funds.

To regulate risky derivatives
Dodd-Frank implemented the regulation by the Securities Exchange Commission (SEC) or the Commodity Futures Trading Commission (CFTC) of things like credit swaps, and other investments considered to be high risk. The rationale was so that excessive risk-taking can be identified and brought to policy-makers' attention before a major crisis occurred.

Prevent banks from using depositors' money
The Volcker Rule bans banks from using or owning hedge funds. Prior to the crisis they would use their depositors' funds to invest on the bank's behalf in hedge funds they owned or wished to invest in. Banks can now only invest in hedge funds at the request of their customers. Dodd-Frank gave banks seven years to divest the funds and regularise their positions which all had to be completed by July 2015.

To Bring Transparency into Hedge Fund trading
Prior to 2008, hedge funds and other financial advisers were not regulated, so no one knew what they were investing in or how much was being invested into these products. Dodd-Frank requires hedge funds to register with the SEC and provide data about their trades and portfolios so the SEC can assess overall market risk.

Oversee credit rating agencies
Dodd-Frank has resulted in the creation of an Office of Credit Ratings at the SEC to regulate credit ratings agencies like Moody's and Standard & Poor's. The SEC can require agencies to submit their methodologies for review, and can deregister an agency that gives faulty ratings which misleads investors.

Increase supervision of insurance companies
It created a new Federal Insurance Office (FIO) under the Treasury Department, which identifies insurance companies which may pose a risk to the entire system.

Regulation of credit cards, loans, and mortgages
The Consumer Financial Protection Bureau was introduced to centralise the functions of many different agencies. This office is now responsible for oversight of credit reporting agencies, credit and debit cards, as well as payday and consumer loans. The CFPB sits under the US Treasury Department.

Increase supervision of insurance companies
It created a new Federal Insurance Office (FIO) under the Treasury Department, which identifies insurance companies which may pose a risk to the entire system.

Reform the Federal Reserve
The Government Accountability Office (GAO) was brought in to audit the Federal Reserve's emergency loans during the financial crisis. It can review future emergency loans when needed.

15. Foreign Account Tax Compliance Act

The Foreign Account Tax Compliance Act (FATCA), was enacted in 2010 as part of attempts by the US Government to combat tax evasion by US persons holding investments in offshore accounts.

Under FATCA, certain types of US taxpayers holding financial assets outside of the US must report those assets to the Inland Revenue Service (IRS). In addition, FATCA placed an obligation on foreign financial institutions to report directly to the IRS about certain information on financial accounts held by US taxpayers, or by foreign entities in which US taxpayers hold a substantial ownership interest.

This means that any funds which have US investors will potentially be subject to reporting under FATCA in relation to those investors.

15.1 Reporting by US taxpayers holding foreign financial assets

FATCA requires certain US taxpayers holding foreign financial assets with an aggregate value exceeding $50,000 to report certain information about those assets. Reporting applied for assets held in taxable years beginning after 18 March 2010. Failure to report foreign financial assets results in a penalty of $10,000 (and a penalty up to $50,000 for continued failure after IRS notification). Therefore, there is a significant deterrent in failing to declare reportable financial assets.

15.2 Reporting by foreign financial institutions

FATCA requires foreign financial institutions (FFIs) to report directly to the IRS on certain information about financial accounts held by US taxpayers, or by foreign entities in which US taxpayers hold a substantial ownership interest. In accordance with the agreement, a participating FFI will be obligated to:

- undertake certain identification and due diligence procedures with respect to its accountholders;
- report annually to the IRS on its accountholders who are US persons or foreign entities with substantial US ownership; and
- withhold and pay over to the IRS 30% of any payments of US source income, as well as gross proceeds from the sale of securities that generate US source income, made to either a non-participating FFI, individual accountholders failing to provide sufficient information to determine whether or not they are a US person, or foreign entity accountholders failing to provide sufficient information about the identity of its substantial US owners.

Financial institutions must report the information they gather to the US. However, where countries have an inter-governmental agreement (IGA), the financial institution will send the US person's data to the local government first. Guernsey and Jersey have an IGA in place with the US and therefore reporting is to the local tax authority who will then pass that data to the US IRS. However, in a non-IGA country, such as North Korea, the North Korean financial institution will gather that data and then have to pass it directly to the IRS.

FATCA data either received via IGAs or directly from FFIs is used to cross-check a US person's self-reported data. FATCA therefore allows detection of persons who have not self-reported, enabling collection of large penalties.

In order to asses US indicia for an investor, the following will need to be considered:

- A citizen of the US, including someone born in the US but living in another country, who has not renounced or otherwise relinquished their US citizenship.
- A lawful resident of the US, including a US green card holder.
- A person residing in the US.
- Someone spending a specified amount of time in the US, potentially including 'snowbirds' who spend winters in the Florida or other warm climes.
- A green card holder who never formally handed in their green card upon leaving the US (even though the green card in no longer valid for US immigration purposes).

- The child of a US citizen, provided a parent lived in the US period for a specified time period.

Financial Institutions will also look for indicia to indicate a US connection and reporting obligation including:

- A US place of birth.
- A current US residence or mailing address (including a US PO Box).
- A current US telephone number.
- Standing instructions to pay amounts from a foreign (meaning non US) account to an account maintained in the US
- A current power of attorney or signatory authority granted to a person with a US address.
- A US 'in-care-of' or 'hold mail' address that is the sole address with respect to the account holder.

Chapter summary

- Even though offshore centres are not directly impacted by the issue of directives in the EU or legislation that is enacted elsewhere in the world, in order to continue to access both the European and global marketplace or provide services to investors around the world, there needs to be an understanding of the regulatory framework that is in operation at EU level, as well as member states' own regimes, and that being enacted by significant market participants.

Chapter thirteen
International regulators

List of topics

1. Moneyval
2. International Organization of Securities Commissions (IOSCO)
3. Country review
4. Thematic review
5. Road maps
6. International Monetary Fund (IMF)
7. Financial Action Task Force (FATF)
8. European Securities and Markets Authority (ESMA)
9. Securities and Exchange Commission (SEC)
10. Cayman Islands Monetary Authority (CIMA)
11. Monetary Authority of Singapore (MAS)
12. Sharia law

Introduction

In this chapter, you will learn about the different bodies around the world which impact upon the funds sector. As part of an increasing globalisation of oversight of financial markets, international bodies and regulators have been established to ensure standards in certain industry sectors are applied consistently around the world. The remit of these bodies will vary dependent on their specific purpose, but all have an overarching purpose of prevention of market abuse, investor protection and prevention of financial crime. You will understand by the end of this chapter the specific remit of each of these bodies and how they came into being.

1. Moneyval

1.1 Background

Moneyval
An EU body whose full name is the Committee of Experts on the Evaluation of Anti-Money Laundering Measures and the Financing of Terrorism, responsible for analysis and oversight of a jurisdiction's compliance with international standards to prevent money laundering and terrorist financing.

Financial Action Task Force on Money Laundering (FATF)
Established by the G7 Summit that was held in Paris in 1989.

Moneyval is an EU body whose full name is the Committee of Experts on the Evaluation of Anti-Money Laundering Measures and the Financing of Terrorism. Established by the Council of Europe, it is responsible for analysis and oversight of a jurisdiction's compliance with international standards to prevent money laundering and terrorist financing. It does this in a number of ways, including visits to the jurisdiction and evaluation of their legislation with follow-up reports.

The offshore centres of Guernsey, Jersey and the Isle of Man have all received visits from Moneyval in the last two years. Each jurisdiction then received a report back which analysed the compliance with a predetermined selection of the **Financial Action Task Force's (FATF)** 40+9 recommendations.

1.2 Remit of Moneyval

AML/CFT
Anti-Money Laundering/Countering the Financing of Terrorism rules which apply within each jurisdiction to comply with international standards.

International Monetary Fund (IMF)
International body whose stated aims are to facilitate global monetary cooperation, secure financial stability, facilitate international trade, promote high employment and sustainable economic growth, and reduce poverty around the world.

Moneyval has the following activities within its remit:

- assessing compliance with all relevant international standards, including evaluation as to the effectiveness of the measures that have been implemented by the jurisdiction in relation to its regulatory and enforcement framework;
- issuing findings and recommendations on improvements to the jurisdiction's **AML/CFT** regime;
- conducting thematics on money laundering and terrorist financing methods, trends and evolution of new methodologies, their potential impact, and issues reports on their findings;
- making recommendations to the Committee of Ministers on enhancements to the AML/CFT legislation in Europe; and
- working in conjunction with other international bodies engaged in the fight against financial crime such as the FATF and the **International Monetary Fund (IMF)**.

Moneyval oversees those EU member states which are not members of FATF, or member states that subsequently become a member of FATF, but still wish to continue under the remit of Moneyval. The member states which are currently evaluated by Moneyval are:

Albania	Georgia	Russian Federation
Andorra	Hungary	San Marino
Armenia Lithuania	Latvia	Serbia
Azerbaijan	Liechtenstein	Slovak Republic
Bosnia and Herzegovina	Malta	Slovenia
Bulgaria	Monaco	'The former
Croatia	Montenegro	Yugoslav Republic of
Cyprus	Republic of Moldova	Macedonia'
Czech Republic	Poland	Ukraine
Estonia	Romania	

In addition to these member states, there are a number of other territories which either by special resolution or extension of the Statute on Europe are also evaluated by Moneyval:

Guernsey	The Holy See (including Vatican City)	Israel
Gibraltar	Isle of Man	
Jersey		

1.3 Representatives

The representatives in Moneyval of a member state are comprised of individuals who are:

- senior officials and experts with responsibility for regulation and supervision of financial institutions;
- senior officials in law enforcement and financial intelligence units; or
- senior legal experts from ministries of justice and/or judicial and prosecutorial bodies.

Those put forward are therefore experts in their field, which assists Moneyval in fulfilling its functions by use of their knowledge and expertise. These individuals who represent the member state have the right to vote on any matter which Moneyval presents for voting.

Moneyval membership also has a category of observer, where individuals can attend meetings representing specific bodies, countries and organisations but, if a vote is held, they do not have the right to vote. At present, in 2016, some examples of observers include Canada, Japan, Mexico and the US or the Secretariat of FATF or the European Bank of Reconstruction and Development.

1.4 Interaction with other regulatory bodies and organisations

Moneyval was originally an observer to the FATF but was promoted to become an associate member from June 2006. As part of international efforts to combat financial crime, Moneyval participates as one of the eight regional bodies in FATF. Moneyval is a separate body to FATF but works closely with it in areas where their interests are aligned or they are working on projects in common. They will also liaise on reporting standards and evaluations helping to reinforce the importance of consistency of global financial crime prevention reporting.

The IMF and World Bank undertake some evaluations on behalf of Moneyval and present the reports for adoption at Moneyval. Examples of cooperation include the review of the Channel Islands, demonstrated by the IMF undertaking visits to the islands in 2010 and then Moneyval using the IMF's report to follow up in 2014. Many local regulators now require their licensee base to identify risks within their business, and now jurisdictions themselves must review their licensee base and products on offer. This is termed a national risk assessment. The World Bank has been tasked with providing technical assistance around national risk assessments in several Moneyval countries. These are key for compliance with the revised set of FATF Recommendations, where the focus on risk is higher than previously.

Moneyval was also tasked with evaluating compliance of all EU Member States and territories covered by the 3rd EU AML/CFT Directive. In addition, Moneyval follows the AML/CFT developments at the EU level and the evolution of European legislation.

1.5 The Committee

The work of the Moneyval Committee, which is the operational arm of Moneyval, is determined by the Bureau. The Bureau sits at the top of the structure and consists of a Chairperson, a Vice-Chairperson and three other members, elected by the Committee from the delegations which are entitled to vote in the Committee. The term of office for the members of the Bureau is two years and it can only be renewed once.

Underneath the Committee there are a number of focused working groups set up to undertake specific tasks. These include, as at July 2016, an Advisory Group on Policy and Evaluations and a Working Group on Evaluations.

1.6 Evaluation cycles

A number of rounds of evaluations have taken place since Moneyval came into existence which can be seen in Table 13.1.

1.7 Evaluation visits

The evaluation team normally consists of a member of the Secretariat and four evaluators, comprising the following areas of expertise; one from legal, one from law enforcement and two financial services industry experts.

In advance of an evaluation visit a detailed pre-visit questionnaire is sent to the jurisdiction. This requires them to provide responses regarding the regulatory, legal and enforcement framework that they have in place in relation to financial crime prevention. During the site visit the evaluation team will meet with those that have contributed to the answers within the questionnaire, which may include representatives of the government, regulators and law enforcement, together with representatives of the private sector such as management of licensed entities. The on-site visits do not normally exceed eight days. The evaluation team then drafts the evaluation report, which will be discussed with the jurisdiction, before being submitted to the Plenary for adoption.

After the third round of evaluation visits to jurisdictions, the ongoing monitoring of jurisdictions in addressing recommendations made in their evaluation report was overseen by Moneyval, who had to be provided with reports from the jurisdiction setting out what action they had taken to remedy identified deficiencies. These progress updates were then tabled and adopted by the Plenary.

Table 13.1: Evaluation cycles

1998–2000	First Round Evaluations	22 Member States were evaluated against the 1996 FATF recommendations.
2001–2004	Second Round Evaluations	Assessment was made against the 1996 FATF Recommendations and the FATF's 2000 criteria for non-co-operative States and territories. 27 Member States were evaluated.
2005–2009	Third Round Evaluations	28 Member States and Israel were assessed against the 2003 revised FATF Recommendations and compliance with certain aspects of the EU's 3rd AML/CFT Directive.
2009–2015	Fourth Round 'Follow-Up' Evaluation	The follow-up round of on-site visits commenced in 2009, with evaluation still being evaluated against compliance with the 2003 FATF Recommendations and the EU's 3rd AML/CFT Directive, as well as progress made in areas identified on the third round evaluation.
2015–estimated 2021	Fifth Round Evaluation	The current evaluations focus on the 2012 revised FATF Recommendations. The first visit of this sort was conducted in 2015 and they are anticipated to continue in this format until 2021.

1.8 Current position

Moneyval introduced three categories for post-visit oversight and interaction as a result of the fourth round visits that it undertook:

Regular follow-up
A rating system is used to benchmark each recommendation and how far it has been complied with. The ratings are compliant, partially compliant and non-compliant. If a jurisdiction receives any partially compliant or non-compliant ratings in any of the six Core Recommendations, or wherever the Plenary considers it appropriate, the jurisdiction is placed on regular follow-up. They then have to report back to Moneyval, the first such report to be submitted within two years from the date of their report being issued, and provide confirmation of the steps that they are taking to rectify matters identified within

the report rated as partially compliant or non-compliant. Moneyval can compel a jurisdiction to report more frequently if they think that that is necessary.

Moneyval has issued guidance that jurisdictions should aim to have concluded their regular reporting process within three years of their fourth round report being approved. Before they can be removed from regular reporting they must provide sufficient evidence to demonstrate that they have an effective AML/CFT framework which covers the FATF Key Recommendations and FATF Core Recommendations on a deemed compliant or largely compliant basis. If they can demonstrate this, then they can be moved onto the biennial update procedure as described below.

Enhanced follow-up

Jurisdictions may be subject to enhanced follow-up where the visit has identified serious non-compliance with FATF recommendations. Moneyval can implement a number of measures to enforce an enhanced follow-up regime. This may include a remediation plan being developed which identifies the outstanding deficiencies and provides timeframes for remediation, the fifth round evaluation may be brought forward or any other measure which they may feel is necessary to ensure a focus on improvement by the jurisdiction.

Biennial update

Where a jurisdiction received a compliant or largely compliant rating in the areas against which they were assessed, they are only obliged to provide a biennial update of their progress in meeting the deficiencies identified, starting two years after their report is tabled.

The biennial report should provide Moneyval with details of any changes or developments in their AML/CFT framework. The biennial update is subject to review by an appointed member state or territory to ensure that progress has been made, as well as to a peer review by Moneyval.

If Moneyval is satisfied with the progress that has been made, it formally adopts the biennial report. However, if the report does not evidence that sufficient progress has been made then the jurisdiction can be referred back onto a higher level of supervisory oversight and reporting.

1.9 Moneyval Plenary

Moneyval's Plenary is its decision-making body. It is responsible for the review and adoption of the on-site visit reports and oversight of the progress made in accordance with the follow-up methods, as well as other reports produced by the Committee (such as typology reports). Plenary meetings are also where ideas and suggestions are shared, or concerns and queries raised as discussion topics for investigation by Moneyval. The Plenary meetings take place in Strasbourg, France, as it is the headquarters of the Council of Europe. There are three Plenary meetings held annually and they consist of delegations of its Member States and territories and two FATF Member States, as well as representatives of observer States, organisations and institutions or bodies.

2. International Organization of Securities Commissions (IOSCO)

2.1 Background

The **International Organization of Securities Commissions** (IOSCO) is an international body of securities regulators generally recognized as the leading regulatory body for the securities sector around the world. IOSCO develops, implements and promotes adherence to international standards for securities regulation. It also liaises with other global and regulatory bodies to ensure that these standards continue to evolve.

International Organization of Securities Commissions
An international body of securities regulators generally recognised as the leading regulatory body for the securities sector around the world.

IOSCO was established in 1983. Its membership regulates more than 95% of the world's securities markets in more than 115 jurisdictions.

In 1998 IOSCO adopted a comprehensive set of Objectives and Principles of Securities Regulation (the IOSCO Principles). IOSCO uses these benchmarks to assess compliance and will then work with the member to ensure that any deficiencies that they identify as part of their review are rectified. IOSCO will provide assistance with the remediation so far as it is able, in helping guide the member on any changes required.

In 2002, IOSCO adopted a template called the **Multilateral Memorandum of Understanding** Concerning Consultation and Cooperation and the Exchange of Information (IOSCO MMoU), which enables effective cross-border cooperation and exchange of information to help ensure IOSCO's objectives are achieved. Members sign up to the MMoU to ensure that information can be passed securely and legally between members to assist in law enforcement and investigations for example.

Multilateral Memorandum of Understanding
Multilateral Memorandum Of Understanding put in place between IOSCO and a member to allow free exchange of information between IOSCO members.

2.2 Objectives

IOSCO members are expected to participate in achieving the overall objectives of the body. These objectives are stated as to:

- Assist in the development, implementation and adherence of international standards of regulation, oversight and enforcement so that the objectives of investor protection, maintaining market integrity and addressing system risk are met.
- Participate in information exchange when dealing with enforcement action and cooperate with other members so that misconduct and oversight of market activities can be dealt with effectively and efficiently so that consumer confidence in the markets can be maintained.
- Exchange information with members on their experiences so that it can be used to assist in the oversight of markets and develop more effective and comprehensive regulation where it is required.

2.3 Principles

When IOSCO was formed, its aim was to produce a set of standards that would be used by members as being the benchmark in regulation of each area being reviewed. IOSCO issued a document dated June 2010, which remains relevant now six years on, which contains the guiding principles and standards that have been adopted by IOSCO:

- The Regulator
- Self-Regulation
- Enforcement of Securities Regulation
- Cooperation in Regulation
- Issuers
- Auditors, Credit Rating Agencies and other information providers
- Collective Investment Schemes
- Market Intermediaries
- Secondary Markets

2.4 The Regulator Principles

In order to be an effective regulator in the eyes of IOSCO, the following principles should be met:

- Responsibilities of the regulator should be clearly stated and enshrined with legal standing.
- A regulator should be operationally independent, in particular in relation to its decision-making processes.
- They must have adequate powers, proper resources and the capacity to perform the functions for which it has been formed and exercise their powers in an appropriate and effective manner.
- Clear and consistent regulatory processes need to be put in place.
- Staff should be appropriately qualified, experienced and subject to appropriate procedures, including standards of confidentiality.
- A system should be in place to monitor, mitigate and manage systemic risk within their licensee base.
- Participate in review and evolution of applicable regulation.
- Procedures for conflicts of interest and misalignment of incentives should be in place to ensure that they are avoided, eliminated, disclosed or managed appropriately.

When applying for membership, these will be the first criteria that IOSCO will use to assess the regulator against in terms of eligibility. Analysis of the way in which each strand of the requirements is met will be reviewed and documented. If any weaknesses are identified these will need to be addressed before membership is permitted.

2.5 Principles for Enforcement

In order for a regulator to be effective, it must have sufficient powers to take action against those who break the legislation in place. In that regard IOSCO states that the following are the criteria expected in relation to enforcement:

- The regulator should have comprehensive inspection, investigation and oversight powers.
- The regulator should have a range of comprehensive enforcement powers.
- The regulatory regime should ensure that there is an effective and credible use of inspection, investigation, oversight and enforcement powers and implementation of an effective compliance program.

Regulators will generally have a range of enforcement powers, varying from fines to preventing people from working in the financial services sector. Some offences may be so serious that criminal charges will need to be brought and therefore the regulator will need to work with local law enforcement. For example, this may include insider dealing, where a regulator may identify the offence, but in most jurisdictions this is a criminal offence and would therefore be taken forward for prosecution by law enforcement. However the legislation is framed within a particular jurisdiction, it is important that the regulator and the law enforcement bodies work together.

2.6 Principles for cooperation in Regulation

A core principle of IOSCO is the interaction between members so that co-operation benefits all and ensures that the IOSCO principles and objectives can be met:

- The regulator should have authority to share both public and non-public information with domestic and foreign counterparts.
- Regulators should establish information sharing mechanisms that set out when and how they will share both public and non-public information with their domestic and foreign counterparts.
- The regulatory system should allow for assistance to be provided to foreign regulators who need to make inquiries in the discharge of their functions and exercise of their powers.

In most cases regulators will put in place a Memorandum of Understanding or similar to enable cooperation and information sharing between themselves and to cover the points as outlined above, whilst ensuring that local confidentiality and data protection legislation is not breached.

2.7 Principles for Collective Investment Schemes

As well as setting out principles for the standards a regulator needs to adhere to, there are specific requirements which relate to the oversight of certain product offerings or services, for example, collective investment schemes, under the supervision of that member. These specifically require that:

- The regulatory system should set standards for the eligibility, governance, organisation and operational conduct of those who wish to market or operate a collective investment scheme.
- The regulatory system should provide for rules governing the legal form and structure of collective investment schemes and the segregation and protection of client assets.
- Regulation should require the collective investment scheme to disclose sufficient information about it in order for an investor to evaluate the suitability of a collective investment scheme and the value of the investor's interest in the scheme.
- Regulation should ensure that there is a requirement for a proper and disclosed methodology for asset valuation and the pricing and the redemption of units in a collective investment scheme.

2.8 Membership

IOSCO has established three categories of membership. These are ordinary member, associate member and affiliate. Currently as at July 2016 there are 126 ordinary members, 20 associate members and 65 affiliates. Ordinary members are the primary regulators of securities and/or futures markets in a jurisdiction, associate members are other securities and/or futures regulators in a jurisdiction, if that jurisdiction has more than one regulator (the lead one will be the ordinary member), and affiliates will be bodies such as stock exchanges, self-regulating organisations or stock market industry associations.

2.9 Structure

At the very top of the structure is the Presidents' Committee which is composed of all Presidents of the ordinary and associate members. Meetings are held once a year for an Annual Conference. Affiliate members are able to attend the Presidents' Committee meeting in order to hear about the work of IOSCO and its future plans.

The IOSCO Board is the part of IOSCO that is charged with setting the standards for IOSCO's regulatory regime. It is currently comprised of 34 securities regulators. Mr Ashley Ian Alder, Chief Executive Officer of the Hong Kong Securities and Futures Commission, is the current chair. The members of the IOSCO Board are the securities regulatory authorities of Argentina, Australia, Belgium, Brazil, China, Egypt, France, Germany, Hong Kong, India, Indonesia, Ireland, Italy, Jamaica, Japan, Kenya, Korea, Malaysia, Mexico, the Netherlands, Ontario, Pakistan, Peru, Quebec, Saudi Arabia, Singapore, Spain, Sweden, Switzerland, Turkey, United Kingdom and the United States.

When the IOSCO Board has identified an area which requires work, it delegates to sub-committees which specialise in particular areas. There are nine committees in total, which deal with areas such as enforcement or investment management. These committees undertake the necessary policy work in relation to any proposed developments or changes.

There is a separate committee for affiliate members called the Affiliate Members Consultative Committee (AMCC). At present this is chaired by Jose Carlos Doherty, the Chief Executive Officer of the Brazilian Financial and Capital Markets Association. This committee has 65 IOSCO affiliate members, representing securities and derivatives markets and other market infrastructures, self-regulatory organisations, investor protection funds and compensation funds, as well as other bodies with appropriate interest in securities regulation. Although there are 65 members, there are 33 jurisdictions represented in the committee.

The committee provides input into the IOSCO policy and standard-setting work as part of its remit. The AMCC also has the power to be able to form task forces to investigate areas which are of specific interest to AMCC members and/or the broader IOSCO membership. For example, in recent years with the emergence of FinTech in securities trading, this has been an area of review.

2.10 Multilateral Memorandum of Understanding

The Multilateral Memorandum of Understanding (MMoU) is a document which sets out the way in which cross-border cooperation will operate. It enables securities regulators to combat cross-border fraud, commercial conduct and market misconduct by sharing of information and intelligence.

The MMoU should consult, cooperate, and exchange information for the purpose of enforcement, both regulatory and potentially criminal.

The MMoU issued by IOSCO sets out the specific requirements for:

- what information can be exchanged and how it is to be exchanged;
- the legal capacity to compel information;
- the types of information that can be compelled;
- the legal capacity for sharing information; and
- the permissible use of information.

In addition, it sets out specific requirements regarding the confidentiality of the information exchanged, and ensures that no domestic legislation can prevent securities regulators from sharing this information with their counterparts in other jurisdictions, so long as certain criteria in relation to the information being requested are met.

Information requests via the MMoU can be made between members who are in the process of investigating offences involving the following activities under the relevant laws and regulations of the jurisdictions in question:

- insider dealing and market manipulation;
- misrepresentation of material information and other fraudulent or manipulative practices relating to securities and derivatives;
- solicitation and misappropriation of investor funds or customer instructions;
- the registration, issuance, offer, or sale of securities and derivatives in contravention of legislation;
- the activities of market intermediaries, including investment and trading advisers who are required to be licensed or registered, collective investment schemes, brokers, dealers, and transfer agents where they do not hold the necessary permissions; and
- the operations of markets, exchanges, and clearing and settlement entities which are not operating in accordance with the legislation or committing any kind of market offence.

Under the terms of the MMoU, the relevant members who can provide information and assistance, including records:

- to enable reconstruction of relevant transactions, including records of all funds and assets transferred into and out of bank and brokerage accounts relating to these transactions;
- of the beneficial owner and controller of an account;
- detailing transactions; and
- providing information identifying persons who beneficially own or control companies.

They can also liaise with the member to request them to take or compel a person's statement or, where permissible, testimony under oath, regarding the potential offence.

paragraph 7 MMoU
Sets out the scope of assistance members will, within the framework of MMoU, provide each other with to ensure compliance with the respective laws and regulations of the member.

The scope of assistance to be made to members is set out under **paragraph 7 of the IOSCO MMoU**. In 2003, 56 requests were made. By 2015, 3,203 had been made in a year.

All governmental regulatory bodies that are ordinary or associate members of IOSCO are eligible to apply to sign the MMoU; of the 140 eligible members, 106 are MMoU signatories as of November 2016.

IOSCO principles
International Organization of Securities Commissions Objectives and Principles of Securities Regulation sets out 38 Principles of securities regulation, which are based upon three Objectives of securities regulation. These are protecting investors, ensuring that markets are fair, efficient and transparent and reducing systemic risk.

2.11 The Assessment Committee

The AC was established to ensure that IOSCO is, and remains, the standard setter for securities regulation globally. It was established in February 2012 to organise and structure a programme to assess implementation of IOSCO Principles and Standards across its membership. It needed to benchmark how its members were complying with requirements.

The AC develops and implements ways in which to benchmark compliance with IOSCO's Objectives and Principles of Securities Regulation (**IOSCO Principles**) and other standards and policies set out in IOSCO reports or resolutions approved by IOSCO.

The objective is to encourage full, effective and consistent implementation of Principles and Standards across IOSCO membership which will ensure:

- investor protection;
- reduction of abuse in markets and reducing systemic risk globally;
- reducing regulatory arbitrage amongst members;
- reducing the costs of conducting business across borders; and
- improving regulatory efficiency and effectiveness.

2.12 Activities of the Assessment Committee

The three main activities of the Assessment Committee are:

- The conduct of Country Reviews. As a starting point the member will have to complete a template Self-Assessment form which requires details of how they have gone about implementing the IOSCO Principles in their jurisdiction. The AC will then evaluate these responses and review the supporting documentation. The aim of these Reviews is to evaluate any gaps in the implementation of IOSCO's Principles and to devise a road map to address any of the shortfalls.
- The conduct of Thematic Reviews of a particular IOSCO Principle or IOSCO Standard. The aim of these Reviews will be to analyse how members have approached the implementation of a particular standard or principle and whether some means are more effective or more efficient than others. This can then be published so that members can review whether they wish to make any changes to their regime to be more efficient or effective in line with the findings of the Thematic.
- Maintenance of the IOSCO Principles and Methodology. This means that the AC will use whatever resources and power they have able to reinforce and support the implementation of the Principles and ensure they continue to be upheld by members.

The responsibilities outlined above are distinct from the provision of technical assistance, which rests with the IOSCO Secretariat. However, the AC does liaise closely with the IOSCO Secretariat to ensure that, following a review, technical assistance is provided to the member if they need it to implement any recommendations.

2.13 Scope of reviews

Who decides on the scope of the reviews?

- **Thematic Review** – The AC is responsible for selecting the thematic topic; it may be one specific principle or it may be a look at the evolution of a new activity in securities and examining how different jurisdictions are dealing with regulation of it.
- **Country Review** – The country is consulted on the scope and Terms of Reference of the review.

- The scope of Country Reviews may be either all of the IOSCO Principles or a specific Principle(s) relevant to the Country.

Test yourself 13.1

Choose a regulator with which you are familiar and assess it against the principles that IOSCO sets for regulators.

3. Country review

3.1 Why would a jurisdiction want a country review?

There are in fact benefits to having a review undertaken. These can include:

- It gives an independent and objective evaluation of how they have implemented the IOSCO Principles and potentially can reaffirm progress which has been made against previous assessments.
- There is a benefit in having the expertise of these individuals in contact with you, helping guide progress.
- Jurisdictions will be offered a road map to assist them in putting together a plan to address any gaps in compliance.
- The report will set out recommendations that the jurisdiction can use to assist in deciding how to go about rectifying any gaps.

Once the scope is agreed upon between the review team and the member, the first step is the preparation by the member of a self-assessment document which sets out how they have implemented the relevant IOSCO Principles which are the subject of the review.

As part of this process, the AC may decide that they should provide technical assistance to help the member prepare the response. The AC then appoints a team to review the self-assessment. The review team will be made up of experts in the relevant area against which the member is being assessed.

The review team will then go through the responses provided within the country's self-assessment. The country may need to provide additional information or relevant data, copies of laws, regulations and supervisory guidance in order for it to be considered fully. This is done via a desk-based process initially, however, the review team may then go on-site if they feel it necessary.

The review team, working with a coordination team within the IOSCO Secretariat, and the country itself, then put together a draft report which sets out each principle against which the country has been assessed and the level of compliance that they have achieved against it. If there are deficiencies, then a road map is prepared suggesting how any gaps might be addressed. The report will be reviewed by the AC. The representatives of the country are invited to participate in the AC meeting to put forward any comments that they may have on it.

Following this, the Final Report (including the road map) will then be submitted to the IOSCO Board for approval and it can then be published.

This overall review process can take anywhere between six and 12 months depending on the complexity of items identified, or the scope of the review.

4. Thematic review

The thematic review programme is intended to:

- Provide best practice guidance in implementing certain Principles and Standards to assist other IOSCO members in implementation.
- Identify areas in which IOSCO Principles and Standards should be considered for revision or where further IOSCO work may be necessary.
- Provide feedback to members on positive implementation of measures balanced with ways in which some measures implemented have not been as effective.

The Terms of Reference (TOR) developed by AC determine what should be considered for a thematic review.

For example, the TOR for the first IOSCO thematic review that was undertaken was on 'Implementation of IOSCO Principles 6 and 7. It was not intended to be a list of members in order of best practice compliance; it was rather designed to ensure that members could share experiences in implementation in these areas and identify pitfalls so that other members could avoid them and assess whether further guidance was needed from IOSCO.

5. Road maps

The AC are responsible for the road maps. They are intended to assist the country in question and are used as guidance for implementation of methods of compliance with the IOSCO principles for that particular jurisdiction.

When being used as a follow up for country reviews, the AC road map will set out areas for improvements and how those improvements might be achieved. The road map will only contain comment on principles where the country has not achieved a 'sufficient progress made' rating or where it has not been assessed as 'fully implemented'. The road map will highlight improvements that are most material in terms of meeting the relevant IOSCO Principles.

6. International Monetary Fund (IMF)

6.1 Background

The International Monetary Fund (IMF) is an international body headquartered in Washington, DC, which now comprises 189 countries working together to 'promote global monetary cooperation, secure financial stability, facilitate international trade, promote high employment and sustainable economic growth, and reduce poverty around the world'. In 2012 its remit was broadened so that any issue that impacts upon a country's financial stability is within its oversight.

It was formed in 1944 at the Bretton Woods Conference but did not come into existence until 1945. At that stage there were 29 countries as members. It now plays a central role in the management of international financial crises.

The IMF's fundamental mission is to ensure the stability of the international monetary system. It does so in three ways: keeping track of the global economy and the economies of member countries, lending to countries with balance of payments difficulties, and giving practical help to members.

Member countries contribute funds to a communal monetary pot from which countries experiencing economic crises can borrow money to help stabilise their financial system.

The IMF works to improve the economies of its member countries in a number of ways, including compiling statistics and undertaking analysis and oversight and review of its members' economies.

6.2 Statistics

- **Membership:** 189 countries
- **Headquarters:** Washington, DC
- **Executive Board:** 24 Directors, representing either a single country or a group of countries
- **Staff:** Approximately 2,700 from 148 countries
- **Biggest borrowers (amounts outstanding as of 31 August 2016):** Portugal, Greece, Ukraine, Pakistan

6.3 Lending

The IMF is able to provide loans to member countries experiencing financial difficulties and destabilisation of its economy. This financial assistance enables countries to rebuild their international reserves, stabilise their own currency and manage its trading activities. However, if funds are borrowed then the country also has to demonstrate to the IMF what measures it is undertaking to correct underlying problems. Unlike a development bank, the IMF does not lend for specific projects that a country may wish to undertake.

6.4 Technical assistance

The IMF also helps its member countries with their economic policies and encourages them to manage their financial affairs more effectively. They will also offer technical assistance and training to the country if they think this will be of benefit. This is an important part of the IMF's work, ensuring training and education within a country so that expertise can be developed and assist in prevention of financial crises within the country, which should prevent future crises recurring.

6.5 Structure

On an operational level, the IMF has a management team and 17 departments that carry out its country, policy, analytical and technical work. There is a whole department dedicated to managing the IMF's resources.

The IMF has a Managing Director, who is head of the staff and Chairperson of the Executive Board. The Managing Director is appointed by the Executive Board for a renewable term of five years and is assisted by a First Deputy Managing Director and three Deputy Managing Directors.

The IMF's employees come from all over the world; they report directly to the IMF and not to the authorities of the countries from where they come. The IMF employees are organised by responsibility: functional, information, liaison, and support.

6.6 Surveillance

Surveillance is used in order to identify risks so that policies can be implemented and preventative measures taken, if possible. Given the accessibility of financial markets in the modern age of technology, if the policies of one country change this can also impact upon a number of other countries, so international cooperation is essential. The IMF, having nearly total global membership of 189 countries, is the body that can ensure that this cooperation happens. There are two main aspects to the IMF's surveillance work: oversight and advice on the policies of each member country and oversight of the world economy.

The IMF employs economists who are constantly monitoring members' economies. Visits to member countries are undertaken to facilitate exchange of views with the local government and consider whether that country has any specific risks in their domestic economy or if on a global level, whether they will impact on global stability. If any areas of concern are identified, then the economists may propose changes in the economic or financial policies as a preventative measure. Usually areas of concern will arise around exchange rates, monetary policy, fiscal treatment and financial policies. IMF delegations on a visit will ensure that they meet with all those who have input into, or may impact upon, the economy of the country.

Following the visit, the staff will prepare a findings report and present it to the IMF's Executive Board for discussion. The result of these discussions are then provided to the country. Most countries who have been subject to such a review publish a press release summarising the views of the Board, together with details of the report. This assists in global transparency of the economic state of a country and can be used to help avoid future financial crises.

In 2011 the IMF published the Triennial Surveillance Review which set out where progress had been made in addressing the weaknesses that it had identified through its surveillance before the financial crisis. It acknowledged there were weaknesses in the IMF's review and surveillance processes. The 2011 review recommended improvements in six key areas to assist in the effectiveness of the IMF's surveillance.

As part of this, in July 2012 the Executive Board adopted a new 'Decision on Bilateral and Multilateral Surveillance' (the Integrated Surveillance Decision), which was put in place to strengthen and make more robust the legal framework under which the IMF can conduct surveillance. In September 2012 further measures were taken and the Executive Board published a new Financial Surveillance Strategy. It proposes additional measures to strengthen the ways in which the IMF can undertake financial surveillance. These measures include the IMF having greater oversight and visibility of members' policies on global stability and visibility of internal economic machinations within the country, better safeguarding the effective operation of the international monetary system, and supporting global economic and financial stability.

7. Financial Action Task Force (FATF)

Following global concern about the increases in money laundering, the Financial Action Task Force on Money Laundering (FATF) was established by the G7 Summit that was held in Paris in 1989. Recognising the threat posed to the banking system and to financial institutions, the G7 Heads of State or Government and President of the European Commission formed the Financial Action Task Force from the G7 member States, the European Commission and eight other countries.

In October 2001, the FATF further expanded its mandate to incorporate efforts to combat terrorist financing, in addition to money laundering.

The FATF has a fixed life span which requires a specific decision by its Ministers to continue. The current mandate of the FATF (2012-2020) was adopted at a Ministerial meeting in April 2012 and therefore will not need to be re-endorsed for another three years at the time of writing.

The stated objectives of the FATF are to: set standards and promote effective implementation of legal, regulatory and operational measures for combating money laundering, terrorist financing and other related threats to the integrity of the international financial system. The FATF monitors countries' progress in implementing its 40+9 Recommendations, reviews money laundering and terrorist financing techniques and counter-measures, and promotes the adoption and implementation of its recommendations globally.

There are 37 Members of the FATF as at November 2016. The FATF currently comprises 35 member jurisdictions and 2 regional organisations, representing most major financial centres in all parts of the globe.

The FATF has developed the series of 40+9 Recommendations that are acknowledged as being the international standard for combating of money laundering and the financing of terrorism and proliferation of weapons of mass destruction. The FATF recommendations were first issued in 1990, and have been subsequently revised in 1996, 2001, 2003 and most recently in 2012 to ensure that they remain up to date and relevant with developments in financial crime and technology.

The FATF monitors member progress in implementing necessary measures, reviews money laundering and terrorist financing techniques and counter-measures, and promotes the adoption and implementation of appropriate measures globally. FATF also works with other international bodies to ensure that any specific national vulnerabilities are identified and addressed, with the aim of protecting the international financial system from misuse.

The FATF's decision-making body, the FATF Plenary, meets three times per year.

7.1 FATF President

The FATF President is a senior official appointed by the FATF Plenary from among its members for a term of one year. The term of the President begins on 1 July and ends on 30 June of the following year. The President convenes and chairs the meetings of the FATF Plenary and the Steering Group, and he/she oversees the FATF Secretariat.

7.2 FATF Recommendations

The Task Force was given the responsibility of examining money laundering techniques and trends, reviewing the action which had already been taken at a national or international level, and setting out the measures that still needed to be taken to combat money laundering. In April 1990, less than one year after its creation, the FATF issued a report containing a set of Forty Recommendations, which set out a comprehensive plan of action needed to further improve the global fight against money laundering.

In 2001, given that it was at the forefront of the minds of governments around the world, the fight against terrorist financing was added to the mission of the FATF. As a result of this, in October 2001 the FATF issued the Eight Special Recommendations to deal specifically with the issue of terrorist financing. A comprehensive review of all standards was later undertaken which led to FATF publishing a Ninth Special Recommendation, further strengthening the agreed international standards for combating money laundering and terrorist financing – these are now known as the FATF 40+9 Recommendations.

The 9 Special Recommendations are kept separate from the earlier 40 as they focus specifically on terrorist financing as opposed to those 40 which focus on the measures against money laundering. The 9 recommendations were expanded to deal with threats at that time such as the financing of weapons of mass destruction. The 40+9 recommendations are now very clear and specific in each area on which they focus.

Figure 13.1: FATF structure

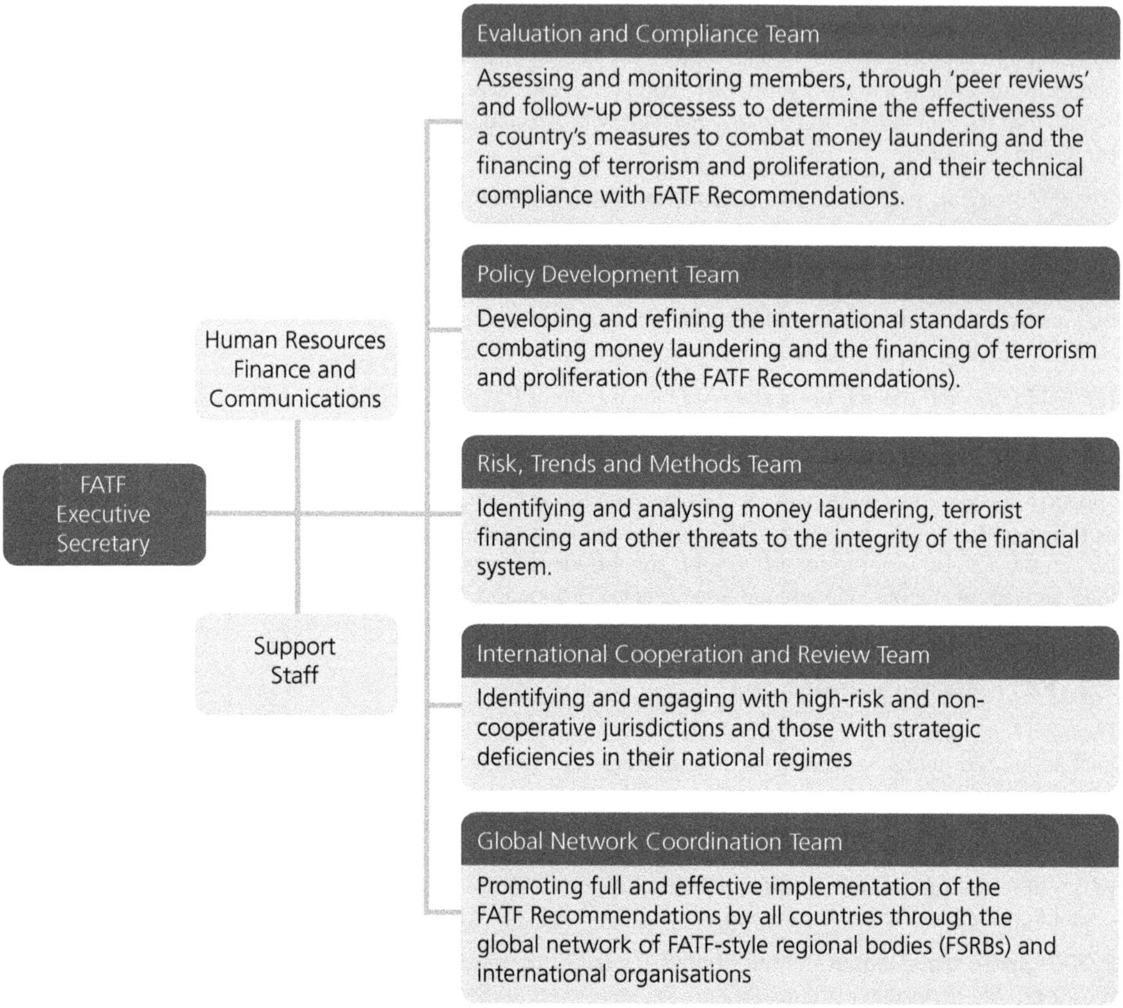

7.3 Non-Cooperative Countries and Territories

The main reason for the implementation of the Non-Cooperative Countries and Territories (NCCT) regime was to highlight certain jurisdictions which had financial systems which had weaker controls, and were therefore more susceptible to money laundering as there were inadequate measures for the prevention, detection and punishment of money laundering compared to those internationally recognised standards applied elsewhere. This list enabled jurisdictions to apply more care when dealing with these countries or territories and to be aware of the risks that engagement with them from a trading or financial perspective may pose.

The NCCT report of February 2000 set out the methodology that was being used for reviewing countries and territories under this initiative. Four regional review groups were established (Americas, Asia/Pacific, Europe, Africa/Middle East) to participate in this project and each review group was made up of representatives from the member governments that were involved in the negotiations and discussions with the country being reviewed.

FATF established a list of reviews to be undertaken, using past reviews and member experience to determine the order in which reviews should be undertaken. Notification of the review by FATF was provided to the country and the review group assigned to the country was then tasked with gathering the relevant legislation, regulations and other relevant information, analysing it all as part of a wider framework review and benchmarking it against the 25 NCCT criteria. Following this review and analysis they prepared a draft report that was sent to the jurisdiction under review for comment. Each reviewed jurisdiction is given the opportunity to provide their comments on draft reports. The comments and the draft report are then tabled in a meeting between the FATF and the jurisdiction concerned, part of which is undertaken via a series of face-to-face meetings. After this process, once the content has been agreed, the draft report is reviewed, and if appropriate, adopted by the FATF Plenary.

47 countries or territories were subject to this process between 2000 and 2001. Of the 47, a total of 23 were listed as NCCTs; 15 in 2000 and 8 in 2001. There have been no further evaluations since then, although there are a number of countries that have to continue to update the FATF on their progress in implementing its recommendations and as updates on their compliance are issued.

8. European Securities and Markets Authority (ESMA)

EU Member States and governments wanted more harmonised regulation and a cooperative form of European supervision to deal with the aftermath of the financial crisis and to provide consistency in the approach to regulation across Member States. As a result of this, an overall European System of Financial Supervision was introduced, and as part of this the European Securities and Markets Authority (ESMA) was formed with the aim of promoting stable financial markets and improving the protection of investors. ESMA replaced an existing regulator, the Committee of European Securities Regulators, whose role was to provide technical advice to the European Commission.

ESMA was tasked with drawing up a single rulebook for the regulation of the EU's financial markets and to then ensure it was consistently applied through enforcement. The rationale for the single rulebook was to demonstrate that all investors, no matter where they are in the EU, receive the same level of protection. It was also beneficial in creating a level playing field for all those in the marketplace as everyone is subject to the same requirements.

8.1 Investor protection

Investor protection is a core objective of ESMA and therefore introduction of the MiFID investor protection provisions and AIFMD all help towards that aim.

8.2 Structure of ESMA

Figure 13.2: Structure of ESMA

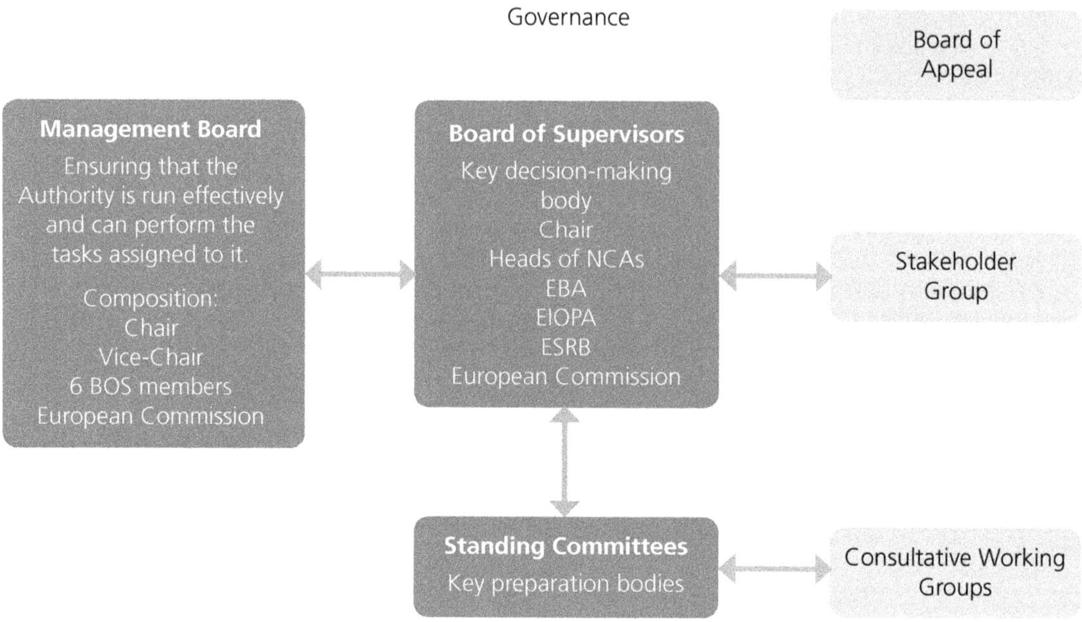

Source: www.esma.europa.eu/about-esma/governance

You will learn more about the work of ESMA in implementing Directives in the EU in the chapter on Directives.

9. Securities and Exchange Commission (SEC)

The US Securities and Exchange Commission (SEC) remit is to protect investors, to maintain fair, orderly, and efficient markets, and facilitate capital formation.

A simple concept sits behind all investment regulation including the SEC's remit: all investors, whether large institutions or private individuals, should have access to certain basic facts about any investment prior to buying it, and while they are holding it.

9.1 Oversight

The SEC oversees securities exchanges, securities brokers and dealers, investment advisers, and mutual funds. The role of the SEC is primarily ensuring disclosure of market-related information of significance, maintaining fair dealing, and protecting against fraud.

The SEC can also use its enforcement powers during the undertaking of its oversight. The SEC is responsible for a significant amount of civil enforcement actions against individuals and companies for violation of the securities laws each year. These range from providing false or misleading information about securities and the companies that issue them, insider trading, and accounting fraud.

9.2 Responsibilities of the SEC

The SEC has the following responsibilities:

- to interpret and enforce federal securities laws;
- to oversee securities firms, brokers, investment advisers and ratings agencies;
- to oversee self-regulating organisations in the securities sector, accounting and auditing fields;
- to issue new securities rules as products evolve; and
- to coordinate US securities regulation with the federal, state and any foreign authorities.

9.3 Organisation of the SEC

The SEC has five presidentially-appointed Commissioners, each of which is appointed for a staggered five-year term. Of these five, one of them is designated as Chairman of the Commission. The agency's functional activities are organised into five Divisions and 23 Offices, each of which is headquartered in Washington, DC. There are currently approximately 4,600 staff located between Washington and 11 Regional Offices throughout the US.

10. Cayman Islands Monetary Authority (CIMA)

10.1 Functions of The Cayman Islands Monetary Authority

The Cayman Islands Monetary Authority has four stated functions which form the basis of its supervisory role.

Monetary
The issue and redemption of Cayman Islands currency and the management of currency reserves.

Regulatory
The regulation and supervision of financial services, monitoring of compliance with money laundering regulations, issuing a regulatory handbook on policies and procedures and the issuance of rules and statements of principle and guidance.

Cooperative
Providing assistance to overseas regulatory authorities, including entering into memoranda of understanding to assist with consolidated supervision.

Advisory
The provision of advice to the Government on policy matters connected to monetary, regulatory and cooperation.

CIMA has a number of obligations given to it under statute that it must meet while undertaking its functions:

- to act in the best economic interests of the Cayman Islands;
- to promote and maintain a sound financial system in the Cayman Islands;
- to use its resources in the most efficient and economic way;
- to have regard to generally accepted principles of good corporate governance;
- to endeavour to promote and enhance market confidence, consumer protection and the reputation of the Cayman Islands as a financial centre;
- to reduce the possibility that financial services businesses can be used for money laundering or other crime;
- to recognise the international character of financial services/markets and the need to be competitive for consumers and suppliers while complying with appropriate and relevant international standards;
- to recognise the principle that a burden or restriction that is imposed should be proportionate to its expected benefits;
- to recognise the desirability of facilitating innovation in financial services business; and
- to be transparent and fair in its activities.

10.2 Supervisory divisions

CIMA is comprised of a Banking Supervision Division, Fiduciary Services Division, Insurance Division and Investment and Securities Division. These four regulatory divisions are responsible for oversight of licensed entities within each of their sectors. This includes processing applications for licences and other relevant authorisations for the provision of those financial services falling within their sectors, making recommendations to CIMA's Management Committee on the issue (or non-issue) of licences, ongoing supervision of licensees through on-site visits in combination with off-site monitoring, and making recommendations for enhancements to the supervisory regime where appropriate.

10.3 Off-site and on-site supervision

Licensed entities must submit quarterly prudential returns which are then analysed, together with annual audited financial statements. Management may also be requested to attend prudential meetings with the division.

On-site visits can take place at the premises of the licensee in the Cayman Islands or in any overseas office. These inspections can be full visits with no restrictions on what may be reviewed, or may be a focus visit on a particular aspect of regulation. The aim of the visit is for CIMA to gain a greater understanding of the operational activities of the licensee and their compliance with the regulations in place.

11. Monetary Authority of Singapore (MAS)

11.1 Background

The Monetary Authority of Singapore (MAS) has a wide ranging remit, which includes acting as the central bank of Singapore, and the associated responsibilities that comes with that, as well as supervision of financial services that are undertaken in Singapore.

MAS was formed on 1 January 1971 and is responsible for enforcing the regulatory laws for banking, insurance, securities and the financial sector in general.

11.2 Banking

There are three Banking Departments which supervise between them all types of licensed and regulated bank. Banking Department I supervises the local banking groups, and certain foreign banks. Banking Department II supervises a mix of retail and wholesale banks, finance companies, money changers and remittance agents. Banking Department III is responsible for the supervision of banks active in treasury and private banking businesses.

11.3 Insurance

The Insurance Department supervises and regulates insurance companies and its main objective is the protection of policyholders' interests.

11.4 Capital markets

The Capital Markets Intermediaries (CMI) Departments, of which there are three, have collective responsibility for the supervision of capital markets intermediaries. CMI Department I supervises intermediaries of Singapore and Malaysian financial groups, CMI II supervises intermediaries of American and UK financial groups, while CMI III supervises intermediaries of Asia-Pacific and other European financial groups.

11.5 Anti-money laundering

The Anti-Money Laundering Department is responsible for drafting and introducing processes to combat money laundering and other financial crime issues, monitor these risks in the financial sector, and provide supervisory oversight of licensed financial institutions with respect to their AML systems and controls.

11.6 Enforcement Department

MAS has a specific Enforcement Department whose aim is to deter licensees from engaging in unlawful and improper conduct. This is primarily done through ensuring effective surveillance of the licensed sector and taking enforcement where necessary. It investigates and enforces breaches of the laws administered by the MAS. The Enforcement Department also jointly investigates market misconduct offences under Part XII of the Securities and Futures Act with the Commercial Affairs Department and provides assistance to overseas regulators under the International Organization of Securities Commissions Multilateral Memorandum of Understanding (see the role of IOSCO above).

12. Sharia law

Sharia law is a body of Islamic law. The term means 'way' or 'path' and is the legal framework within which the public and some private aspects of life are regulated for those living in a legal system based on Islam. It is also a way of instilling communal values into investment.

A Sharia compliant fund is an investment vehicle fund which has been specifically structured to comply with Sharia rules. Sharia funds can be managed as mutual funds, ETFs or hedge funds. They are like a standard fund but with an extra layer of Islamic rules integrated in the investment policies of the fund. While the funds themselves are required to be fully compliant with Sharia rules, the companies which manage or promote the funds do not always have to be Sharia compliant.

12.1 Sharia compliant equity funds

Equity funds can be established to invest in the common shares of companies that operate a halal business. Any such companies, to be eligible, must also comply with Sharia accounting principles. As the number of eligible companies is restricted, this can result in higher volatility.

12.2 Sharia compliant commodities funds

Commodities funds can be Sharia compliant by being structured to buy and resell halal commodities. Commodity compliant funds make use of two types of Sharia approved contracts:

- **Istisna** – A contract where the buyer of an item funds upfront the production of the item. The precise details of the item must be agreed before production of it starts and the cost of production can be paid in stages as part of the manufacturing stages.

- **Bay al-salam** – These can be compared to a forward contract where the buyer pays in advance for the delivery of raw materials at a given date. The end price of the item includes the profit of the person who has purchased the good and the cost of making the product.

12.3 Ijarah

These types of fund will invest in a physical asset (property, vehicles or equipment) and generates profits by leasing them in return for rent. The fund is responsible for the management of the asset and will normally receive a management fee. Any property that is leased must be used in a halal manner.

12.4 Investment restrictions

The payment or receipt of interest is not permitted. Having any form of debt is also not permissible, so investments in debt or leveraged funds is not a possibility. Any compliant funds cannot pay a fixed or guaranteed return on capital. Instead of borrowing and lending, Islamic finance relies on the concepts of sharing ownership of assets.

There are also restrictions on activities of the underlying companies that the fund can invest into. Anything which is connected to the production or sale of alcohol, including pubs and restaurants, pork products, gambling or adult entertainment orientated, are not allowed to be included in a fund portfolio.

Chapter summary

- There are different bodies around the world which impact upon the funds sector.
- The remit of these bodies varies according to their specific purpose, but all have an overarching goal to prevent market abuse, protect investors and prevent financial crime.
- There is a wide range of legislation in place and many different regulators to which any one fund may come under the remit of.

Exercise answers

Chapter 2

Worked example answers

Worked example 2.1
Portfolio A = (18-4)/20 = 0.7

Portfolio B = (22-4)/30 = 0.6

Therefore we can see that, on a risk-adjusted basis, portfolio A has outperformed portfolio B.

The higher a portfolio's standard deviation (risk), the higher its returns need to be to earn a high Sharpe ratio. Conversely, funds with lower standard deviations can still have a higher Sharpe ratio if they have consistently decent returns. A high Sharpe ratio indicates a good historical risk-adjusted performance; however, this doesn't necessarily translate to a low volatility portfolio. A higher Sharpe ratio just means that the portfolio's risk-return relationship is more optimal.

Chapter 3

Test yourself answers

Test yourself 3.1

1 Management of a company is the responsibility of the board of directors.

2 Management of a unit trust is the responsibility of the trustee (sometimes referred to as the managing trustee).

3 Management of a limited partnership is the responsibility of the general partner.

Test yourself 3.2
The three main characteristics of an investment fund are:

- pooling of contributions;
- third party management of assets; and
- spread of risk.

Test yourself 3.3

The key documents investors sign up to when they invest in a fund are:

- The scheme particulars (by whatsoever name), which may include offering document, prospectus and information memorandum.
- Subscription agreement (or application form). This is the long form of application document an investor completes upon subscription.
- Substantive documents of the legal entity, i.e. Articles of Association in respect of a company, trust deed in respect of a unit trust and limited partnership agreement in respect of a limited partnership), along with a form of adherence document (where relevant).

Worked example answers

Worked example 3.1

Your structure diagram may look something like the following:

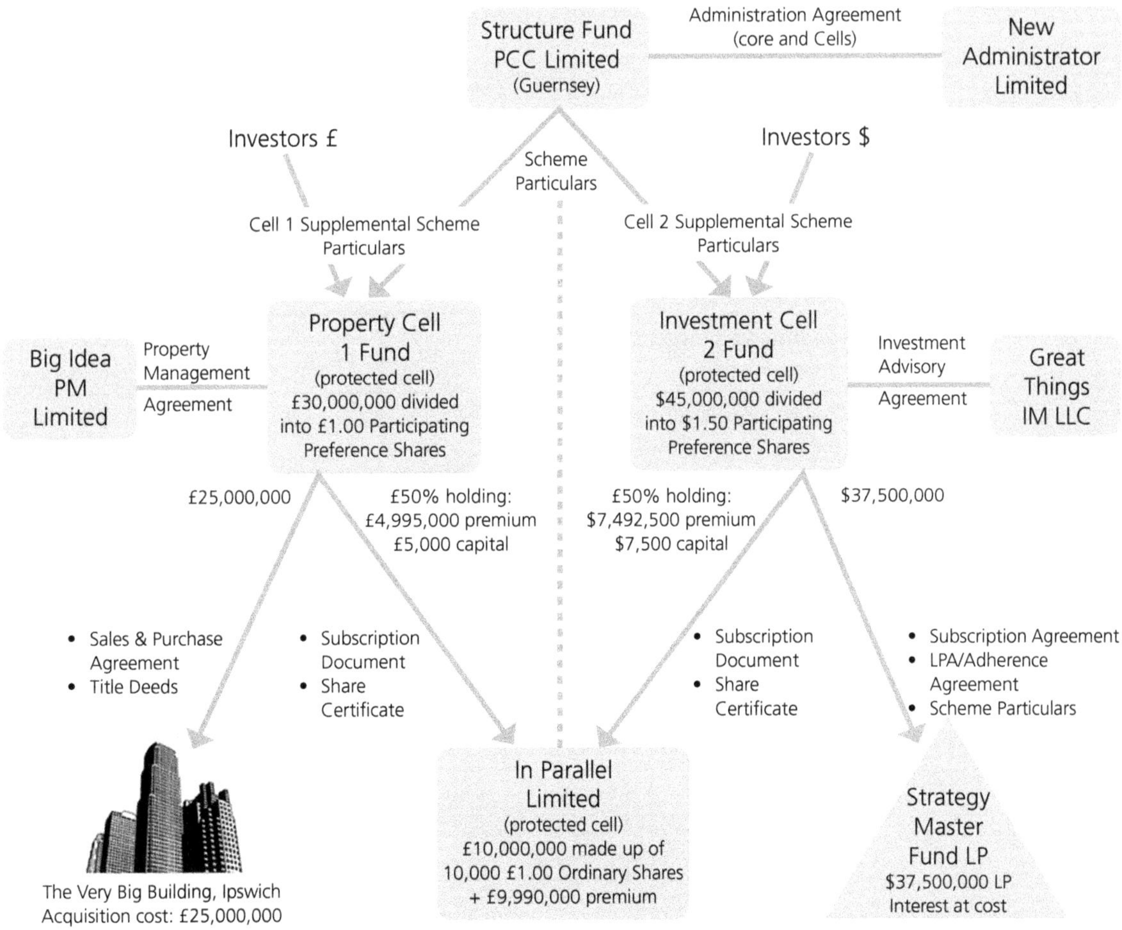

When composing the structure diagram, it is also worth considering the flow of monies (denoted in x on the above chart).

It is also worth considering what legal documents and agreements will govern each relationship identified (denoted in x on the above chart).

Chapter 4

Test yourself answers

Test yourself 4.1

Description	Manager	Administrator	Governing Body
Selecting prospective investments	X		
Acquisition/Disposal of investments			X
Monitoring/ensuring investments remain in line with the terms of the Offering Document[1]	X	X	X
Management of investments	X		
Obtaining investment valuations[2]	X	X	X
Preparation of the NAV of the Fund[3]		X	X
Calculation of Management Fees		X	
Calculation of Performance Fees		X	
Scrutinising all fees payable to the Manager for reasonableness[3]		X	X
Approval of Management/ Performance Fees			X

[1] Ultimate responsibility will always rest with the governing body, which must ensure that assets comply with the fund documentation and are managed in

accordance with them. However, it is important to remember that the manager is bound by contract to ensure that fund objectives, limits and restrictions are adhered to or otherwise find themselves in breach of contract. Finally, the fund administrator provides a useful barrier of scrutiny and so should put in place a mechanism of assessing investments held against the fund's offering document.

[2] The core principle is that underlying asset valuations should be from as independent a source as possible.

For some assets, such as listed securities, finding independent valuations is simply a matter of subscribing to relevant feeds and automatically loading the prices into the administration system; this would ordinarily rest solely with the fund administrator.

However, other asset types are more difficult to obtain independent sources, this increases the more esoteric (alternative) an asset class becomes. As this occurs, the fund manager will be looked to more and more to provide valuation inputs, as they are the party with the most reliable sources of information. In such instances, the offering document will explain how the valuations will be obtained, often utilising set formulae to mitigate the risks associated with less independent sources. The administrator's role in these circumstances will be to scrutinise the valuations information being provided to the extent it is able.

The governing body will always remain responsible for all valuation inputs, including setting approved formulae and, where applicable, hiring independent third parties (such as property valuers). Ultimately, the governing body must satisfy itself as to the robustness of the valuations utilised.

[3] The governing body is the only party that may approve fees paid to the fund manager. However, the fund administrator's role should never be underestimated or downplayed. Part of compiling the fees calculations must include evaluating all of the inputs into the calculations and the results for reasonableness at all times.

Chapter 5

Test yourself answers

Test yourself 5.1

The trend for increased regulation is not likely to decrease. With each new economic crisis, regulation increases and fund administrators have to actively adjust accordingly.

Test yourself 5.2

Funds sectors have grown up in offshore locations for a number of reasons:

- Offshore finance centres present themselves as one-stop shops for fund managers, providing access to structuring experts and legal advice.
- Offshore finance centres have garnered relationships with placement

agents, brokers, fund managers and major fund lawyers.

- Offshore finance centres have demonstrated not only their resilience but also their robustness through the creation of world-leading regulatory frameworks, strong corporate governance regimes and a requirement for true substance to be demonstrated by all of their key players.

Chapter 6

Test yourself answers

Test yourself 6.1

BALANCE SHEET
BRILLIANT PROPERTY FUND

Assets		**2015**	**2014**
Current Assets			
	Cash	7,521	3,253
	Pre-paid expenses	18,255	19,365
	Rent receivable		
Fixed Assets			
	11, Langton Road	210,750	195,500
	3, Park Square	365,500	355,000
	25, Garden Mews	250,000	250,000
	The Shire, Essex	1,350,000	1,245,000
	100 Shares – Equity Fundsmith	45,000	44,000
	Mercedes SLK230	50,000	50,000
TOTAL ASSETS		2,297,026	2,162,118
Liabilities			
Current liabilities			
	Insurance	25,400	21,500
	Short-term finance	15,000	14,500
	Tax payable	28,000	25,000
		68,400	61,000
Long-Term Liabilities			
	Long-term debt	450,000	420,000
Shareholders funds			
	Paid-up capital	2,500,000	2,500,000
	Retained earnings	125,000	110,000
		2,625,000	2,610,000
TOTAL LIABILITIES AND SHAREHOLDERS' FUNDS		3,143,400	3,091,000

The balance sheet has the following issues:

- It does not balance.
- It is not clear if there has been revaluation of the property, and if so, on what basis. Some values have changed, others have not
- It is not clear if there are any creditors.
- Depreciation of any of the assets has not been included.
- Two of the assets do not look like they should be in a property fund.
- The year end is not stated.

Chapter 7

Test yourself answers

Test Yourself 7.1

Whilst the term NAV is often used to mean both NAV and price by the general public, a simple growth in NAV doesn't indicate the fund is performing well. Similarly a reduction in NAV doesn't mean that the fund is doing badly.

Chapter 8

Test yourself answers

Test yourself 8.1

These are the main points to consider in the appointment of a custodian:

- How can they demonstrate the cars are held securely, both in terms of damage prevention and security from theft?
- Do they have any other similar clients?
- What insurance do they have in place?
- Can they provide regular reports to you on the condition of the vehicles?
- Will you need to arrange for external valuations to be done or can they provide this?
- Will they undertake any maintenance, such as starting the cars up regularly to ensure they still work? Are they covered appropriately and qualified to do this?
- How long have they been in business?
- Have the most recent financials been reviewed?
- Have the principals been checked to ensure that they are fit and proper / no criminal convictions of relevance?
- What fees are they charging? Are they in line with the market?
- Has a fully comprehensive draft agreement been provided to review, including their terms and conditions?

Chapter 10

Worked example answers

Worked example 10.1

1. The Scheme Particulars place a restriction on the amount of cash held such that 'no more than 5% of the Fund may be held in cash or near-cash. The fund is not permitted to invest in derivatives or any financial asset'

Clarity will need to be sought as to whether the 5% refers to NAV or to AUM, as this will impact significantly. If 5% of NAV, the maximum cash permissible would be £12,750,000 (5% of £255,000,000) if 5% of AUM this would equate to £32,500,000 (5% of £650,000,000). However, in this example, whatever measure used, the amount of cash held significantly exceeds either level.

2. The Scheme Particulars state that 'leverage must not exceed 65% of the total acquisition costs of an investment'.

Property	Acquisition Cost	Leverage	Leverage as a Percentage	Compliant with Restrictions?
57, Cavendish Walk, City of London	£95,000,000	£70,000,000	73.68%	No
Wow Skyscraper, Canary Wharf, London	£270,000,000	£235,000,000	87.04%	No
The Truncheon Building, Kensington	£39,500,000	£10,000,000	25.32%	Yes
Landmark Tower, Edinburgh	£103,000,000	£60,000,000	58.25%	Yes

3. Consider each property in respect of the following statements taken from the Scheme Particulars as to the type of property that is suitable for the Fund–

- 'the acquisition and active management of Grade A office property';
- 'predominantly in the City of London';
- a maximum of 25% of the Assets Under Management of the Fund (at the time of such investment) may be allocated to any one particular investment;
- 'Property may only be England, Wales or Scotland situs and no more than 15% of the total property portfolio at any one time shall be situated outside of the City of London.'

Property	Acquisition Price/ Audited Value	Grade A office property	Concentration Limits breached?	Geographical location permitted?	Geographic limits breached?
57, Cavendish Walk, City of London	£95,000,000/ £160,000,000	YES	At the time of purchase, this may have breached the limits. Often an exempted period will be permitted to allow the Fund to buy sufficient assets.	Yes – City of London	N/A
Wow Skyscraper, Canary Wharf, London	£270,000,000/ £300,000,000	YES	In the absence of an exempted period, this purchase would have represented 74% of AUM at the time of purchase.	Yes – City of London	N/A
The Truncheon Building, Kensington	£39,500,000/ £50,000,000	YES	9.77% at the time of purchase; compliant	Yes – however, this is outside of City of London	8.29% – alone, this complies with the geographic restriction.
Landmark Tower, Edinburgh	£103,000,000/ £93,000,000	YES	20.30% at the time of purchase; compliant	Yes – Scotland	15.42% – alone this breaches the restriction. When added to the Kensington property, these equate to 27.71% and so the Fund is in breach.
Total Value	£603,000,000				

Chapter 11

Test yourself answers

Test yourself 11.1

The answer will depend on your risk appetite and what your desired returns may be. A five-year gilt which is backed by the UK Government will be a more secure bond than one issued by a corporate, but the rates may be lower as a result.
A three-year corporate bond issued by a public listed company means that the information available to you to research the company and its profitability will enable you to assess the level of risk you are taking. It will also potentially offer higher rewards and you are not committed for such a long period, therefore the risk of inflation impacting upon returns is less than a five-year bond.

Test yourself 11.2

Inflation risk is likely to be a significant consideration. Given that the bond is to be of such a long duration, the erosion of capital value or the dividends that are being paid over time may decrease in comparison to the increase in cost of living in that period. However, risks of a bond also need to be looked at on a case-by-case basis, and in this instance, more information may be required to determine other applicable risks, such as, if issued as a corporate bond by a relatively new company, then this may be a greater risk than the risk of inflation. It is important to consider all aspects of the bond that may carry a risk, not just the one which would appear to be most apparent on first review.

Chapter 13

Test yourself answers

Test yourself 13.1

Using the criteria as set out in Section 2.4, you should take each strand of the principles and assess how the regulator you have chosen meets them. This would include, for example:

- Details of the legislation under which the regulator has been formed and has its powers.
- Set out the decision-making processes and how it has the ability to assess and take action independent of any government or state body.
- Consider their staffing levels and financial resources in terms of their ability to fulfil their role. For example, can they visit licensed entities frequently enough to enable meaningful oversight of their licensee base, given the staff they have available to do such visits?
- Set out the processes in place to apply for a licence in terms of minimum criteria and how the process works.

- Details of the risk mitigation that the regulator has in place, such as regular face-to-face meetings with licensees, or if it has a specific methodology to risk assess their licensee base.
- Evaluate the conduct of business or ethics rules put in place by the regulator for licensees to adhere to and whether they adequately require disclosure and management of potential conflicts of interest.

Directory of web resources

Professional bodies

Cayman Islands Monetary Authority
www.cimoney.com.ky

The Financial Action Task Force
www.fatf-gafi.org/

International Monetary Fund
www.imf.org/external/index.htm

International Organization of Securities Commissions
www.iosco.org/

Monetary Authority of Singapore
www.mas.gov.sg

Moneyval
www.coe.int/t/dghl/monitoring/moneyval/

US Securities and Exchange Commission
www.sec.gov

Bibliography

(2009) *4 stages in the life of a private equity fund*
Available online at: www.seekingalpha.com/article/172992-4-stages-in-the-life-of-a-private-equity-fund

About the IMF
Available online at: www.imf.org/external/about.htm

(Sep 2012) *Exploring the emerging potential of Africa*
Available online at: www.investmauritius.com/ezine_sep12/article2.html

(2013) *The changing landscape of private equity fund formation*
Available online at: www.empea.org/research/legal-regulatory-issues/the-changing-landscape-of-private-equity-fund-formation-2013/

Hempel, C., Mungall, S., and Olsen, C. *Private equity in the British Virgin Islands: market and regulatory overview*
Available online at: www.us.practicallaw.com/0-610-9225

Jersey funds: at a glance
www.jerseyfunds.org/overview

JP Morgan private equity fund services expands in the Channel Islands, Europe
Available online at: www.globalcustodian.com/Fund-Administration/JPMorgan-Private-Equity-Fund-Services-Expands-In-The-Channel-Islands,-Europe/

Lee, T. (10 Feb 2016) *A list of venture capital firms in Singapore*
Available online at: www.techinasia.com/directory-of-early-stage-venture-capital-seed-funds-and-angel-investors-for-startups-in-singapore

Lee, V. (25 Oct 2013) *Private equity in Singapore*
Available online at: www.preqin.com/blog/0/7709/private-equity-singapore

Ozannes, M. (Aug 2015) *Comparison of offshore private equity holding structures*
Available online at: www.mourantozannes.com/media/1355405/comparison-of-offshore-private-equity-holding-structures.pdf

(1 Mar 2016) *Private equity in Guernsey: market and regulatory overview*
Available online at: wwwuk.practicallaw.com/7-564-8905

(28 Oct 2008) *Private equity funds in Jersey*
Available online at: www.mondaq.com/jersey/x/68266/offshore+financial+centres/Private+Equity+Funds+In+Jersey+An+Overview

Raftopoulos, S. (2015) *Private equity transactions offshore 2015*
Available online at: www.applebyglobal.com/publication-pdf/thought-leadership-report/private-equity-report-2015.pdf

Smith, L. (22 Feb 2016) *Cayman Islands Private Equity Funds and the use of Exempted Limited Partnerships*

Available online at: www.lexology.com/library/detail.aspx?g=1bc19bb4-6dfa-4e90-9c76-9b17b07a5ef2

Weaver, A. (2015) *A rise of private equity in Jersey*
Available online at: www.applebyglobal.com/publication-pdf/article/2015/a-rise-of-private-equity-in-jersey-(aweaver)-march-2015.pdf

Why the British Virgin Isles? A guide to setting up and doing business
Available online at: www.withersworldwide.com/system/files/2123/original/25_BVI_setting-up_bus_8jan2015.pdf

(15 Jul 2013) *Why private equity keeps on choosing Guernsey*
Available online at: www.hedgeweek.com/2013/07/02/186763/why-private-equity-keeps-choosing-guernsey

Glossary

Acquisitions for expansion When a PE firm buys out a successful company to enhance the likelihood of the success continuing and facilitating growth through the provision of additional capital as required.

Administration Providing any administrative, secretarial or clerical services in relation to an investment.

AML/CFT Anti-Money Laundering/Countering the Financing of Terrorism rules which apply within each jurisdiction to comply with international standards.

Bookkeeping Ensuring that the books and records are maintained.

Business companies A business company (BC) incorporated under the BVI Business Companies Act (as amended) (BC Act) and often incorporated to act as the general partner of a fund entity.

Buy-outs When PE firms seek out struggling privately owned companies and purchase the shareholding.

Callable A type of bond which can be redeemed by the issuer prior to the bond term expiring.

Capital asset pricing model (CAPM) Describes the relationship between systematic risk and expected return for assets.

Capital base Capital within an institution that is considered in relation to the financial stability of a custodian, especially for private equity funds.

Capital raising The stage of the life cycle that involves sourcing institutional investors or wealthy investors to invest large sums of money into a fund.

Corporate bonds Debt securities issued by private and public corporations.

Corporate governance Refers to the mechanisms, processes and relations by which corporations are controlled and directed.

Class Q Scheme Registered funds in Guernsey established solely for investors who are considered to be qualifying or sophisticated investors.

Closed-ended funds When NAV and the price are linked but not in the same way and not with the same absolute correlation. A closed-ended fund issues a number of shares, invests the cash and generally expects to hang onto it for the life of the fund, often seven or eight years.

Diversification How risk in a portfolio is reduced.

Duration The length of time for which a bond will be live, such as ten years.

Eligible Investor Fund A certified fund which is suitable for eligible investors (professional or experienced investors) and which can be authorised expeditiously by the Jersey Financial Services Commission subject to certain requirements, as set out by them, being met.

Equity Funds that invest in stocks (equity securities).

Esoteric An unusual and out of the ordinary asset class for a fund.

European Commission The European Commission is the EU's decision-making body. It represents the interests of the European Union as a whole, rather than the interests of individual Member States.

European Council The European Council is responsible for defining the EU's overall political agenda. It is made up of the heads of state or government of the Member States, along with the President of the European Council and the President of the European Commission.

European Court of Justice The highest court in the EU in determining interpretation of EU legislation and ensuring its consistent application across Member States.

European Parliament The elected parliamentary institution of the EU. Together with the Council of the European Union and the European Commission, it exercises the legislative function of the EU. The Parliament is composed of 751 (previously 766) members.

European Union Consists of 28 Member States, predominantly in Europe. The aim of the European Union is to implement policies to ensure the free movement of people, goods, services, and capital within its Member States.

Exiting This is the disposal of investments usually through sale or an initial public offering (IPO) on a recognised stock exchange.

Fair value Fair valuations tend to be provided to support the audited financial statements/valuation of the fund, with reliance on other methods in intervening periods.

Financial Action Task Force on Money Laundering (FATF) Established by the G7 Summit that was held in Paris in 1989.

Financial or Capital Markets Where governments and companies raise finance via the sale and purchase of fixed income securities, often called bonds or equities, more commonly known as shares via a stock market.

Fixed income funds Also known as bond funds that are invested in corporations or governments by way of loan, for which they receive an agreed amount of interest on regularly agreed dates for a set period of time.

Fund sectors Specific locations associated with highly developed fund infrastructures.

General Principles As set out within the COMMISSION DELEGATED REGULATION (EU) No 231/2013 within section 8 to comply with in relation to the delegation of functions under the AIFMD.

Gilts Bonds which are issued by some national governments. The term originally referred to the debt securities issued by the Bank of England on behalf of Her Majesty's Treasury, whose paper certificates had a gilt (or gilded) edge.

Hedge Fund A hedge fund, whilst still pooling investor funds together is targeted more towards sophisticated investors with substantial sums available to invest.

High-yield bonds Have a lower credit rating, implying higher credit risk, than investment-grade bonds and, therefore, offer higher interest rates in return for the increased risk an investor must take on.

International Limited Partnerships These are established under the Partnership Act 1996 (as amended) (Partnership Act) and have at least one general partner and at least one limited partner.

International Monetary Fund (IMF) International body whose stated aims are to facilitate global monetary cooperation, secure financial stability, facilitate international trade, promote high employment and sustainable economic growth, and reduce poverty around the world.

International Organization of Securities Commissions (IOSCO) An international body of securities regulators generally recognised as the leading regulatory body for the securities sector around the world.

IOSCO Principles International Organization of Securities Commissions Objectives and Principles of Securities Regulation sets out 38 Principles of securities regulation, which are based upon three Objectives of securities regulation. These are protecting investors, ensuring that markets are fair, efficient and transparent and reducing systemic risk.

Investment-grade bonds Have a higher credit rating, implying less credit risk, than high-yield corporate bonds.

Key staff Are those staff to whom the remuneration policy of the firm should apply to and will also include staff of the firm to which portfolio management or risk management activities have been delegated by the AIFM.

Limited partnerships A long-recognised legal structure which has been replicated, to a greater or lesser degree, in multiple jurisdictions.

Managing the investment portfolio When the fund has sufficient investments in their portfolio, these investments must be managed in accordance with the agreed strategy.

Market portfolio Deemed to hold a proportion of all investments in the market.

Member State Each Member State is a party to the legal treaties which founded the European Union and thereby subject to the benefits as well as the obligations of being a member.

Mergers When PE firms buy companies successfully trading or otherwise in order to merge them with companies that the firm already has in its portfolio in order to gain an advantage over competitors.

MiFID Rules Markets in Financial Instruments Directive Rules issued pursuant to the Directive to provide more detail on compliance with certain requirements of the Directive.

Modern Portfolio Theory (MPT) An investment framework that is useful in diversifying the risk when allocating assets in a financial, liquid (tradable) portfolio in order to maximise the potential return given a specified level of risk appetite or tolerance.

Moody's A ratings agency which assesses the credit rating of debt instruments and securities.

Money market funds A type of fixed income fund, they are open-ended funds that invest solely in short-term securities, primarily treasury bills and certificates of deposit.

Moneyval An EU body whose full name is the Committee of Experts on the Evaluation of Anti-Money Laundering Measures and the Financing of Terrorism, responsible for analysis and oversight of a jurisdiction's compliance with international standards to prevent money laundering and terrorist financing.

Multilateral Memorandum of Understanding (MMoU) This is put in place between IOSCO and a member to allow free exchange of information between IOSCO members.

Mutual funds These pool together the funds of several investors in order to invest these funds in specific markets.

Net Asset Valuations (NAV) A fundamental element of pricing funds and also for calculating performance, but in themselves they are neither the price nor the measure of a fund's performance.

Open-ended funds A daily dealing fund where NAV and price are directly connected, which can be good for investors because they can put money in or take it out whenever they like, and receive or be charged the value mostly dictated by the underlying NAV per share.

Objective Reasons Within section 76 of the COMMISSION DELEGATED REGULATION (EU) No 231/2013. The objective reasons under which justification for delegation must be made are set out.

Paragraph 7 MMoU This sets out the scope of assistance members will, within the framework of MMoU, provide each other with to ensure compliance with the respective laws and regulations of the member.

Portfolio variance A measurement of how the aggregate returns of a number of securities making up a portfolio fluctuate over time.

Private equity Funds that invest in the equity securities and debt of operating companies that are not publicly traded on a stock exchange.

Private equity funds Investment schemes funded through substantial amounts of pooled capital obtained from institutional investors such as pension funds, insurance companies and also high net worth individuals.

Publicly quoted The benefit of a public quotation (i.e. IPO) may be that liquidity for investors can be created even where a fund itself is closed-ended.

Rating A bond fund can be rated from high to low credit quality.

Real estate Can include many different types of property for many different purposes, such as residential, office space and commercial property as well as funds investing in care homes or student accommodation etc.

Registration Comprises two components: (a) recording particulars of a specified investor; (b) issuing a certificate or policy to a specified investor or to bearer.

Remuneration Guidelines Guidelines issued by ESMA explaining how firms may comply with the Annex II Principles to the Alternative Investment Fund Managers Directive in relation to remuneration policies.

Reporting and systems The level and standard of reporting and access to information that is available for the fund administrator from the custodian will assist in determining suitability.

Restructuring A PE firm buying a struggling company and restructuring it completely to try and turn around its fortunes and bring it into profit.

Return The potential amount back that the investor will receive back in dividends or interest, ordinarily quoted as a percentage basis.

Securities Market Line The line which shows the relationship between relative levels of risk (β) and expected returns.

Segregated Portfolio Company (SPC) A BVI SPC is a single company that contains a number of segregated portfolios.

Sourcing investment opportunity When the firm ensures that it has the right human capital in place in order to manage the investment portfolio and identify the right business opportunities in which to invest the capital held in the fund in order to give the fund the best chance of success.

Sovereign debt or government bonds Debt securities issued by governments and have set period to return of capital. Short-term securities generally mature in under five years, medium-term bonds mature within ten years and long-term bonds typically mature in excess of 20 years.

Standard and Poors A rating agency which provides financial research and analysis on stocks, bonds and commodities.

Subscription In relation to regulatory requirements, receiving funds or assets for the purposes of investment.

Third country Reference to a jurisdiction which is outside of the EU but may wish to engage in trade with the EU.

Track record When appointing a guardian of assets, it is important to know what experience they have in already providing that service, both as a business and the key individuals involved within that business.

Unit Trusts A unit trust is an unincorporated fund structure that allows funds to hold assets and provide profits that go straight to individual unit owners instead of reinvesting them back into the fund. The investment fund is set up under a trust deed. The investor is effectively the beneficiary under the trust.

United States Treasuries Government debt instruments issued by the United States Department of the Treasury to finance the national debt of the United States.

Venture Capital Funds that invest into private companies with a view to financing and managing their growth, improvement etc.

Index

www.ingramcontent.com/pod-product-compliance
Ingram Content Group UK Ltd.
Pitfield, Milton Keynes, MK11 3LW, UK
UKHW051923100926
8556IPUK00021B/1338

9 781860 727009